FROM SUFFERING TO GOD

Also by Santiago Sia

GOD IN PROCESS THOUGHT
CHARLES HARTSHORNE'S CONCEPT OF GOD (*editor*)

From Suffering to God

Exploring Our Images of God in the Light of Suffering

Marian F. Sia and Santiago Sia

St. Martin's Press

First published in Great Britain 1994 by
THE MACMILLAN PRESS LTD
Houndmills, Basingstoke, Hampshire RG21 2XS
and London
Companies and representatives
throughout the world

A catalogue record for this book is available
from the British Library.

ISBN 0–333–61638–3

Printed in Great Britain by
Ipswich Book Co Ltd
Ipswich, Suffolk

First published in the United States of America 1994 by
Scholarly and Reference Division,
ST. MARTIN'S PRESS, INC.,
175 Fifth Avenue,
New York, N.Y. 10010

ISBN 0–312–12185–7

Library of Congress Cataloging-in-Publication Data
Sia, Marian F.
From suffering to God : exploring our images of God in the light
of suffering / Marian F. Sia and Santiago Sia.
p.   cm.
Includes bibliographical references (p.   xxx–xxx) and index.
ISBN 0–312–12185–7
1. Suffering—Religious aspects—Christianity.   2. Theodicy.
3. Image of God.   I. Sia, Santiago.   II. Title.
BT732.7.S53   1994
231'.8—dc20   94–25373
                                                          CIP

To
the memory of

INNA

(Gregoria B. Sia)
mother and mother-in-law

whose counsel and life
taught us
to turn to God
in times of suffering

CONTENTS

ACKNOWLEDGEMENTS

One of the satisfactions of completing a piece of work is being able to acknowledge one's indebtedness to those who made it possible. The present work is no exception, and we gladly take this opportunity to express our gratitude for all the help and encouragement we received in the course of writing this book.

First of all, we would like to thank the very many individuals and groups—the oppressed, the victimised and the poor—who shared with us their experiences of suffering and challenged us to reflect on the topic of this book. Although we have not documented their stories and testimonies, they will recognise in these pages the lessons we have learned from them. We want to thank our families and friends whose example and counsel in the midst of suffering have been a constant inspiration to us. We would also like to express our gratitude to our numerous students and colleagues in the Philippines, Ireland, England, Poland, Belgium and the USA with whom we discussed many of the things which we say in this book. Their questions, comments and suggestions helped improve the manuscript. The institutions we have been associated with during the writing of this book also deserve our gratitude for their support: Terenure College, Dublin, Ireland, and Loyola Marymount University, Los Angeles, USA.

Many of the ideas in this book were first presented in papers or talks given at different locations and to various groups: St. Scholastica's Priory, Petersham, Massachusetts, USA; Catholic Teachers Federation in Birmingham and Coventry, England; Center for Process Studies, Claremont, California, USA; International Conference on Process, Peace and Human Rights, Kyoto, Japan; Second European Congress of URAM, Leuven, Belgium; Second Yoko Civilization International Conference, Takayama, Japan; International Symposium on Process Thought, Tokyo, Japan; Mater Dei Institute of Education, Dublin, Ireland; East Asian Pastoral Institute, Quezon City, Philippines; Katholieke Universiteit

Nijmegen and Rijksuniversiteit te Utrecht, The Netherlands. We are grateful for the invitations and for the opportunity to interact with those who attended these presentations. We also wish to express our thanks to Rev. Prof. Boleskaw Bartkowski, Prorector of Katolicki Uniwersytet Lubelski, Lublin, Poland for the honour of giving public lectures based on the subject matter of this book at their university. Discussions with their faculty and students, following each of the four lectures, helped us immensely. We are most appreciative of the Senior Research Fellowship awarded by the Katolieke Universiteit Leuven, Belgium, which gave us the opportunity to share our work with the faculty and graduate students of the Hoger Instituut voor Wijsbegeerte and to complete the manuscript. It certainly was an honour to do research in such a renowned academic institution.

Some of the chapters in this book were based on sections of articles of ours published in various journals but revised for this work. Our thanks to the editors of *Spirituality Today, Ultimate Reality and Meaning, New Blackfriars, Modern Theology, Process Studies, American Journal of Theology and Philosophy, The Clergy Review* (now *Priest and People*) and *Nederlands Theologisch Tijdschrift* for permission to make use of material which originally appeared in their journals.

Several individuals in one way or another facilitated the preparation of this book for publication. We want to thank them all, but especially Charles Hartshorne and John B. Cobb, Jr., who read the entire manuscript. We feel especially encouraged by their comments. Schubert Ogden, Jan Van der Veken, David Griffin, Mary Elizabeth Moore, Dermot Lane, Piotr Gutowski, Vincent Brümmer and others provided us with constructive comments and helpful suggestions on early drafts of parts of the manuscript. We have tried to incorporate them here. We appreciate the interest shown in our work by Belinda Holdsworth, Annabelle Buckley, John Smith and the staff of Macmillan. Their encouragement supported us along the way. This work and many others have benefited from Richard Morris' expertise with computers. We are truly grateful to him. We want to thank Julie Morris for the time spent poring over different drafts of the manuscript and for her insightful comments on it. We are also grateful to Edna Hastings, Bernadette Bernard, Margaret Edwards and Rita Dehaes for secretarial assistance. Our thanks also go to Gil Braganza and Eric

Young for their valuable help and to the library staffs of Loyola Marymount University, L.A., and of Katholieke Universiteit Leuven, Belgium, for getting many of our sources.

Our deepest gratitude, however, is reserved for Inna (Gregoria B. Sia), whose courage and vision in the midst of the trials and tribulations of life have taught us valuable lessons. This book is lovingly dedicated to her memory. We hope that in this small way, to paraphrase a saying, what she has left behind in our lives may help others find the way.

Before Another Dawn

by *'Marisan' Sia*

that awe-some sunrise here—
ever noticed it, Lord?
how the light streams out,
penetrating every nook,
passing out new cheer,
dissipating old fear
as the sun slowly rises!

> *well, it's like that, Lord.*
> *I mean, we human beings*
> *are searching for that sun in our lives—*
> > *to put meaning into our daily lives,*
> > *to bring cheer to us all.*

if we don't grasp it—
this meaning, that is—
nothing will look bright to us
*nothing will **ex-sist** for us.*

take away the sun—
you know what happens.
we turn to substitutes:
> *lighting candles*
> *switching on electricity*

> > *and we are contented—*
> > *at least for a time,*
> *knowing the sun will re-rise*
> *re-brightening*
> > *our world.*

and so we are given courage
to face another morn.

yes, Lord, that's what we are searching for
          meaning
          real meaning
to lace together all the seemingly
     in sig
          ni
       fi cant
     de
          tails
to re-make them into a whole.

for otherwise, we shall reach out for
evanescent substitutes.

as we grope about
we feel restless
dis contented
               lonely.

but
could it be that restlessness
frustration

loneliness

are woven so intimately into the cloth of life
that if we dare pull them out
we would be ruining the whole weave of an intricate pattern?

are they really the shady colours
balancing the light and loud-coloured ones?

     tell that to us, Lord, when things are bright—
     we'll agree perfectly with you.

     but explain that to us
     when these colours really dampen us
     and we'll just wonder—
     in unbelief, perhaps.

                    Ah, men!

INTRODUCTION

THINKING ABOUT GOD

It may sound like an extravagant claim, but it is probably true to say that each and every one of us has a certain image of God. This is not to say that we all accept the existence of a personal reality to whom various believers have given the name 'God'. But insofar as that word evokes a certain response from us, it must mean something. And behind the particular reaction, including rejection on the part of those who profess to be atheists or indifference on the part of those who regard themselves as agnostics, must lie certain preconceptions which explain the reaction. But like many others, our own images of God sometimes remain unexplored. Or more often we take them for granted because we do not appreciate the need to scrutinise them any further. Nevertheless, they often account for the way we conduct our lives or the way we try to make sense of life. Now and then the presumptions underlying certain images of God surface when we are confronted by situations which force us to look much more closely at the way we imagine God to be. We do not always welcome these 'confrontations,' but they serve the purpose of making explicit what we do not always advert to.

One such confrontation which can provoke us into making explicit certain presumptions regarding God is the phenomenon of atheism. The reasons behind someone's rejection of God require further exploration. Why does the atheist deny that there is a God? What model of God is operative in his or her mind? For it is not untrue to say that many times atheism is the rejection not of God but of certain claims being made by some believers, claims which should be examined more critically.[1] Again it is not unknown for theists to align themselves with atheism so as to remove many idolatrous misconceptions about God. As Voltaire once remarked, human beings have a tendency to fabricate God according to their image. Thus, it is alleged that 'in order to believe in God we must first disbelieve in the gods that we have contrived; we must begin by being atheists.'[2] But how can we know the difference between these idols and the living God?

Another situation which brings into the open certain presuppositions that we have regarding God occurs when we reflect on the relation between so-called secular matters and religious affairs. The excesses of religious leaders who insist that governments be run along theocratic lines have made us wary of linking politics with religion. And yet situations such as those in developing countries where Christians, including clergy and nuns, are taking an active role in political matters, make us question or at least take a second look at this separation between the secular and the sacred. Does it not betray an image of God whose domain is outside worldly affairs? But if God is being described as a liberating God, does that not imply that God uses every resource, even political action, to free people from all types of oppression and degradation? Such an understanding of an involved God has implications for our own conduct in the face of social injustice.[3]

More recently, we have been confronted by the accusation that the image of God being perpetuated by Western theism supports racial and gender bias. Theodore Walker, for instance, blames classical Western theism and its concept of God as abiding peaceably with, and even of being very supportive, of such oppressive activities as the enslavement of Africans and the genocide of native Americans.[4] Others have complained that the classical doctrine of God contains implicit and even explicit biases and vested interests and thus poses a threat to full human liberation. In 1973 Mary Daly wrote: 'when God is male, the male is God.'[5] It has been argued more recently by Sallie McFague and many others that the so-called patriarchal and white image of the divine being is not merely irrelevant and idolatrous, but it is also oppressive and dangerous since it may work against the continuation of life on earth.[6] Consequently, she calls for the development of new metaphors or models of God. As she puts it, 'in order to be faithful to the God of its tradition—the God on the side of life and its fulfillment—we must try out new pictures that bring the reality of God's love into the imaginations of the women and men of today.'[7]

These situations—and there are many others—bring to the fore certain claims which require further clarification.[8] We could, of course, ignore the demand to probe deeper into our images of God. After all, facing up to perplexing issues which demand a lot of thinking can be an onerous task. For some it may seem to be a useless exercise since it could lead nowhere; that is to say, it results in no clear-cut answers or any so-called significant conclusions.

But the danger with unexamined assumptions or claims is that they have the greater tendency to lead us astray. This is especially true with our images of God. As Terence E. Fretheim puts it, 'The images used to speak of God not only decisively determine the way one thinks about God, they have a powerful impact on the shape of the life of the believer.'[9] Although the pursuit of truth does not always lead to indisputable conclusions, we can at least be less unclear and inconsistent if we make the effort to reflect on our assumptions. We may discover that all along we have entertained beliefs which have to be discarded because they do not stand up under scrutiny or that given more information we may have to reshape our understanding of those beliefs. Or we may even continue to uphold them, but at least this time on more solid grounds.

As has already been pointed out, there is a need to clarify for ourselves our assumptions about God, whether these are religious or not. Life, with its ups and downs, has a way of presenting awkward questions about the kind of God we can or cannot believe in. And if we are serious about the intellectual credibility of our faith, then we should face up to the challenge to reflect on these matters. Michael Langford expresses this point well in his *Unblind Faith*: 'Unfortunately the history of Christianity and of many other religions is sprinkled with the dire consequences of blind faith and it is the horror of this spectacle that helps in large measure the rejection of all religion by many thoughtful people.'[10] While religious belief is not a purely rational enterprise, it does contain elements which require careful, deliberate, and logical thinking.[11]

Those of us with responsibility for the upbringing of the young, be it in our professional or domestic capacity, have an added reason for taking seriously the challenge to think through our presuppositions about God. The young have the habit of raising questions about life, questions which can at times be rather unnerving because they are penetrating. One such set of questions deals with our ideas of God. In their own way, for instance, many children ask about the problem of evil, about death and about God's involvement in life. It is a pity, not to say disastrous, if what is passed on to children are answers which have not been fully thought out. We are not referring to conclusive judgments (can we come up with any on these matters?) which we can convey to children but to ideas which have been given our personal attention. For unlike the passing on of information or the development of skills, educating the young in this context involves us much more personally.

Educators know that we have to deal with these questions at the children's level. And so we try to explain through stories, symbols and concrete examples. But it seems that what is sometimes overlooked is the development on the children's part of the awareness that our talk of God, hence our understanding of God, undergoes various stages. The initial stage when we resort to particular stories and very concrete representations of God is an important stage. Nevertheless, it is only *a* stage.[12] A time should come when we can outgrow many of the things we are taught about God at a very early age.[13] One wonders whether children as they grow up ought not to be encouraged to put aside their childish images of God which were called for at a certain stage of their development but which have now become irrelevant. That is to say, those beliefs and those ways of describing God, having served their purpose, should now be discarded.

The reason why it is important for us to bring home this awareness to those whose upbringing lies in our hands and why it is essential for us adults to do the same is that too often we forget that like every aspect of our life, there is a need to mature in the way we think about God. It is disappointing to come across people who have developed intellectually in other spheres but still cling to infantile images of God. It is not surprising when they feel bound to abandon a certain understanding of God which they cannot reconcile with their more developed ways of thinking. We are beginning to appreciate that education does not end with schooling, but we often ignore that this applies too to the way we describe God.

THE CHALLENGE OF SUFFERING

Perhaps the most significant challenge to our thinking about God occurs when we are faced with the reality of suffering and pain. The absurdity of the situation, especially if those who are in agony are clearly innocent victims, makes us wonder what kind of God would allow it. How can a God who is supposed to be all-loving and all-powerful tolerate so much misery in creatures? Thus, the problem of evil has challenged the minds of people down the ages. But what is causing more concern today, particularly in countries where there is wide-spread poverty and deprivation, is another dimension to this problem: the suffering of the innocent or in Adolphe Gesche's terms (and used by Gustavo Gutierrez) 'the evil of misfortune' (rather than the 'evil of guilt').[14] The existence of suffering continues to make us more conscious of the need to reconcile the idea of a provident and omnipotent God with the existence of so much unnecessary and often clearly unmerited misery in the world.

Thus, suffering challenges the way we describe God. In fact, suffering or the feeling of pain, whether mental or physical, has always been a source of serious and often perplexing questioning. We cannot help but wonder why there is so much suffering in the world. At times we may know the immediate cause, for instance, someone's foolish act; but this is small consolation because the knowledge of how something has resulted in a person's affliction is not sufficient to justify his or her plight. In other words, the reality of suffering demands not just an explanation but a justification. This is why the traditional distinction between moral evil (the consequence of human free acts) and natural evil (natural disasters which are considered to be outside reasonable human control) can sometimes be unhelpful. Even when we know how the suffering came about, its very existence will continue to trouble us. For it does not make sense that creatures should be prey to so much suffering.

A Theistic Problem

But why does suffering cause such existential questioning? Why is it problematic? Usually the reality of suffering is presented as a theistic problem in that, as has already been noted, its existence is irreconcilable with the belief in a truly benevolent *and* omnipotent God. It is held that an entirely righteous and loving God who has the power to abolish suffering would not wish to inflict it on creatures. Hume is commonly credited with formulating the problem in this way although earlier thinkers had already shown that suffering or evil in general is incompatible with the belief in a God possessing perfect goodness and power.[15] Theists, therefore, have felt particularly threatened on this point. As John Hick puts it, the problem 'sets up an internal tension to disturb [their] faith and to lay upon it a perpetual burden of doubt.'[16] To non-believers it stands as a major obstacle to religious commitment. It is understandable then that Jürgen Moltmann would claim that the question 'why do I suffer?' is the rock of atheism.[17] If indeed there is a God, how can God remain silent and inactive in the presence of such misery in the world? Accordingly, the problem of suffering has generally been discussed in the context of a theodicy. That is to say, explanations which are forthcoming are seen as attempts to defend God, not in the sense that God needs defending but rather in the sense that the be-lievers' portrayal of their God requires validation, i.e. that despite the presence of suffering one could justifiably continue to believe in such a God. Suffering has, therefore, been an issue among many philosophers and theologians.

But it is not only philosophers and theologians who have grappled with the question of belief or unbelief amidst suffering. David Jaspers' observation that 'literature and religion are never far apart'[18] is particularly true in this case. Literary writers have also dealt with this issue in their writings. Fyodor Dostoyevsky's novels are well-known for their religious themes. In *The Brothers Karamasov*, in particular, Dostoyevsky's characters represent different attitudes to the presence of so much misery in the world. Varying reactions, including belief and unbelief, are also illustrated by the characters of Albert Camus' *The Plague*. The novels of the Japanese writer Shusako Endo address the deep feelings of the suffering of his people. Similarly, the Korean poet Kim Chi-ha in his poem 'Declaration of Conscience' articulates the suffering of the minjung. Rejecting the false image of God perpetrated by the ruling classes, Kim shows God to be on the side of the minjung.

Perhaps another kind of protest to the theistic claim to a

provident God can be seen in Santiago's experience in Ernest Hemingway's *The Old Man and the Sea* and in Kino's life in John Steinbeck's *The Pearl*. In both books, the main characters start with an implicit belief in a caring God. Their recourse to that God seems initially to provide the answers to their hopes and aspirations only to have them dashed again. Santiago in Hemingway's novel manages to catch the giant marlin he has prayed for; but the long journey home, the struggle with the sharks and the gradual disintegration of his great prize do not suggest a benevolent God but one who is determined to make fun of the human individual's valiant efforts. In Steinbeck's work Kino's pearl seems to be the longed-for response to his request for help to pay for his son's medical treatment. But the consequences of obtaining such a miraculous gift are tragic: he loses his home and simple possessions, he becomes an outcast and he finally loses his son, though cured of his illness, to a pursuer-turned-killer. Both writers, therefore, question the theistic description of God as one who *truly* cares for us. Once again the onus has been laid on the shoulders of theists to defend their portrayal of God.

A Human Problem

But while theists should indeed expect to feel threatened on this point, it ought not to be forgotten that whether we believe in a God or not, we will still find suffering problematic and to a large extent absurd. We will still ask the same fundamental question simply because suffering cuts across our understanding of 'how things ought to be.' Human nature is such that we are sensitive to and disposed towards certain standards, e.g. moral or aesthetic. We may not always pursue these standards or even want to do so especially since we are not always clear as to what they are. But basically we are creatures who can distinguish between what we believe *ought to be* and what *in fact is the case*. It is this capacity to distinguish between the two and the realisation that suffering is an impediment to the fulfillment of that which ought to be that makes us wonder why it is not otherwise. Even the atheist or non-believer who challenges the theist sees the problem in terms of this distinction. Hence, we all ask: what stops the fulfillment of what ought to happen? What is the reason for its non-fulfillment?

Why is the situation the way it is and not otherwise?

That the reality of suffering is just as much a human as a theistic problem should help us to see that some theistic explanations, such as that suffering is part of God's plan as if it were deliberately willed by God, are not only misguided but also insensitive. They are misguided because they give the wrong idea of God and insensitive because they belittle the tragedy of suffering. Or to regard suffering as punishment from God as Edgar in *King Lear* does to justify the blinding of his father who had an illegitimate son[19] is to commit an injustice to God and to ourselves. In any attempt therefore to meet the challenge of suffering we should be conscious that suffering poses difficulties for us all insofar as we are humans and not merely because some of us believe that there is a God. Suffering mars our understanding of how reality should be, an understanding that arises from being the kind of creatures that we are.

Suffering as a Theoretical Issue and a Practical Demand

For theists and non-theists alike, therefore, the reality of suffering creates difficulties. Its existence is to some extent an intellectual puzzle for human beings. Because human beings are thinkers, they are being called upon to resolve certain inconsistencies caused by the reality of suffering. Hence, we need to find an answer.[20] In this sense the search for an answer is really a search for a solution, i.e. an explanation that would establish the logical soundness of our claims. David Griffin is perfectly right in arguing that 'a great amount of evil is aggravated by the thoughts and feelings that we have by virtue of our rational capacity for generalizing and comparing what is with what might have been' and in stressing that 'questions about evil always implicitly contain theoretical affirmations.'[21]

But we are not just thinking beings who have the need to reconcile contradictions in our thinking, to untangle the knots, as it were. We are also agents. This is why the reality of suffering demands a practical answer from us; that is, a response to change the situation. We are being challenged to take effective measures, if not to eliminate it completely, at least to minimise it. Neglect of this side of the problem can result, as indeed it unfortunately has, in an endeavour to meet the intellectual challenge of suffering by saying that we need not be overanxious about its presence here because everything will be rectified in the next world.[22] Although this may not have been intended by the belief in an afterlife, it conveys nevertheless the mistaken impression that we do not have to face up to our responsibility to make this world a happier place for everyone to live in. As agents, we ought to do something about the suffering, misery and sad plight of countless individuals. And many times we are in a position to remove the causes of such suffering. We should—because often we can—reduce the gravity and extent of suffering also brought about by the action of other creatures and by natural phenomena.

At times, however, taking up the practical challenge of suffering will take the form of siding with the victim. For Tarrou in Camus' novel, *The Plague*, this is the only possible response to the suffering in the world. For Job's friends, the silent sharing in his misfortune showed an attitude of respectful compassion and a manifestation of fellowship.[23] The amount of good that results from the way some people react to tragedies is another way of meeting the practical challenge of suffering and of rising above its absurdity. Solidarity with those who are suffering, victimised or alienated is not an empty gesture. The lives of many people are an eloquent testimony. It is to their credit that what initially was a handicap became the means for transforming their own and other people's lives.

EXPLORING ANOTHER DIMENSION OF THE PROBLEM

Over the years the existence of suffering in the world we live in and its challenge to our images of God have engaged our attention. Our interest in this topic has been stimulated by the experiences of those with whom we worked and lived or whom we taught. Often their lives were shattered by the 'slings and arrows of outrageous fortune' but they found in their God not only comfort but also the motivation to transform the situation. The commitment and dedication of these individuals and groups inspired us when we ourselves were caught up in the maelstroms of life. We felt, and continue to feel, challenged by people like Victor and Irene Chero who said to John Paul II: 'We suffer affliction, we lack work, we are sick. Our hearts are crushed by suffering as we see our tubercular wives giving birth, our children dying, our sons and daughters growing up weak and without a future. But despite all this, we believe in the God of life.'[24] Countless others have made and continue to make the same profession of faith. Sharing in their concerns, we have reflected on their questions. We have listened to their answers and developed them by bringing to bear on their insights the academic disciplines we had been trained in. As we tried to learn from them, they also heard and sometimes heeded our voices. This work, therefore, is a result of that interchange. Each chapter in this book was initially written by one of us, but since we have read and revised each other's work, we regard this book as a joint undertaking.

We are interested in exploring another dimension of the challenge of suffering brought to our attention by the experiences of those ordinary believers we mentioned above. Whereas atheism, given the presence of considerable misery and evil in the world, protests against belief in God, our aim is to give due regard to the experiences of many people who continue to believe in God despite suffering, impoverishment and oppression. But unlike traditional theism, this work starts not with a developed concept of God but with reflections on the experience of suffering and asks what it can disclose about God. This approach has led to a conceptualisation, different from that of classical theism, of the images of God which emerged from these reflections.

Our explorations start with literary works because we believe that these are particularly rich in imagery. They capture the concreteness of the questions many people ask. More significantly, we concur with David Jasper's claim regarding the value of literature for theological reflections: 'In literature we glimpse, at times, the fulfilment of our nature, cast in the imaginative genius of great art, and continuing to persuade us of the value and ultimate truth of the theological enterprise as a seeking for utterance of the divine mystery as it is known and felt in our experience.'[25] We then turn to theology and philosophy to articulate the issues and to develop possible answers. In this context we agree with what Whitehead has said: 'Philosophy is akin to poetry. Philosophy is the endeavour to find a conventional phraseology for the vivid suggestiveness of the poet. It is the endeavour to reduce Milton's "Lycidas" to prose, and thereby to produce a verbal symbolism manageable for use in other connections of thought.'[26] In this way we would like to think that this effort on our part contributes to an interdisciplinary approach to a theme of common interest to literature, theology and philosophy. Our present use of these disciplines follows the way we understand the relationship between them. [27]

A book on suffering always raises certain expectations. It is important, therefore, at the outset, to be clear about the limitations of this work. It is *not* our intention here to prove, despite the reality of evil, that there is a God. That issue is beyond the scope of this work and of our capabilities. Nor is it our plan to provide yet another solution to the problem of evil, as least as it is understood traditionally, nor to suggest strategies to eliminate evil in its diverse forms.[28] We wish we were in a position to do that. We do not pretend to be able to offer comfort to those afflicted or in sorrow for whatever reason nor to put on record the experiences of those whose sufferings we have come to share. Their experiences are much too concrete and painful for us to do them justice. Our aim in undertaking this work is a more modest one but, we hope, no less significant. As we have already stated, because we continue to admire the many believers who have suffered and undergone persecution yet have persisted in belief in their God we want to pursue the question: what kind of God can we continue to believe in despite all the suffering around us? The title of this work 'From Suffering to God' indicates the particular perspective adopted throughout as well as the context while the subtitle 'Exploring Our Images of God in the Light of Suffering' suggests both our intention and our approach.

Liberation theologies, particularly in Latin America, have acknowledged the centrality of this topic by claiming that knowledge of God today is discerned in the midst of suffering.[29] Gustavo Gutierrez expresses this very forcefully:

> How are we to talk about a God who is revealed as love in a situation characterized by poverty and oppression? How are we to proclaim the God of life to men and women who die prematurely and unjustly? How are we to acknowledge that God makes us a free gift of love and justice when we have before us the suffering of the innocent? What words are we to use in telling those who are not even regarded as persons that

they are the daughters and sons of God? These are key questions being asked in the theology that has been forming in Latin America and in other places throughout the world where the situation is the same.[30]

Juan Luis Segundo's *Our Idea of God*, Gustavo Gutierrez' *On Job: God-Talk and the Suffering of the Innocent* and *The God of Life* and many others have focused on this very issue. Other books coming from that part of the world such as Antonio Perez-Esclarín's *Atheism and Liberation*, Victorio Araya's *God of the Poor*, the collective volume titled *The Idols of Death and the God of Life,* and Ronaldo Muñoz' *God of Christians* have likewise shown the urgency of the task, to paraphrase Gutierrez, of speaking of God amidst wide-spread suffering, deprivation and oppression.[31] Asian theologians, for whom suffering too is a felt reality, have likewise been reflecting not only on the challenge of poverty but also on the religious answers which arise from a plurality of religions in Asia. Aloysius Pieris' *An Asian Theology of Liberation* is a fine example of the work being done by Asian theologians in this area. The publication of *Minjung Theology* showed how Korean Christians are dealing with the relationship between oppression and their Christian faith by turning to their own cultures. The proceedings of the 1979 Asian Theological Conference, edited by Virginia Fabella as *Asia's Struggle for Full Humanity* and A.A. Yewangoe's book, *Theologia Crucis in Asia: Asian Christian Views on Suffering in the Face of Overwhelming Poverty and Multifaceted Religiosity* provide an overview of the reflections of a number of Asian Christians on the challenge of suffering to the Christian faith. We have profited from reading these books as well as many others. Moreover, we have become more aware of the importance of the issues being raised in the present work.

Contemporary christology, characterised by the recovery of the importance and centrality of the resurrection of Jesus brought about by the renewal in biblical studies, is once again turning its attention to a theology of the cross. This is fortunate since the neglect of this theological thinking could lead to certain distortions of aspects of Christian belief, not least of these being the doctrine of the resurrection itself.[32] It could also deprive us of an important source for thinking about God for as some theologians like

Walter Kasper, Jürgen Moltmann, Aloysius Pieris and Jon Sobrino maintain, the cross of Christ is the final self-revelation of God. There is a need, therefore, to inquire into what we can know about God through and in the Cross of Christ. As Aloysius Pieris puts it, 'The crisis in the modern world is not the lack of prayer but its advocacy of a fictitious Christ, a Jesus minus his cross, thus seeking him where he is not found. Instead, Jesus can be found in the real, i.e. unjust, world where he hangs crucified, calling us to join his struggle.'[33] While the present work is not specifically a work in christology (nor incidentally, in trinitarian theology), we hope that it addresses some of the issues which need to be worked out in what Dermot Lane calls 'a theology of the darkness of the Cross.'[34]

In line with what has been said above regarding the relationship between literature, theology and philosophy, the book is divided into two parts:

Part I contains literary and descriptive reflections on the experiences of suffering. Here we present and analyse the concerns, fears and hopes as expressed in selected literary and theological sources.

In Chapter 1 'Reflections on Job's and Hopkins' Question' we focus on the question raised by these two authors as they come to grips, because of their suffering, with the nature of the God on whom they had relied. In Chapter 2 'Literary Meditations on Death and Christian Hope' we follow up on their question within the context of the reality of death. No doubt, for many people the greatest source of suffering is the inevitability of death, theirs as well as that of others. After citing some attitudes to death, we concentrate on selected poems (making use of literary explication to bring out the meanings of various lines) by Vaughan, Donne and Herbert and listen to them as they ponder on their fears and their hopes. The symbols and metaphors they use point to a certain Christian understanding of a God who liberates them, thus giving them hope. Chapter 3 then draws the previous chapters together by articulating and developing the issues implied by these reflections and meditations. Called 'What Kind of God?: an Inquiry into the Challenge of Suffering' this chapter serves as the focus of this book. Here we try to show that an important challenge that needs to be investigated and met, given the presence of suffering, is discovering the kind of God in whom we can credibly continue to believe. This chapter also discusses further our approach in this work: we look into the practical responses often made by theists to the existence of suffering and inquire into the theoretical affirmations about God underlying such responses. In other words, the question for us is: what images of God lie behind the concrete responses to suffering? We discuss the image of God as co-sufferer (because often the response to suffering in others is through sympathetic participation in their plight) and as liberator (since many times what is required is to liberate others from their miserable situation). Towards the end of the chapter we briefly set out the methodology that informs our task of developing these images (or any other images) of God.

Part II is a theological and philosophical attempt to think through the issues which have emerged in the previous Part. In putting forward our position and developing some answers, we turn primarily to Hartshorne's neoclassical philosophy and Latin American liberation theology.

Chapter 4 examines the possibility of using human reason for this task. This chapter is called for because of the objections brought up by many regarding the role of reason in religious matters. We discuss how and to what extent one can use reason in trying to develop our descriptions of God. In setting out our view, we interact with Hartshorne's metaphysical God-talk. We then inquire in Chapter 5: 'The Concept of an Immutable God' into the adequacy of the classical theistic concept of an immutable God, dominant in Western theism, to make sense of the images of God specified earlier. We cite the objections put forward by Hartshorne and the Latin American liberation theologians. In their view, such a concept of God fails to do justice to our experiences of suffering. In the next two chapters we then discuss an alternative which draws on both Hartshorne's conceptuality *and* Latin American liberation theology. Chapter 6: 'Reformulating the Meaning of God's Compassionate Love' suggests how one can more meaningfully develop the image of God as co-sufferer. But since it is not sufficient to talk of God's compassion, Chapter 7: 'Participating in God's Liberative Act' turns to the issue of God's work of liberating us from suffering. We find the symbol of God as liberator affirmed by Latin American liberation theologians to be particularly appropriate. Moreover, we suggest that it can be developed further by turning to Hartshorne's concept of universal creativity. Basically, we argue that the creativity of human beings is the reason why all of us must feel obliged to transform the world. We also try to show that our creativity enables us to participate in God's liberative act. By interacting with both Hartshorne's neoclassical theism and Latin American liberation theology we hope to show not only the complementarity of these two schools of thought but also the conceptual development they can offer to the images which we focused on in Part I.

The final chapter entitled 'Some Concluding Remarks' sums up our findings regarding the key issues of the book: the problem of evil, the task of developing our images of God, and the role and status of concepts of God.

Part I

FROM SUFFERING...

Reflecting on Our Experiences

of Suffering

Chapter 1

REFLECTIONS ON JOB'S AND HOPKINS' QUESTION

QUESTIONS

A question is revealing: it not only asks for information, but often also discloses what is going on in the mind of the questioner. From the questions that are being posed we are given some insight into the questioner's thoughts. This is even more true if we pay attention to the very way the questions are phrased.[1] A question, furthermore, sometimes shows up the questioner's prior knowledge of what he or she is asking about. Hence, there can really be no 'stupid' question, only perhaps an idle one, for a question bears within it an implicit answer, no matter how vague it may be when the question is asked. For if the questioner had no knowledge at all of the answer, he or she would not have been able to raise the question in the first place. To ask 'Why?' for instance, presupposes a knowledge of an observed fact, that something is, so that the question 'why?' is really a progression, an explicitation.[2]

A question also points to an inquiring mind. To ask a question means to search for more; it shows that one has perceived behind the apparent and has gone beyond instinct. Perhaps this is why human beings are regarded as questioners; humans are always searching for answers. (Significantly, *question* and *quest* are related.) Because they are endowed with the capacity to wonder, they have reflected. This has caused them to look for deeper meaning, to be unsatisfied with what is transitory, and to seek what lasts.

Raising a question usually leads one to new and deeper knowledge or, at times, to a new awareness of what one had known previously. The latter is best exemplified in the often-heard expression, 'Oh, of course, I knew that before!' It is a sudden recognition of what one already knew. Sometimes, however, a question is not meant to be answered, perhaps not directly. Sometimes we search even if we can expect no answers, at least no immediate answers. This is because there are some questions to which no answers are at hand, though only for a while, but the answers may emerge later if we chance to glance back.

There are times when in raising questions one is transformed. Then the questions, viewed in the light of one's transformed state, become irrelevant. Perhaps this is because one becomes aware of the 'wider context.' Such an experience, for example, occurs when one is 'plunged into the depths.' Profound questions about the meaning of life are often asked in moments of distress, anxiety, and suffering. But strangely enough, when one is back in 'good form,' everything seems clear again and the questions that were so pressing before lose their urgency and even their importance. This is so because one has been transformed rather than because one has simply returned to one's usual self. One has not gone back but gone further. One's answer came in the form of a transformation.

EXISTENTIAL QUESTIONS

But what questions do we raise? Humans, it may be argued, have the distinction of being perhaps the only kind of creatures who can ask fundamental questions about existence. While requiring basic items such as food and drink in order to survive, humans nevertheless are often made aware that the fulfillment of human existence needs more than these. Shakespeare expresses this well when he makes Hamlet cry out: 'What is a man,/ If his chief good and market of his time/ Be but to sleep and feed? A beast, no more.'[3] It seems that humans ask for more. Unfortunately, the answer to these existential questions is rarely clear. What is less unclear is a certain uneasiness or even dissatisfaction with merely satisfying one's immediate needs.[4] Hence, questions like: what makes us truly human? is life worth living? is there a purpose to life? are asked. Humans, unlike other living beings, can and sometimes do wonder about the significance of being alive and interacting with others. In short, a specifically human concern is whether life itself has any ultimate meaning.

It would be naive to think that we humans always ask these questions in such an explicit way. Nor do we address the issue of ultimate meaning with uniform concern and interest. Moreover, an examination of our list of priorities in life would hardly reveal such in-depth existential values. In fact, we generally seem to be contented with setting ourselves certain goals, striving after them and, when attained, with looking for others.[5] Nonetheless, the question as to how life can have any meaning at all is a human one not only because, as far as we know, humans alone are capable of reflecting on it but also because every human being—although at times implicitly rather than explicitly—is confronted by it.[6] As a matter of fact, we more or less presume the meaningfulness of life by carrying on with our daily routine. We assume that there is some sense to life by engaging in the various activities that we do. Otherwise, we would not do them. This is not to say that when queried we can always provide an adequate or enlightening reason. Yet the fact that we are actually carrying them out implies some confidence in the meaningfulness of our specific tasks and even of life in general.[7]

JOB'S QUESTION

Job is a very good example of someone who asks such existential questions when he finds himself in a situation where he is forced to speak out and hurl accusing questions at God.[8] He raises one of the most difficult questions. Because of his unique experience, he is unsatisfied with the usual answers to the suffering of the innocent. He cries out for a more satisfactory solution. In fact, he comes to the point of challenging the Almighty. Job's questioning illustrates the kind of questioning that results in a transformation. In his questioning, Job is changed radically. He is brought to a certain experience that reduces his previous questions into insignificance.

The question that is usually made to appear as the question with which Job is grappling is the suffering of the innocent: How can one reconcile the idea of a good God, without whose will and knowledge nothing can happen, with the idea of a person who has not committed a sin and yet is made to suffer severely and for a prolonged period? To maintain that this is the theme around which the Book of Job revolves is certainly true. The author takes pains to point out that not only does Job claim that he is innocent but also that Yahweh regards him so (1:8, 2:3; cf. 1:1). With this consciousness of his innocence, Job cries out for the reason of his affliction because it appears to him utterly nonsensical that he, an innocent man, should be made to suffer.

Job's question goes much deeper, however, as the very analysis of the question of suffering will indicate. It raises the associated question of the nature and character of God and how human beings stand in relation to God. Job's suffering, then, is more than just the physical agony he is experiencing. He is racked and torn mentally as well. He is in mental agony not just because he is searching for the meaning of his sufferings, but more because he cannot comprehend the nature of this God he is dealing with.

His friends propose some reasons for his sufferings. These are the traditional answers to the question of suffering. One reason given is that suffering or punishment is traceable to a guilty deed. Especially in the case of a monstrous human crime, it was believed that sooner or later disaster would return to the person who had committed it. For this reason Job's friends insist that he examine his conscience to find out what guilty deed he has done (4:7-9; 8:20; 11:6) and to renounce it (11:14). Only then would he find peace again.

The explanation of suffering as corrective is also brought up. Sometimes suffering comes to people for apparently no reason; that is to say, there seems to be no recognisable sin. Yahweh was believed in this case to be secretly but, in the end, clearly pursuing the task of correcting men and women. Job is reminded of this (5:17-27; 33:15-30) and urged to return to God, to prayer, and to cultic confession. What is presupposed here is that Job's life was not in order. For suffering, according to this explanation, was being offered in order to 'turn man aside from his deed and cut off pride from man' (33:17).

Job's friends also recall the doctrine of the sages, the doctrine of material rewards and punishments. They assert the correlation between the morality of people and their well-being: good people are prosperous and the prosperous are morally good. If the wicked appear to prosper, this is only for a while. Their prosperity cannot endure; hence, to them death is dreadful, for it means leaving behind their possessions. Disaster always lurks for the wicked (20:4-29).

Job's friends maintain the connection between sin and suffering. In their view every person who suffers has sinned; there was no such thing as a good person whose situation is evil. Job, who claims to be innocent, was a contradiction because, according to the traditional understanding of which his friends are exponents, innocence and suffering together are impossible. The blame must be on Job, the friends argue, for it could not be on God. God is righteous, whereas human beings are not (5:6-7; 34:12). Hence, his friends ask him to submit to God's correction so as to win God's favor again.

Job insists otherwise. He protests his innocence (9:20-21; 27:5-6, chapters 29 and 31). He is not aware of any crime or misdeed. His friends are accusing him of an imagined, or cleverly deduced, wickedness. He believes he is in the right with regard to his relationship with God because he feels himself unable to admit in his own case the correspondence which is asserted by his friends between guilt and punishment. If indeed his suffering comes from God, then it must have some other reason or purpose, but not his guilt. He wants his claim of standing in a right relationship to God, however, not to be based on his own estimate of himself. He wants to find some reassurance in a declaration from God. It was a reassurance which had been available to him long before, enough to enable him to claim himself to be innocent. But Job is aware that it is the justificatory verdict of God that matters, not his own protestations of innocence.

A DEEPER QUESTION

If it is not Job who is at fault, then it must be God. Cost what it may, he must force God to speak since he cannot make sense of his afflictions. This distress leads him to an even deeper problem: what kind of God is he involved with? His experience seems to contradict his belief in a just God. For how could there be such a God when it is obvious that there is no justice in a world where the wicked prosper and the just suffer and suffer intensely?

He could not reconcile this God of his experience with the God of tradition who was very much involved in human history and had in fact entered into a relationship with the people of Israel. The God of old was always identified as being on the side of the poor and the sick. God was their saviour. To those who had been deprived of justice, God was their defending counsel. Yet this God whom Job is experiencing now seems to be capricious, to be toying with him, an innocent person, and acting more like Thomas Hardy's 'Vast Imbecility,' a mighty builder but impotent caretaker, who 'Framed us in jest, and left us now to hazardry'[9] or Pietro's God who plays a cruel dice game with creatures in Morris West's novel, *Lazarus*.[10] Gloucester's description of the gods also seems to be more applicable to this God he is experiencing: 'As flies to wanton boys, are we to th' gods;/They kill us for their sport.'[11] Is God truly capricious? Job comes to the point of accusing God of appearing as a sinister enemy. Instead of caring for a creature, God is like a capricious tyrant (9:18-19), a savage beast (16:7, 9), a treacherous assailant (16:12-14). In a display of wild imagination, Job likens himself to the mythical sea-monster (Tiamat or Rahab), the arch-enemy of God, over whom God has set a watch (7:11-12).

Job's question, therefore, assumes larger proportions: How credible is God? What does God mean to him, to Job? This is what has become problematical. Perhaps there is no essential difference between good and evil. God seems to destroy both the blameless and the wicked; the same fate seems to await both (9:22-23). And yet, being a believer, Job cannot accept this. He believes in the supreme moral will of the Lord. But why the apparent ineffectiveness of this moral will in human life? If the will of the Lord is for good, and if the divine power is supreme, then why does not the good that God wills come into being and why does God not remove evil?

Job demands an answer. He cannot understand and with desperation he complains: 'I cry to thee and thou dost not answer me' (30:20), and again: 'Oh, that I had one to hear me! Here is my signature! Let the Almighty answer me!'(31:35). Yet God seems to turn a deaf ear.

But God *does* answer. The answer given is not to the question why the innocent Job is suffering, but to the more profound point which Job had raised: God's nature and the human being's relationship to this God. The response is at the same time a rebuke and a challenge to Job. Instead of a clear-cut reason for his suffering, Job is brought to an existential awareness of how he stands with God: the God who is wise enough and powerful enough to be able to govern the universe in all its complexity must be great enough to direct the course of human events. Human beings cannot comprehend God's purpose; they cannot penetrate the secrets of God's providence. Human wisdom consists in serving God, not in being equal to God in the knowledge of divine providence. In the face of this experience, Job's response is one of faith and humility (42:1-6).

The answer which Job receives is not in the form of words but in the form of an experience; that is, a realisation of creaturely existence in the presence of the Creator.[12] It is not the time for questions but for faith and humility. Job comes to the stage where his original question of why he is suffering in spite of being innocent becomes irrelevant. He has been transformed and in the context of his changed state, that question slips into obscurity. He has learned that 'the beginning of wisdom is the fear of the Lord.' Thus he withdraws his question because he has grasped that he is a creature and his destiny is well protected by this mysterious God who demands complete surrender on Job's part.

'I HAVE HEARD OF THEE BUT NOW I SEE'

The Book of Job offers many points worth reflecting on. It is no wonder that it seems to have a lasting significance. Whoever wrote the book—and did it with such style that commentators refer to its literary merits[13]—had remarkably sensitive insights into human problems. The author deals with these as one who really appreciates the complexity of human nature.

In raising the problem of suffering, the author touched upon one of the most bothersome human questions. The problem is even more acute for somebody who, like Job, believes in an all-good and all-powerful God, because the reality of evil and suffering is a direct challenge to that belief. As Gustavo Gutierrez puts it, 'The problem of speaking correctly about God amid unjust suffering is not limited to the case of Job, but is a challenge to every believer.'[14] Theists, therefore, have turned to the Book of

Job for an answer to this question. Their reactions have varied depending on how acceptable or unacceptable they have found the response that the author gives to the question of Job's suffering.

But, as we have noted, the author of Job seems to have been concerned with a much more fundamental question: what is one's relationship with God? Job's suffering had provoked that more basic question. Perhaps this is the reason why what is offered to Job is not an explanation of his miserable plight but an experience that enables him to cope with it. The series of questions that Job raises leads him to an existential awareness that the God who is able to govern the entire universe with much care and wisdom certainly provides for human beings as well as the rest of creation. This awareness does not really 'solve' the problem although to some extent it 'dissolves' it, as it were. In the greater insight into the kind of relationship that he has with God, Job's original question somehow fades into the background. Now he can truly claim that he is in touch with God, not just that he has heard of God. In his suffering Job experiences God differently. He wanted to know why he was suffering, but he ends up relating more to his God. He was dissatisfied with the answers provided by his friends because these were attempts to justify suffering, but what matters more is his relationship with this God.

HOPKINS' QUESTION

Gerard Manley Hopkins asks his God a question similar to Job's. In his sonnet 'Thou art indeed just, Lord' Hopkins explains his wretched plight to God.[15] He seems much worse off than the wicked despite his efforts. Thus, he remonstrates with God who seems to permit the wicked to prosper and thrive while all his own efforts are thwarted. Hopkins finds himself unable to accept this situation; having devoted himself to God's service by becoming a priest, he expects more from God. Although he is complaining, his tone like Job's nevertheless expresses reverence rather than utter despair. Knowing God's goodness and trusting in God's ability to rectify things, he can pray that God would inspire him to achieve something of value.

The Latin quotation at the very beginning of the sonnet is

taken from the Vulgate and comes from Jeremiah 12:1.[16] In fact, Jeremiah 12 seems to be the basis of the entire sonnet:

> Thou indeed, O Lord, art just, if I plead with thee, but yet I will speak what is just to thee; why doth the way of the wicked prosper: why is it well with all them that transgress and do wickedly? Thou has planted them, and they have taken root: they prosper and bring forth fruit: Thou art near in their mouth and far from their reins. And thou, O Lord, has known me, thou has seen me, and proved my heart with thee (Jer. 12:13).

Right from the beginning Hopkins asserts his belief in God's justice. He is convinced that if he should 'contend' (line 1), i.e. debate a matter with God, God would listen and be fair. Accordingly, he has the courage to make his plea which he believes to be 'just' (line 2). Paul Mariani describes Hopkins as 'pleading in the role of a skillful *advocatus* before the *dominus*.'[17] Hopkins is seeking an answer to his question: 'Why do sinners' ways prosper? and why must/Disappointment all I endeavor end?' (lines 3 and 4). In putting his case so directly to God, Hopkins shows his willingness to believe in a fair system.

His reverence for God is noticeable in his use of 'sir' (line 2). This reverence remains in evidence when he addresses God: 'O thou my friend' (line 5): there is love between the speaker and his Lord. If God were his enemy (judging by the way God treats him as friend), could God possibly mistreat Hopkins any more than God seems already to be doing? Behind these lines one can hear the echo of the familiar saying: 'With friends like you, who needs enemies?' The extent of Hopkins' suffering is coming to the fore.[18] Since one justly expects better treatment from one's friends than from one's enemies, Hopkins becomes more hurt when he realises that those who do wrong prosper while he who has committed his whole life to God's service does not. At this point in the poem Hopkins' feelings are so intense that the structure of the poem reflects them. The lines cannot contain the feelings and they run on with an enjambed line carrying the speaker's protest into the sestet: '...Oh, the sots and thralls of lust/Do in spare hours more thrive than I that spend,/Sir, life upon thy cause...' (lines 7-9). Hopkins conveys his frustration and disgust that 'the sots and thralls of lust,' i.e. drunkards and slaves, prosper without even trying while he fails despite his best endeavours.[19]

The poem was written in spring in Dublin (17 March 1889), a few months before Hopkins' death. The season of spring as well as the plant imagery in the Jeremiah passage may account in part for Hopkins' turning to nature in the sestet of the poem:

> . . . See, banks and brakes
> Now, leavèd how thick! lacèd they are again
> With fretty chervil, look, and fresh wind shakes
>
> Them; birds build—but not I build, no, but strain,
> Time's eunuch, and not breed one work that wakes.
> (lines 9-13)[20]

Here Hopkins is once more taken up with the beauty and bounty of nature, a sentiment which can be seen in many of his poems (for example, 'God's Grandeur,' 'Pied Beauty,' and 'Spring'). This shift from religion to nature in this part of the sonnet enables Hopkins yet again to combine two of his great strengths in this one poem—the power of his religious poetry and the beauty of his nature poetry. The image of nature in this poem is one of lushness and great productivity and contrasts starkly with the poet's own unproductive stasis. As John Pick puts it, Hopkins 'contrasts his own interior desert with the fecundity around him.'[21] Hopkins points out that the leaves are being shaken by the 'fresh wind' (line 11). His use of the adjective 'fresh' gives the picture of energy, movement and newness in nature unlike his own stale plight. We sense the essence, i.e. the 'whatness'—inscape, of the wind and its power breathing new life into things. Nature is thus renewed.

But Hopkins returns to his frustration. While birds build, he himself does not.[22] The nesting image augments the fertility and creativity of nature and underscores Hopkins' frustration in not being able to achieve or accomplish such security for himself. He is trying hard, but all his efforts leave him straining as 'Time's eunuch' unable to 'breed one work that wakes' (line 13).[23] His enslavement, unlike that of 'the sots and thralls of lust,' does not produce any success.[24]

Hopkins makes a final plea: 'Mine, O thou lord of life, send my roots rain.' Calling the Lord 'mine' and 'lord of life,' Hopkins indicates his close relationship with God and his belief and trust in God. Hopkins is like a plant without water.[25] This desire for 'rain' is a desire for the life-giving force of water, so necessary to nature for spurting growth in spring. Spiritually, it is a desire for grace which can rejuvenate. Divine inspiration will help Hopkins' priestly and poetic life.

The last line is distinct from the rest of the sonnet. It encapsulates a plea from his heart to God to justly reward the just. It reinforces the theme of the poem—justice—and reaffirms the poet's belief in his opening assertion: 'Thou are indeed just, Lord, if I contend/With thee; but, sir, so what I plead is just' (lines 1-2).

A QUESTION WITHOUT AN ANSWER?

It would be presumptuous to conclude that Job and Hopkins answer the question of suffering in its various forms.[26] Being assured of God's providence or justice will not silence our questioning. The question will continue to bother us again and again because suffering, especially that of the innocent, seems irrational and unjustifiable. Like Pietro we will still ask: 'Why, why, why? We live in faith and hope, we are the givers of love. Why is this torment visited upon us and upon our children?'[27] The reality of suffering is one of the facts about life that may escape a solution but not an investigation. Hence, one may rightly suspect any allegation that the existence of suffering is a pseudo-problem or the wrong question. It is a real problem. When one experiences excruciating pain or watches helplessly the agony and misery of others, then one realises how genuine the problem of suffering is. Anybody who tries to make light of someone else's miseries through well-intentioned interpretations should try exchanging places with the sufferer.

It ought to be pointed out, furthermore, that we have the obligation to remove the causes of suffering whenever possible. Especially where suffering is the consequence of injustice and selfishness, then we must not only alleviate suffering but also actively seek to root out its causes. Accepting the fruits of people's wicked deeds will only strengthen their greed and perpetuate their crime. We should feel obliged to make this world a happier place in which to live for everyone. Human creative powers are meant to be used to reduce the gravity and extent of suffering brought about by evil people or by natural causes. Although this world may never be perfect, it can be less imperfect, thanks to what women and men, individually and collectively, can do.

But there is another side to this quest for an answer to suffering. It may account for the change of direction in the mind of the author of Job when he dealt with that question and for Hopkins' firm belief in God's justice. For it seems that the question of suffering is one of those questions mentioned at the beginning of this chapter to which we can expect no ready answers, yet they can transform us. The change that comes about in us makes us look back only to realise that the questions we have raised now appear so superfluous.

When the 'chips are down' (as they were for Job and Hopkins), when our sufferings make us see only a very hazy future, then we tend to ask whether life has meaning at all. At times like this the meaninglessness-of-it-all makes its painful presence felt. Then we are tempted to call it quits, wondering whether the struggle is worthwhile. When port and home seem distant and the boat we are in is rocked by angry waves and tossed about by strong gales and rough seas, then we can get sick and feel tempted to jump overboard. Only the stout-hearted will want to hang on and sail on. And yet when everything is calm again, when the stormy weather breaks up to give way to sunny spells, then life again becomes not only bearable but exciting and the light that glows from life seems to dispel the gloom. Everything stands out again so clearly that we begin to wonder why we had questioned whether there was any meaning in life itself. Everything is so buoyant once more, everything is so meaningful again.

Some would call this experience simply the 'different moods' or the 'ups and downs' of life. But it is more than that. Instead, it is a matter of coming to grips with the reality of life rather than being simply carried by life's currents, now into still and calm waters, now into churning waters. Neither the author of Job nor the poet Hopkins was giving us an analysis of 'moody' human beings. They were debating the very existential question that is still being asked today: how do human beings stand in relation to their God? Job's suffering and Hopkins' plight are situations that really cause such a question to arise. Both of them underwent an experience that many of us at one time or another have undergone or are now undergoing. Like them, we are confronted by suffering, ours as well as that of others. But for many of us it stands in the way between God and ourselves or sours any personal relationship with God. In other words, the question of suffering leads us to call our relationship with God into question, sometimes angrily. Such a reaction is understandable given the baffling aspect of suffering.

LEARNING FROM JOB AND HOPKINS

But the message that the author of Job and the poet Hopkins have for us even today is that it need not lead to that. But why not? Because the irrationality of suffering is not everything about it, even if the fact of suffering appears to militate against the belief in a just and powerful God. The writer of the Book of Job wants to show us that Job wrestled with the same problems, but instead of turning his back on God, he made the question his route to God. Hopkins wondered and even complained but still found God just. It may be that suffering, disappointments, the roughness of life are our opportunity of feeling closer to our Creator, just as they were for those two. They could turn out to be shady colours which balance the lighter ones so that the intricate pattern of life will come more fully into view and hence be more valued. They could become, as it were, punctuation marks at significant places of life so that we can properly read and understand God's message or the pauses in the musical score of life so that the music may be better appreciated.[28] Much depends on us. We may not understand why there is suffering (sometimes one is at a complete loss to explain it, never mind justify it), but we can transcend the situation by letting it lead us to a more authentic relationship with God. Job may have been a fictional character, but there have been too many concrete examples of people who have refused to allow suffering to become a barrier between God and themselves for us to ignore this point. Someone once said that in moments of distress and loss we experience God first as an enemy, then as a void, and finally as a friend. Our sufferings could be the very factor which will enable us to experience God's compassion, something which one finds only in a true friend. It could be that the rough side of life will be our means to say to God: 'I had heard of thee by the hearing of the ear, but now my eye sees thee' (*Job* 41:5). It may even, despite appearances, still enable us to cry out with Hopkins: 'Thou art indeed just, Lord.'

Chapter 2

LITERARY MEDITATIONS ON DEATH AND CHRISTIAN HOPE

Job's and Hopkins' question becomes more poignant when one considers the reality of death. In this chapter we shall continue to probe into certain literary meditations on suffering. We shall do this by explicating specific poems, arguably an effective way of presenting their insights while preserving the rich imagery and the concreteness of their language. Although these poems were written by different poets, they form a certain unity of thought.

ATTITUDES TO DEATH

What is troubling about the moment of death, thereby causing much distress and anxiety, is that we all know that one day each of us will die; yet there is much uncertainty about death. Consequently, the thought of it grips our whole being, leaving us bewildered. Or it could be the parting with loved ones or perhaps leaving behind an unfinished task which makes death a sad and unwelcome moment. John Keats' poem 'Terror of Death' certainly expresses the tragedy of being separated from loved ones or being unable to complete a piece of work. Maybe it is the fact that there is no turning back after—to use Alfred Tennyson's words—one has 'crossed the bar' that terrifies us. Dylan Thomas' advice, therefore, is:

Do not go gentle into that good night.
Rage, rage against the dying of the light.[1]

We are afraid that death may reveal our lives to have been a sham, and it would render us powerless to change them.

Nevertheless, there are some for whom death is welcome. Just as there are varied reasons for fearing it, there appear to be different reasons for welcoming it. To some death will be the longed-for break from life's toils. As Shakespeare puts it:

Fear no more the heat o' the sun
   Nor the furious winter's rages;
Thou thy worldly task hast done,
   Home art gone, and ta'en thy wages;[2]

It will be like the respite that one looks forward to after a hard day's work. Then again there will be those for whom death marks the end of an absurd existence, enabling them to slip into oblivion. For these life has had no meaning; what better choice than to cut it short? Others will have a rather stoic attitude towards death. Caesar in Shakespeare's play wonders: 'It seems to me most strange that men should fear,/ Seeing that death, a necessary end,/ Will come when it will come.'[3] Humans are destined to die; hence, the best that one can do, it is claimed, is to put up with it. Still others, like John Donne in his poem 'Death, be not Proud,' challenge death and maintain that it does not in fact have power:

One short sleepe past, wee wake eternally,
And death shall be no more; death, thou shalt die[4]

THE SYMBOL OF LIGHT AND THE MEANING OF DEATH

The different literary passages cited above articulate what possibly various individuals feel about death. There is no doubt that the reality of death is a source of much suffering even if for some it is something not to be feared. But someone once claimed that death is a tragedy only when we know nothing about it. If this is true, then just how much do we know of death? If we had some idea of its significance, would there be less fear in us?

Would we be less scared at the prospect of it since it would not be a plunge into the unknown or a leap into the dark?

A poet whose attitude toward death is worth looking into is Henry Vaughan. In his poem which has been given the title of 'They are all gone into the world of light!' he uses the symbol of light to reflect on the meaning of death for him.[5] In this poem he also voices his hope for liberation.

Light has always been an illuminating symbol in religion and literature since it is capable of embracing many meanings, thus helping us gain an insight into what is otherwise difficult to comprehend. Henry Vaughan certainly finds the symbol of light useful. In the poem referred to above the proliferation of words and images associated with light underlines the importance of this symbol for him: *star, kindle, flames, burn, bright, fair, glows, glitters, jewel.* Furthermore, by contrasting these with terms connected with darkness, such as *dark, sad, gloomy, cloudy, dull, hoary, mists, blot,* the impact of the symbol becomes greater. For Vaughan, light represents God, heaven, immortality, happiness, knowledge, vision, freedom; whereas darkness stands for damnation, mortality, misery, absence or separation from God, ignorance, blindness, bondage.[6] Commenting on Vaughan's use of these two images or groups of images, S. Sandbank writes that they 'serve to re-enforce a dramatic world-picture in which the opposition between heaven and earth, Grace and nature, is a very basic distinction.'[7]

The imagistic contrast of darkness and light gives unity to Vaughan's poem.[8] One can clearly see this contrast in the very first stanza:

> They are all gone into the world of light!
>   And I alone sit lingring here;
>   (lines 1-2)

The word 'they' refers to those people who have died (including his younger brother William and his own wife, Catherine); they have passed from this world into the world of light (in another work of his, 'The World,' he also describes the next world in terms of light: 'I saw Eternity the other night/ Like a great *Ring* of pure and endless light,' lines 1-2). The radiance of that 'world of light' makes this earthly world very dark, adding to the isolation of the

poet (speaker), which we can sense in the phrase 'I alone.' From
such a dejected state the poet would like to escape.

The next two lines reinforce the contrast by repeating the
pattern of opposition:

> Their very memory is fair and bright,
> And my sad thoughts doth clear.
> (lines 3-4)

Their 'fair and bright' memory is set off against his 'sad thoughts.'
At the same time, however, the poet seems to want to introduce
a less sombre note. While the word 'sad' is not one to be associated with light but with darkness, the sad thoughts are 'clearing.' In
addition, the opening of the second stanza describes his memory
of them (and hence, by implication, his thoughts) in this way:

> It glows and glitters in my cloudy brest
> Like stars upon some gloomy grove,
> (lines 5-6)

The alliteration in 'glows' and 'glitters' highlights the dazzling
power of the departed even in his 'cloudy breast.' The imagery of
light and darkness—condensed in one line—has the effect on him
of stars on a gloomy grove. The light of the stars, more obvious
and appreciated, dispels the darkness and gloom. The poet
continues his thoughts with references to 'faint beams' which
shroud the hill after 'the Sun's remove' (lines 7-8).

The third stanza directs our attention to the gulf which exists
between the quality of his mortal life and the immortal life of the
departed. They walk 'in an Air of glory,/ Whose light doth trample
on [his] days' (lines 9-10). In contrast, he lives in an earthly life
which is very imperfect: he feels his days are 'dull and hoary' at
best. James Simmonds notes that, 'Implicit in this contrast
between two kinds of life which the speaker "sees" is a contrast
between two kinds of knowledge, one that sees the surfaces of
things and one that sees beyond them'.[9] In this world, Vaughan
appears to be saying, we do not have the fullness of knowledge
nor sight.

Vaughan believes that it is through death that we can be
raised 'High as the Heavens above!' (line 14). Death is a necessary

stage through which we must pass to reach the higher plane (or as Donne puts it: 'And soonest our best men with thee doe goe,/ Rest of their bones and soules deliverie.')[10] The imagery of light is seen once again in the word 'kindle' (line 16). Death kindles in Vaughan's heart a passion: it is now 'beauteous death' (line 17). It is 'the Jewel of the Just,/ Shining no where, but in the dark;' (lines 17-18). Making use once more of the contrast between light and darkness, he describes death as leading us to the brightness of immortality. But we cannot see beyond this world because of our limited light (here the symbol of light has evolved to mean understanding and vision). Thus, post-mortem mysteries remain unsolved while we are in this world:

> What mysteries do lie beyond thy dust;
> Could man outlook that mark!
> (lines 19-20).

Vaughan is expressing a wish or desire for greater understanding and insight—to see things as they really are. His wish echoes verses 12-13 of 1 Corinthians: 'For now we see in a mirror dimly, but then face to face. Now I know in part; then I shall understand fully, even as I have been fully understood.'

In the next stanza Vaughan shows us what it is to see as mortals, emphasising once more the difference between that sight and true vision or understanding. He illustrates it by citing our limited knowledge and range of sight on seeing that the bird has flown the nest. We do not have enough 'light' (that is, intelligence, understanding) to see 'what fair Well, or Grove he sings in now,' (line 23). We are in the dark about these things (incidentally, the reference to 'grove and well' is, according to E. C. Pettet, to details of the Old Testament landscape[11]).

But even in such darkness, there is a glimmer of hope. The phrase 'And yet' (line 25) introduces it. Just as Angels call to the soul in brighter dreams when we are asleep, so 'strange thoughts'—flashes of light, divine inspiration—help us to 'transcend our wonted theames' (line 27), giving us a peep into glory. At times with God's help we overcome our limitations and catch glimpses of 'glory' (line 28). In another work, Vaughan makes a similar point:

When on some *gilded Cloud*, or *flowre*
My gazing soul would dwell an houre,
And in those weaker glories spy
Some shadows of eternity;
. . . .
But felt through all this fleshly dresse
Bright *shootes* of everlastingnesse.[12]

Returning to the poem 'They are all gone into the world of light!'
one can see that the symbol of light is further evident in these
lines:

If a star were confin'd into a Tomb
　Her captive flames must needs burn there;
　　　　　(lines 29-30).

The burning flames encased in a tomb represent the soul enclosed
in our mortal body. The longing of the soul for freedom is fulfilled
by the death of the body (opening of the Tomb) since it releases
the soul whereupon 'She'l shine through all the sphaere' (line 32).
As he puts it in another poem entitled 'Ascension Hymn,' souls
'must be undrest' (line 6). The soul, once liberated from the
captivity of the body, will join all those who are 'gone into the
world of light' (line 1). Each soul adds its own star, a light to the
world of light.[13] E. C. Pettet observes that this reference to the
Tomb confining a star (in line 29) has intimations of the Resurrection.[14] Immortality for us mortals was brought about by Christ's
Resurrection, which has ensured Vaughan's 'liberation from the
tomb' and entrance into 'the world of light.'

　　The ninth stanza is an appeal to God to release the spirit from
this world of slavery into true freedom. The stanza thus conveys
more explicitly Vaughan's attitude to this life and to the next. He
affirms his faith in God, recognising God as the 'Father of eternal
Life' and of all creation.

　　Believing that we will not be truly liberated until we understand
fully and can see clearly, Vaughan presents in the final stanza two
ways of being liberated:

Either disperse these mists, which blot and fill
　My perspective (still) as they pass,
Or else remove me hence unto that hill

Where I shall need no glass.
(lines 37-40)

In these lines Vaughan indicates the forms of liberty he desires. Again, he pursues the light-and-darkness imagery: mists result in diminished sight, which 'blot' the clear or total picture. The true brightness is not seen by mortals because of the darkness and the cloudy nature of 'mists'—ignorance, mortal understanding, mortal sight. Thus, he asks God to 'disperse these mists.' One is reminded here of Emily Dickinson's 'Of all the Souls that stand create':

And this brief Tragedy of Flesh—
Is shifted—like a Sand—
When Figures show Their royal Front—
And Mists—are carved away,
(lines 7-10)

Vaughan's second choice is to be removed from this world (dark vale) to that other world of heaven (bright hill) where all is revealed. Only then will he be enlightened and join those who are already stars in the world of light. This option of being taken out of this mist-obscured world into the illumination of heaven neatly ends the poem. Thus, for Vaughan 'to lose this life is, in fact, a gain, the shedding of the dross which is the material world and the gaining of the pure light of God and eternity.'[15] Or, as Vaughan himself puts it in '[Silence, and stealth of dayes!]:' 'But those fled to their Makers throne,/ There shine, and burn;' (lines 24-25).

One can easily see that in Vaughan's work the symbol of light with its rich connotations of heaven, immortality, happiness, knowledge, full vision, freedom (and often contrasted with the symbol of darkness) pervades the whole meditation on the meaning of death for him. It is a symbol capable of bearing simultaneously several kinds of interpretation.[16]

THE DEATH OF JESUS[17]

In his meditation on death Vaughan mentions the liberating effect of Jesus' death. The fact that Jesus died on the cross seems to make a difference to the way Christians view death. They believe that Jesus' death enables them to see meaning in their own deaths and this gives them hope. For them part of the significance of that historical death some 2000 years ago lies in their being able to untangle some of the knots that surround death. Because of that event, death for the Christian is not a plunge into the unknown or a leap into the dark. The reality of death assumes a meaning which comes from Christ's meritorious death on the cross: the process of dying becomes a participation in Christ's saving act. And because death is made meaningful, then life itself is seen as an important challenge since it is the situation where the Christian is given all the opportunities of fulfillment at death. It is in this sense that contemporary Christian theology talks of life as 'death in anticipation'.[18]

To regard Christ's death as giving meaning to our own death is not, however, to ignore the deep-seated dread of death that Christians share with other people.[19] Death, more than anything else brings before us the radical finitude of our existence. It threatens to nullify everything. In the document 'Church in the Modern Word,' Vatican II stated that 'it is in the face of death that the riddle of human existence becomes most acute. Not only is man tormented by pain and by the advancing deterioration of his body, but even more so by a dread of perpetual extinction.'[20] There is an instinctive desire in everyone of us to want to live forever. Hence, we feel restless and anxious as we become painfully aware that like everything else, we too must pass away. Death is the most tangible expression of human finitude. It is a real threat. No wonder it has been described as life's sharpest contradiction, the absurd arch-contradiction of existence.

GOOD FRIDAY AND EASTER

Two poets who meditate on the Christian understanding of the death and subsequent resurrection of Jesus are John Donne and George Herbert. In a poem entitled 'Good Friday, 1613, Riding Westward' Donne reflects on the meaning of that event while Herbert brings out the significance of Christ's resurrection in his poem 'Easter.' Both of these works are full of images of the God they believe in and of their relationship to that God.

The title of Donne's meditation 'Goodfriday, 1613, Riding Westward' arrests our attention for a number of reasons. The poem commemorates the crucifixion and death of Jesus Christ, but the date '1613'—so prominently positioned in the title—reminds us that Donne is concerned with his own observance of the anniversary of that event and its implications for him rather than with the actual historical occurrence.[21] The phrase 'Riding Westward' implies a journey but one in the opposite direction from that expected in relation to Good Friday and its Eastern connections.[22]

The first line of the poem sets up a hypothetical analogy: 'Let mans Soule be a Spheare' (line 1). As a sphere, the soul is subject to the principles which govern the other spheres—here we are introduced to Donne's 'conceit' which sees the movement of the soul in terms of the movement of the spheres.[23] Man's soul, like the other spheres, has a guiding Intelligence. Devotion should be its guiding principle. Its movement should be towards devotion (especially on Good Friday); but, like the other spheres, the soul is also subject to 'forraigne motions' (line 4) which cause it to lose its own direction.[24] The soul as sphere is buffeted everyday and rarely obeys its 'naturall forme' (line 6). The next lines state clearly what interferes with the progress of the soul towards devotion:

Pleasure or businesse, so, our Soules admit
For their first mover, and are whirld by it.
(lines 7 and 8).

Distracted from its true course, the human soul gets caught up in the attractions and demands of this world and is no longer moved by devotion to God. In thus likening the soul to a sphere, subject to the movement of other spheres, Donne has given us a striking comparison.

This comparison also explains the direction of his journey. Like a mathematical problem clearly demonstrated—if we have followed his argument so far—Donne's reason for taking this direction becomes explicit:

Hence is't, that I am carryed towards the West
This day, when my Soules forme bends toward the East.
(lines 9 and 10).

Today of all days (emphasising the significance to Donne of Good Friday, and his wish to observe it properly) his 'Soules forme bends towards the East' in devotion and gratitude to his Saviour. Yet, he is moving towards the West. Temporal attractions exert a great force on him (he is going to Montgomery Castle in Wales) preventing the soul from obeying its 'naturall forme.'

Donne knows what he should see at Calvary in the East:

> There I should see a Sunne, by rising set,
> And by that setting endlesse day beget;
> But that Christ on this Crosse, did rise and fall,
> Sinne had eternally benighted all.
>   (lines 11-14)

Through his use of paradoxes he shows his Christian belief that the salvation of human beings was brought about by the setting of a 'Sun'.[25] The imagery of the sun is effective in depicting what Jesus Christ accomplished by his death and resurrection: he begot 'endless' day and immortality for mortal humans. The absence of the sun is conveyed by the words 'eternally benighted' stressing that without Christ's death on the Cross (setting sun) and his resurrection (rising sun) we would not have been redeemed and sin would have permanently covered all in darkness. Here again Donne is contrasting East and West (rising and setting sun), thus connecting the second movement of the poem (lines 11-32) with the first.

Yet Donne is almost glad not to see the crucifixion. It is a 'spectacle of too much weight' for him (line 16). He would not be able to face up to the horrifying spectacle of the tortured, crucified Jesus. To look at God's face is tantamount to death: 'Who sees Gods face, that is selfe life, must dye;' (line 17—a reference to Exodus 33:20). But how much worse to view God die: 'What a death were it then to see God dye?' (line 18). It is not surprising that Donne finds 'that spectacle of too much weight' (line 16) for him since it had such profound consequences on nature, as seen in this metaphor:

It made his owne Lieutenant Nature, shrinke,
It made his footstoole crack, and the Sunne winke.
(lines 19-20)

These lines are reminiscent of Isaiah 65:1 and Matthew 27:51-55. The enormity of the event (crucifixion) is mirrored in disturbing phenomena—an earthquake and eclipse of the sun.

The difficulty he experiences in facing the crucifixion is further brought out in his rhetorical question: could Donne look on 'those hands which span the Poles,/ And turne all spheares at once' (lines 21-22) and witness the marks of the nails in Jesus' hands stretched out on the Cross? Once again the idea of opposites and extremities (North-South poles and the right-left arm of the Cross) and the movement of the spheres are kept before us. God is given the role of turning all spheres. Thus, this section of the poem is linked with and reinforces the opening movement (lines 1-10). Donne wonders whether he could bear to look on Jesus Christ—humbled, suffering the ignominy of the crucifixion:

Could I behold that endlesse height which is
Zenith to us, and our Antipodes,
Humbled below us? . . .
(lines 23-25)

It is a terrifying contemplation which reminds one of another Christian paradox—the greatest shall be least.

Donne's next rhetorical question asks if he could behold that blood which is:

The seat of all our Soules, if not of his,
Make durt of dust, or that flesh which was worne
By God, for his apparell, rag'd and torne?
(lines 26-28)

He focuses on the shedding of Christ's blood and its mingling with the earth and on the tortured state of Christ as his flesh is injured and mutilated by human beings—paradoxically, for their salvation.

In his meditation Donne considers next the possibility of reflecting on the suffering of Mary 'Who was Gods partner here, and furnish'd thus/ Halfe of that Sacrifice, which ransom'd us?'

(lines 31-32). Perhaps he can relate to Mary and appreciate her suffering (as parent) and the sacrifices demanded of her as Mother of God. Her sufferings also helped to win our salvation.

Throughout the second section of the poem (lines 11-32) we are kept aware of the religious implications of Good Friday and of the paradoxical notion that the West (setting sun-Christ's death) leads to East (rising sun-resurrection and immortality). All the ideas and images are thus held together.

Donne then informs us that since he is riding westward, he cannot actually see these sights (suffering, crucifixion, resurrection) before him; nevertheless, he is mindful of them. Thus, he can make an appropriate act of meditative devotion even as he rides westward. The sights which are 'present yet unto [his] memory' (line 34) — traditionally located at the back of the head, according to A. C. Partridge[26] — enable him to contemplate his sinfulness and the ever-watchful presence of Christ. His 'memory' is looking East even as he rides towards the West. Therefore, God (in the East) is looking towards him. It is at this stage in the poem that God becomes personal for Donne:

> . . .thou look'st towards mee,
> O Saviour, as thou hang'st upon the tree;
> (lines 35-36)

He feels unworthy. Maintaining the metaphor of his movement to the West, Donne points out that his back is towards God not because he is rejecting God but because he wishes to expose his back to receive God's punishment which will clear him of his unworthiness:

> I turne my backe to thee, but to receive
> Corrections, till thy mercies bid thee leave.
> (lines 37-38)

Donne wishes to suffer his own scourging personally from God to atone for his wrongdoings[27]   He wants to be punished so that he can get closer to God:

> O thinke mee worth thine anger, punish mee;
> Burne off my rusts, and my deformity,
> Restore thine Image, so much, by thy grace,
> That thou may'st know mee, and I'll turne my face.
>
> (lines 39-42)

Donne realises that he is tarnished by sin and that unless he is cleansed and purged he cannot be united with God.[28] Only when he is made free of sin through punishment will he be able to turn his face towards God. This turn at the end of the poem reiterates the conceit of the movement of the sphere (soul) obeying its 'naturall forme' and turning to devotion—he will turn his face from the West to the East. The poem's thought has, as it were, gone full circle: just as West meets the East, the human individual who emanates from God returns to God.

George Herbert's poem 'Easter,' beautifully complements Donne's poem since in Christian thought Good Friday and Easter are not separated. Thus, Herbert's reflections can be said to develop further the significance of Jesus Christ's death.[29]

The structure of the poem is worth a mention. The poem consists of thirty lines, grouped in six stanzas. The first three stanzas, comprising six lines each, form the first movement of the poem while the remaining twelve lines, divided into three 4-line stanzas, form the second movement of the poem. The line-length is irregular—long and short—in the first movement, and the lines rhyme in couplets. In contrast, the line-length is much more regular in the second movement, and the lines rhyme alternately. It is no wonder that in some editions of this poem it is printed in two separate parts as 'Easter I' and 'Easter II.'[30] A probable reason for this is that the two movements or parts of the poem look distinct, at least on first sight. But a closer examination of the poem reveals a certain unity: the second movement answers the first. That is to say, 'Easter II' is the speaker's response to the call in 'Easter I' for his lute to awake.[31] Furthermore, both appear to be hymns, making it more credible to refer to the underlying unity in this work.[32]

The first movement begins with a formal call to praise:

> Rise heart; thy Lord is risen. Sing his praise
>   Without delayes,
>   (lines 1-2).

Herbert bases this movement on Psalm 57, one of the Proper Psalms for Easter matins:

> My heart is fixed, O God, my heart is fixed: I will
>   sing and give praise.
> *Awake* up my glory, *awake* Lute and Harpe: I my selfe
>   will *awake* right earely.
> I will give thanks unto thee, O Lord, among the people:
>   and I will sing unto thee among the nations.
>   (lines 8-10, italics added)

According to Chana Bloch, in the first stanza of his poem, Herbert transforms the biblical sequence of verbs, 'awake, awake, I will awake,' into a new Christian sequence—'*Rise* heart, thy Lord is *risen*, thou mayst *rise*.' Herbert's use of the word 'rise' takes on three different senses: wake up, Christ has been resurrected from the dead, you may be reborn to a new life of the spirit.[33] The reason for singing and giving praise is that Christ's saving deeds in the Crucifixion and Resurrection guarantee immortality for us mortals. We are restored to eternal life and have just cause to celebrate and sing:

> Who takes thee by the hand, that thou likewise
>   With him mayst rise:
> That, as his death calcined thee to dust,
> His life may make thee gold, and much more just.
>   (lines 3-6)

Mere 'dust' has been transformed into 'gold.' Christ has justified us.

Now that the heart is ready to sing, Herbert calls—at the beginning of the second stanza—on the lute:

> Awake, my lute, and struggle for thy part
>   With all thy art.
>   (lines 7-8).

It is not an easy task. Because of the importance of the event, one needs to exert effort to celebrate this Easterday in an appropriate manner. Herbert continues:

> The crosse taught all wood to resound his name,
>> Who bore the same.
> His stretched sinews taught all strings, what key
> Is best to celebrate this most high day.
>> (lines 9-12)

Christ's sinews were stretched taut on the Cross. Likewise, the strings on Herbert's lute must also be stretched to the correct tension to achieve the proper key.[34] It was by his suffering—'stretched sinews on the cross'—that Christ conquered death. However, Herbert focuses not so much on the pain but on the results of it: the liberation, resurrection, eternal life. Consequently, Easter is a time of joyous celebration. Herbert proclaims that the wood of the cross has shown how all wood, including the wooden bridge of his lute, should give praise to God. For his own part he will use his talent to praise God. As he expresses it in another work, 'The Thanksgiving':

> My musick shall finde thee, and ev'ry string
>> Shall have his attribute to sing;
> That all together may accord in thee,
>> And prove one God, one harmonie.
>> (lines 39-42)

Indeed in still another poem 'Providence' he considers praise of God to be our chief function.

In the opening line of the third stanza of this first movement of 'Easter' Herbert joins the 'heart' of stanza 1 and the 'lute' of stanza 2 together:

> Consort, both heart and lute, and twist a song
>> Pleasant and long:
>> (lines 13-14)

He also announces the song, which seems to extend from line 19 to line 30.[35] Music is made up of three parts; if he is to produce such music, a third part must be supplied. This third part is the 'blessed Spirit,' often associated with inspiration:

> O let thy blessed Spirit bear a part,
> And make up our defects with his sweet art.
> (lines 17-18)

Human efforts are not sufficient; hence, God's role remains essential. This third 'component' takes our 'dust' and once again turns it into 'gold.'

The three stanzas taken together thus form what Anthony Low calls a 'paean celebrating the most joyful of the Church's feasts.'[36] The first movement of the poem, with its three stanzas, is somehow evocative of the Trinity, especially due to the reference to the Spirit. Moreover, the movement resembles a musical arrangement. In the first stanza the heart rises and sings while in the second the lute enters, playing counterpoint to the singing heart. In the last stanza the Holy Spirit like another musical instrument plays his part, thus completing the three-part harmony to round off the concert. As Low again observes: 'The poem, constructed on this musical metaphor, seems also to provide us with a program for its musical setting.'[37]

The second movement of the poem begins with line 19 and runs to the end of the poem. This movement also consists of three stanzas, thus linking it to the structure of the first movement. But the regularity of the lines by contrast is immediately noticeable. Low refers to this part of the poem as 'the simplest and most lyrical of Herbert's songs.'[38] The measure, four lines in tetrameter or Long Meter, could be sung to many established tunes and was thus a favorite of hymn and psalm writers. Its simpler style, compared to that of the first part of the poem, meant that music would bring out the harmonious contrast.[39]

The fourth stanza, which initiates the second movement of the poem, opens with the following lines:

> I got me flowers to straw thy way;
> I got me boughs off many a tree:
> (lines 19-20)

It is clear that Herbert is anxious to do something, to do his part. But God does not need the flowers nor the boughs:

> But thou wast up by break of day,
> And brought'st thy sweets along with thee.
>   (lines 21-22)

These lines echo Mark 16:1-6: the women had brought sweet spices to anoint Christ's body in the tomb, only to find that he had risen from the dead. Richard Strier notes that in this same stanza one can see that the shift in pronoun emphasis—from I, to thou and thy—is significant because it puts the focus on Christ, his Resurrection, his independent nature.[40]

The fifth stanza contrasts the rising of the Sun with the Resurrection. The difference is immense: the Resurrection is unlike the rising of the sun and everything else in nature. Herbert expresses it thus:

> The Sunne arising in the East,
> Though he give light, & th'East perfume;
> If they should offer to contest
> With thy arising, they presume.
>   (lines 23-26)

The Sun and the East mentioned in the first line of this stanza are united in the 'they' of the third and fourth lines. The rising of the sun in the east ushers in the day; but the Resurrection, which brings about the first and last everlasting Day, is far superior to the sun's day. It would be presumptuous of them to think that they could outshine the Resurrection.

The sixth and final stanza clarifies this point by asking:

> Can there be any day but this,
> Though many sunnes to shine endeavour?
>   (lines 27-28)

The answer is, of course, *No*: 'There is but one, and that one ever' (line 30). Our futile efforts and calculations are again referred to: 'We count three hundred, but we misse:' (line 29). Herbert's 'I' and 'they' become joined in 'we.' He, like many sons (suns), endeavours to shine, only to realise that human attempts are finite and fallible.[41] Our notion of time, punctuated by sunrise, is not able to make us comprehend the essential magnificence of the Resurrection and the Infinite, Infallible One.

The chords of Herbert's hymn have, as it were, struck a chord as it dawns on him that 'There is but one, and that one ever' (line 30). That one everlasting day is the Resurrection. Richard Strier maintains that 'this ending is one of the most astounding moments in Herbert. A vista opens up in relation to which all our "countings" like all our acts of "natural piety" (getting flowers) fail, but we are here left contemplating the vista itself rather than our failures in relation to it.'[42]

In this poem then, which consists of two movements, Herbert unites himself with God. The first stanza is devoted to the heart, the second to the lute. In the third, the heart and the lute unite with the Holy Spirit. Having completed the first movement with an expectation of a song on our part, Herbert introduces the second movement. This movement is also composed of three stanzas—'since all musick is but three parts vied/ And multiplied;' (lines 15-16). With God's help the song is complete. Herbert contemplates the Resurrection in stanza 4. In stanza 5 he considers how the Sun and the East cannot rival the glory of the Resurrection. Finally, he proclaims the mystery of the Resurrection.

DEATH, SIN AND CHRISTIAN HOPE

So far we have been listening, as it were, to the poets, who despite their fears and anxieties continue to express their Christian hope. The significance of their work for theological reflection is well brought out by David Jasper: 'The poet speaks in metaphor and analogy; theology itself cannot abandon the language of similitude and speak of the mystery of God in the language of science and analysis, for God is no analysable system. The poet is always there to remind theology of this, and of the reticence, obliquity and indirection of its Truth.'[43] On the other hand, there is a sense in which poetry needs theology for 'theology meanwhile works upon the language of religious faith, straining in its careful way beyond poetic analogy and poetic inspiration ....Poetry itself then finds in doctrine and the language of belief a precise means by which to apprehend the human mystery.'[44]

Donne's and Herbert's poems reflect Christian theological tradition which regards death as the consequence of original sin affecting all people and leading to their fall from the gift of immortality. Death in Christian terms is punishment for sin. 'Death spread to all men because all men sinned' (Rom 5:12). Edward Schillebeeckx describes death as 'a sentence of doom that man because of his sinfulness called down upon himself and all mankind.'[45] Since it was sin that brought about death, we have a genuine reason to be afraid of dying. For death may unveil our lives to have been lived in falsehood, thus sealing us off in a monument of folly.

But there is another side to the reality of death and sin, one that is not clearly brought out in the Christian interpretation presented above but of particular relevance to our exploration. In many places one cannot but speak of a situation of death caused by what has been referred to as 'sinful structures.' Certain structures or policies have directly or indirectly contributed to the utter wretchedness of life so much so that people get no chance at all to participate in what life has to offer. Sometimes even the opportunity to hope is taken away from them. It is not surprising then that we hear of individuals, governments or societies being given the label of 'perpetrators of death.' In an ironic twist the explanation of death as the consequence of sin is certainly true since it is their sinful actions which result in the horrible and unnecessary deaths of many.

But, as we have noted in the poems by Vaughan, Donne and Herbert, Christians also believe that the tragic aspect of death is not everything about it because Christ's death has conquered sin. Indeed Christian theology clearly affirms that by overcoming sin, Christ has won over death which is the result of sin. What Christ has achieved was victory not in the sense that humans will no longer die, i.e., not that we will no longer undergo physical death, but in the sense that our death has taken on a new meaning. The punishment attached to death because of sin becomes meritorious penance. Schillebeeckx explains: 'So by the fact that Christ as a holy man who is God entered lovingly into it, death has obtained a redemptive worth. Death remains a punishment for and a consequence of sin as a result of which Christ died; but the punishment now becomes reparation, satisfaction and meritorious penance. The punishment is now a constructive, salutary punishment; it receives something that of its own self it could not possess and has got only through God's merciful intervention—a positive saving worth.'[46] Thus, Christ's death has given us hope.

In the same tone Karl Rahner writes: 'What was the manifestation of sin becomes, without its darkness lifted, the manifestation of an assent to the will of the Father which is the negation of sin. By Christ's death his spiritual reality which he possessed from the beginning and actuated in a life which was brought to consummation by his death becomes open to the whole world and is inserted into this whole world in its ground as a permanent determination of a real ontological kind.'[47] In other words, Christ's death has radically altered our own. His acceptance of death has turned a natural phenomenon into a significant one. It has enabled the Christian to reject the claim made by people like Sartre that our death is the absurd last chapter of our absurd book of life. Christ's death gives meaning to our own in that our own deaths could be the culmination of our daily attempts to turn to God. Instead of being merely the end of our existence, it could be the very occasion of our meeting with God. Death, Christ has shown us, could be looked upon as our final encounter with God.

Christians regard Christ as the fulfillment of all the Father's promises to us. Salvation history sees in him the fullness of God's actions on God's people. All along it was Christ who had been foretold by the prophets of old as the Messiah, the One who would bring redemption to his people. He accomplished this through his death: by his death and subsequent resurrection we are saved. As St. Paul puts it: 'But God shows his love for us in that while we were yet sinners Christ died for us. Since, therefore, we are now justified by his blood much more shall we be saved by him from the wrath of God'(Rom. 5:8-9). Paul saw the death and resurrection of Jesus as the work which freed us from slavery to sin and death and raised us to new life in the Spirit.

Thus, according to Christian thinking, Christ's death removes the meaninglessness of our deaths and of our lives. But in what sense is it liberating? Vaughan, Donne and Herbert have shared with us their interpretations. We have also looked at a theological answer. These have shown us that Christ's death gives us a purpose, a goal to work for. Those of us who have had the experience of grappling with the senselessness-of-it-all, of searching for answers to the existential questionings which inevitably are raised by thinking animals and of discovering some of those answers will know how liberating that last step is. It is more than a passing relief. There is nothing more pitiful than a serious questioner for whom an answer is fundamentally necessary but who is left with a question mark. He or she is like a clock which continues to tick but has lost its hands, or a person who extends a hand in anticipation of a handshake which never comes. To Christians, these situations do not arise because of Jesus' death. We are not, of course, claiming that it is only the Christian who finds meaning in life or in death. Rather the death and resurrection of Christ provide meaning to the Christian and this is liberating.[48]

Within the Christian context, the decisions one makes in life can participate in Christ's redemptive act because life has been thoroughly transformed by his death on the cross. Furthermore, it is an invitation to us to also participate in the process of liberating others from a meaningless existence and death-causing situations. To the Christian the world as a whole and as the scene of personal human actions has become different from what it would have been had Christ not died. Genuine possibilities have been opened up for the personal action of humans, individually and collectively, which would not have existed without that most eventful death. Although that death happened at a given time in the past, it continues to save us at all times so long as the possibilities he has bestowed on us are genuinely appropriated by us. Christ's act is continually being made present so that it happens, not literally or factually but nonetheless truly, over and over again in the experiences of people throughout history.[49] We are saved by our actualising within us those possibilities provided to us by Christ when he died on the cross.

Thus, the Christian, despite experiencing the uneasiness of knowing that he or she must die or that loved ones will die, believes that dying is not really 'a sailing into unknown horizons.' Moreover, the Christian realises that dying may after all be the final affirmation of a life in which one has responded affirmatively to the many invitations Christ has offered us so as to save ourselves and others.

Chapter 3

WHAT KIND OF GOD?:
AN INQUIRY INTO
THE CHALLENGE OF SUFFERING

SUFFERING AND THEISM

As we have seen in the previous chapters, tragedies, suffering and especially death raise difficult problems. In fact, their occurrence is said to constitute a classic argument against those who uphold a theistic explanation of life.[1] One would therefore expect that atheism would generally be regarded as a more credible option in life. What is surprising, however, is that not only do theists continue to believe in their God—Job, Hopkins, Vaughan, Donne and Herbert do represent a strong theistic viewpoint—but they have also developed arguments to try to resolve the contradictions in their beliefs caused by the dark side of life.[2] It has even been pointed out recently that we must hope that there is a God for only then can there be meaning to the suffering of the innocent.[3] The testimonies of those who have suffered considerably and who continue to uphold their faith or who have even discovered God in their suffering seem to give the lie to atheism.[4] For them far from being the occasion when they turn their back on God, suffering becomes the vehicle which brought them to know the kind of God they had always relied on. It would appear then that suffering, though a challenge, does not necessarily contradict the theistic interpretation of life—at least, for these people.

Such a positive understanding of suffering, however, does not mean that for these theists there is no absurdity in some kinds of suffering. The sight of people in agony, the unexpected loss of a loved one or the fate of a starving nation where thousands are condemned to die horribly remind us that this kind of suffering goes contrary to what we can reasonably expect of life. We then realise that what is happening ought not to happen. Nor should we belittle the pain, whether physical, mental or emotional, that many individuals have had to experience. Comforting them by showing that others are worse off than they are can be more hurtful than helpful. It is also unfortunate when the victim is told to bear the burden patiently either because it is alleged to be a punishment from God or because there is a greater reward awaiting him or her after life. Such comments neglect to take into account that there is much undeserved misery in the world and that we cannot rule out the issue of injustice. Moreover, we should be particularly alert to any attempt to cover up the miserable plight of people and other creatures which is the consequence of the greed and malice of others. Violation of human rights, for instance, has to be checked. Perpetrators of policies which cripple others, individuals or nations, have to be made aware of their crime. For the form of suffering that results from their actions cannot be justified. We are challenged, therefore, to remove the causes of much of the suffering in today's world just as much as to face the threat that suffering brings to a meaningful existence.

OUR IMAGES OF GOD

The claim that suffering has been a route to God for some people together with the observation that we also have the obligation to remove the causes of certain forms of suffering highlight a side to the problem of evil which does not often get much attention. Earlier on we noted that what has generally concerned theists and unbelievers alike is the threat presented by the reality of evil to the belief in an all-good and almighty God. It is regarded as a stumbling-block to theistic belief and has therefore led to some people denying God's existence.[5] But it seems that there is a more fundamental need to explore further our images of God insofar as, contrary to atheism, God continues to be real to many victims of suffering and oppression.[6] Without denying the validity of questions such as why there is suffering in the first place nor the need to scrutinise further the reasons why believers continue to believe in their God, we do have to address the question: what kind of God can we still believe in despite the presence of so much suffering?

The author of the Book of Job, as we have seen, had wrestled with this problem (closer to our time we have noted the question that Hopkins asked). He presents the character Job as starting out with certain presuppositions about the God of his tradition. But his experience of undeserved suffering made him not only doubt the truth of traditional claims but also articulate with more urgency and force a different question: who is this God he was dealing with?   For Job God was real, but he needed to discover the character of this God. The answer to Job's question came in the form of a revelation: the God he was involved with was a mysterious person whose ways are not our ways. Thus, for Job the proper attitude in the face of undeserved suffering towards this God can only be one of humility and faith.

What calls for more attention now is not Job's conclusions but his (and Hopkins') question. Some will find Job's conclusions rather unsatisfactory. Should we be resigned to the mysteriousness of God? Can we not say more about this God? Who is this God in whom people like Vaughan, Donne and Herbert continue to hope? What does the evidence of suffering tell us about God's nature? Having reflected on some experiences of suffering in the first two chapters we now want to direct our attention to the theological and philosophical implications of those experiences.

In wanting to pursue these questions, one is, of course, taking certain debatable issues for granted. Not only is one assuming that there is a God, but one is also presupposing that we can talk about God. But it seems that an investigation into our claims about God's nature is just as necessary as the issue regarding God's existence because much atheism actually revolves around questionable concepts of God. The challenge confronting many of us today is to outgrow or overthrow these false notions of God.[7] The presupposition that we ought to or that we can describe God's nature is a more delicate one (we shall address this point more fully in the next chapter). There are some who would view the task to be preposterous since it would be dragging God down to our level. According to them, whatever we can say about God would be anthropomorphic. We should be contented with symbols and images of God. Others will even argue that the finite nature of human language makes the exercise a futile one. While acknowledging these difficulties, we still think that we do not have much choice. We *do* make attempts to describe God. Even the concern to preserve God's transcendence and otherness is one description of God. Or the appeal to revelation is itself an endeavour to say something about God. The limitations of human resources, however, should make us cautious about our claims regarding God. Any such claim made will always be provisional and subjective. The pursuit of statements about God is a continuous one.[8]

But can the experience of suffering, our own or that of others, disclose anything about God? In focusing on this question, we are trying to explore another dimension of the problem of evil. While the existence of evil is traditionally interpreted as a theoretical problem or a practical demand (as explained earlier) what concerns us here are the theoretical issues *which emerge because of* the practical responses which theists make to suffering. In other words, by taking into account the ways in which they deal with suffering in us and around us, we want to explore the theoretical affirmations which lie behind those responses. More specifically, the question is: what images of God underlie the practical responses of different believers to suffering?

HUME'S CHALLENGE

In a sense David Hume, whose *Dialogues Concerning Natural Religion* is a fine example of a literary, theological and philosophical approach to a common problem, had referred to this issue. Hume is usually portrayed as the philosopher whose writings on religion gravely undermined Christian belief. He had argued, among other things, against the principle of causality on which the traditional proofs for the existence of God had been based. He pointed out that if the principle were valid, the kind of God which emerges is a rather undesirable one for Christian theism: an imperfect or finite God or even gods. Hume is thus often presented as challenging the classical theistic idea of God as all-good *and* almighty, an idea which did not fit in with the reality of evil. It led theists therefore to think that what was demanded was a justification of their belief in God's existence.[9]

But Hume it appears was actually presenting another challenge through the character of Philo. Philo's reference to Epicurus' questions[10] and Philo's own statement,[11] which are usually cited as expressing the problem of evil, must be interpreted within the context of Philo's argumentation. In his narrative Philo states that he accepts that *if* we had another way of knowing that it is indeed true that God is omnipotent and benevolent then it may be possible to reconcile these attributes with the suffering in the world. As he puts it: '...I will allow, that pain or misery in man is *compatible* with infinite power and goodness in the Deity, even in [Cleanthes'] sense of these attributes....'[12] But Philo insists that if one proceeds from human experience of the world, one would be mistaken in attributing these traits to God. His direct challenge then to Cleanthes is: 'You must *prove* these pure, unmixed, and uncontrollable attributes from the present mixed and confused phenomena, and from these alone.'[13] In short, it is a question of inference.

Philo of course was adopting the position that not only is it not possible to reach the classical theistic conclusion but that an inference from human experience yields the opposite results. Not even an acknowledgement of the limitations of human knowledge can help the theist's case. Philo's exact words are worth quoting here:

> But supposing, which is the real case with regard to man, that this creature is not antecedently convinced of a supreme intelligence, benevolent, and powerful, but is left to gather such a belief from the appearances of things; this entirely alters the case, nor will he ever find any reason for such a conclusion. He may be fully convinced of the narrow limits of his understanding but this will not not help him in forming an inference concerning the goodness of superior powers, since he must form that inference from what he knows, not from what he is ignorant of.[14]

To strengthen his own case, Philo marshalls the evidence against the theistic position. He calls these 'the four circumstances, on which depend all, or the greatest part, of the ills that molest sensible creatures.'[15] He accepts that these may be necessary and unavoidable, but, given what human reason can know, Philo doubts their necessity and unavoidability. These 'circumstances' are: 1) capacity for pain 2) the general laws of nature 3) the frugality of Nature 4) the inaccurate workmanship of Nature.[16] Philo then considers what he regards as the most probable conclusion to the process of inferring from what can be observed from the state of affairs in the world: the first causes of the world have neither goodness nor malice.[17] In other words, one cannot know the moral character of God *in this way*.

Granting that Philo is right in arguing that the state of affairs in the world militates against the theistic claim of a benevolent and omnipotent God, are there areas of human experience, accessible to human reason, which could be more fruitfully explored in the interest of Christian theism? It seems that Philo focuses mainly, and even exclusively, on 'how things are and how they ought to be.' What we are suggesting is that we look elsewhere: at what theists are doing in response to the reality of suffering.[18] In other words, by taking into account the ways in which they deal with suffering in us and around us, we want to make explicit what is implicit in those responses. The problem then, taking into account Hume's challenge is: what descriptions of God emerge as we reflect on Christian *praxis*?

GOD AS CO-SUFFERER

Let us now turn to these responses. As has been pointed out, the existence of suffering challenges us in many ways. One practical response to that challenge is to show solidarity with the victims. The Jobs and Hopkinses of this world—and we all are at one time or another—call for some comfort. Being united with them can be a healing process for both the comforter and the sufferer. It is surprising that many times tragedies do unite people and bring out the good in them. Even when a kind gesture does not always last, the instantaneous response of good-will has a way of easing the burden. When it is followed by practical measures, the relief can be more effective. There is much truth in the belief that much comfort is derived from the realisation that one is not alone in one's distress. Psychologists tell us that the deepest need of a human person is the need to overcome separateness. That need is intensified in moments of misery. The lack of companionship in affliction adds greatly to one's unfortunate situation whereas when others come to one's aid, the burden is less onerous. One is given hope. Because people can be touched, much good work occurs. If love means caring about what happens to others, then caring implies being affected by them. Our feelings for them motivate us to respond positively.

Communities, whether primitive or sophisticated, have realised the value of putting people in touch with one another at times of misfortunes. For example, various rituals, religious or not, taught people to share experiences with one another at times of sorrow, such as someone's death.[19] As Rabbi Kushner explains, the Jewish custom of sitting *shiva*, the memorial week after a death, like the Christian wake or chapel visit, grows out of our need to share our fears and our grief. It reminds us in our moments of need that we are part of a community, that there are people who care about us.[20] In his poem 'Felix Randal' Hopkins shows the positive effects that tending the sick has on priest and patient.

The knowledge that others care, made explicit through rituals or concrete help or mere presence, can be therapeutic. All this is made possible because we can sympathise, that is, share the unpleasant feelings that others are experiencing and the pain that they are undergoing even if not always on the same scale or intensity. We are after all co-sufferers. Hence, the more we have suffered, the more we can sense the agony of others and the more likely we are to help.

If we put so much value on sympathetic compassion as a way of dealing with the suffering around us, could we also say that God ought to be conceived as capable of sharing in our sorrows?[21] Sympathy is usually distinguished from empathy. Empathy means putting ourselves into the inner world of others, recognising their needs but without letting their suffering overwhelm us. In so distancing ourselves we are said to be in a position to help. This distinction is often employed by some defenders of God's impassibility. God is said to empathise rather than sympathise with us. According to them, to claim that God sympathises with us is to bring God down to our level. Thus, the idea of God, at least in some Western theists, tended to exclude sympathetic suffering in God.

For example, Anselm's concept of a perfect God made him rule out any passion in God. Yet he wanted to uphold the belief that God is compassionate. Anselm then considers how God can be both. He formulates the paradox in this way:

For, if thou art passionless, thou dost not feel sympathy, thy heart is not wretched from sympathy for the wretched; but this is to be compassionate. But if thou art not compassionate, whence cometh so great consolation to the wretched?[22]

Anselm answers his own query by stating that God is compassionate in terms of our experience, but not so in terms of God's being. While we experience the effect of God's compassion, God does not.

Commenting on this passage, Charles Hartshorne and William Reese write that Anselm's analogy with experience fails to illumine in that he has merely shifted the difficulty since the question of how God 'beholds our wretchedness' has still to be faced. They ask: 'How can a being know what wretchedness is if no shadow of suffering, disappointment, unfulfilled desire or wish, has ever been experienced by that being?'[23] Anselm's description of God, it would appear to these critics, does not give us the right to believe that God sympathises with us. It is a mockery to claim that we feel the effects of God's compassion since the supreme effect of compassion is to give the awareness that someone really and literally responds to our feelings with sympathetic appreciation. Compassion implies that one is truly, and not merely apparently, moved by our plight.

If compassion, i.e. sympathetic suffering, is a value which prompts us to alleviate the suffering of others, it is hard to see why ascribing it to God is seen by Anselm as limiting God. Rabbi Kushner makes an eloquent point:

I don't know what it means for God to suffer. I don't believe that God is a person like me, with real eyes and real tearducts to cry and real nerve endings to feel pain. But I would like to think that the anguish I feel when I read of the sufferings of innocent people reflects God's anguish and God's compassion, even if His way of feeling pain is different from ours. I would like to think that He is the source of my being able to feel sympathy and outrage, and that He and I are on the same side when we stand with the victim against those who would hurt him.[24]

Kushner believes that his offer of sympathy became acceptable when people realised that he too had suffered (from the death of his son) whereas as a young rabbi, healthy, gainfully employed, his efforts to aid people in sorrow were resisted. Now that he was really a brother in suffering, they were able to let him help them. There is a strong tendency in us to think that those who have had similar experiences are in a better position not only to understand us but also to offer help.[25] Why then is there a reluctance to extend that observation to our understanding of God's character?[26]

Kazoh Kitamori in his book *The Theology of the Pain of God* writes that there is something in Japanese culture which allows for a fuller understanding of divine suffering insofar as even common people are appreciative of tragic themes in their drama. For example, the idea of *tsurasa* is realised when one suffers and dies or makes his beloved son suffer and die for the sake of loving and making others live. Moreover, the impact of Buddhism on Japan (with its concern for alleviating human suffering) has led to an understanding of 'the sickness of great mercy'. Consequently, Kitamori's Japanese background has led him not only to affirm divine sympathy but also to talk of divine pain, different from human pain, but just as real. He argues that pain is the essence of God, not merely in the sense of sympathy or empathy with the miseries of human beings, but in the sense that it is constitutive of the Godhead. Moreover, divine pain, he says, is God's response to human sin. Jung Young Lee, a Korean, maintains that the idea of a God who suffers is the logical conclusion of an Asian metaphysics. In his *God Suffers for Us*, therefore, he develops the idea of divine empathy based on the *I Ching* (Book of Changes). He writes that God does not merely feel with (sympathise) the human situation. God feels into (empathise) the human situation and actively participates in it.

The relevant point here is that since one valuable response that we make to the presence of suffering in others is to have sympathetic feelings towards them, then ought we not to say that God too must be affected by all the suffering around us? If indeed we are to portray God as one of love, God must be said to be capable of identifying with our plight to the extent that God too suffers. This should not, however, be mistaken to mean that God suffers in exactly the way we do.[27] After all, even our own sympathetic feelings vary in accordance with the kind of person that we are. God is affected in a way which corresponds to God's nature, as the worshipful reality.[28]

A possible objection here is that we seem to be implying that even God must accept the inevitability of suffering. Surely God's perfection is being threatened. Is God not competent to abolish it in the first instance? As Schillebeeckx observes, 'A God who only shares our suffering leaves the last and definite word to evil and suffering.'[29] The question then which demands our further attention is: how can a sympathetic God also be said to abolish suffering?

Another possible criticism is that by conceiving God as affected by suffering, we are conceding that there is such a definite reality capable of making God suffer. This is an objection that requires a nuanced answer. There is no such thing as suffering itself as if it had an independent existence challenging God in the way some dualistic systems portray the reality of evil. It is people and other creatures who suffer (as well as rejoice). Insofar as they are real, they are capable of touching God in their sorrows and in their joys.

But how can one develop this image of God as co-sufferer? How can we make sense of the claim that God is truly a compassionate God? These are some of the questions that we need to answer in the next chapters.

GOD AS LIBERATOR

Before proceeding with the development of the image of God as co-sufferer, let us first examine the issue of God's work of liberating us from suffering. In chapter 7 we shall try to develop a possible interpretation of God's work of liberating us. Here we shall be concerned with the question: Why should a sympathetic God also be said to abolish suffering? Job and Hopkins wanted to be taken out of their misery. Vaughan, Donne and Herbert turned to the liberating effect of Christ's death and resurrection. To some extent their suffering was an individual experience and many of us undergo that kind of experience. But the suffering of countless others is quite different and calls for still another form of liberation.

Previously it was pointed out that certain forms of suffering

accelerated pace of development, but it benefits only a small minority. They speak therefore of the need to liberate those who are its victims, the oppressed majority.[32] It is understandable that in these countries there is a conscious effort to respond to suffering in terms of 'setting the poor free.' Gustavo Gutierrez puts this point across:

> The poor person is the byproduct of the system in which we live and for which we are responsible. He is the oppressed, the exploited, the proletarian, the one deprived of the fruit of his labor and despoiled of being a person. For that reason the poverty of the poor person is not a call for a generous act which will alleviate his misery but rather a demand for building a different social order.[33]

The experience of Latin Americans (and various groups in different countries who are experiencing oppression and exploitation) has helped focus on the image of God as Liberator. The challenge for them—but one may add, to us all no matter where we are—is 'how to find a way of speaking about God that springs from the situation created by unjust poverty in which the great majority of the people live' and 'to find language that talks of hope which buoys up a people struggling for its liberation.'[34] They have turned for an answer to God the Liberator who favours the poor and the oppressed and assists in their struggle. Such a turn necessarily entails the repudiation and removal of false gods.[35]

The reality of poverty and oppression, it seems, demands that we go further than Kitamori's and Lee's answer to the question of how God liberates us from our suffering. For Kitamori, a recognition of the pain of God will overcome human pain. He writes: 'When the pain of man becomes the symbol of the pain of God, man's pain is in turn healed. What heals our wounds is the love rooted in the pain of God.'[36] Lee holds that God overcomes our suffering through God's suffering. 'Faith,' he maintains, 'emancipates us from suffering *alone* to be suffering *with*.'[37]

As we have already noted, there is a sense in which such a reaction to suffering can be liberating, particularly if its prevention is beyond our reasonable control. However, it could also lead to the kind of passivity and even fatalism that characterises the thinking of some who regard suffering to be inevitable since it balances the good to produce harmony.[38] Unfortunately, the reality in Latin America and in Asia (and in other countries) is that much of the suffering is counterproductive. According to Virginia Fabella, Peter K. H. Lee and David Kwang-sun Suh, even though Asians have known suffering to be conducive to spiritual growth, 'suffering becomes a constructive element in liberation spirituality only if it strengthens the character and spirit of the one who suffers, and at the same time transforms the forces that cause the pain.'[39] Noting that in Asia there exist two worlds, that of the privileged and that of the marginalised, these writers correctly note that:

> No spirituality that claims to be Asian can disregard the plight of these marginalised and suffering millions, for they are the majority of Asia's people. To be relevant, spirituality in Asia cannot be an elitist or a 'pie in the sky' spirituality, but one that responds to people's needs and situations. It must concern itself with people's struggles against dehumanising economic and political conditions, as well as with their aspirations for a more humane and egalitarian society. It must concern itself with countering those cultural and psychological elements that demean and subjugate, and with creating new patterns of relationships that make life worth living. In a word, spirituality in Asia must be a liberating spirituality.[40]

Given these realities, what is implied when we speak of God as Liberator, as one who gives life and hope in the midst of suffering? It seems to us that it is to recognise that a task lies ahead of us to change the situation whenever it cripples and even kills rather than frees people. Theodore Walker makes this point from the perspective of black theology: '...black theology knows, from the data of human experience, that the experience of suffering from oppression entails a desire to be liberated from such suffering. Hence, it follows that the God who experiences the suffering of the oppressed also desires their liberation.'[41] It means that siding with the victims of suffering does not mean inaction. Instead, it should spur us on to participate in God's work of liberating us from all kinds of oppression. Or as Gustavo Gutierrez puts it, 'Yahweh too has limits, which are self-imposed. Human beings are insignificant in Job's judgment, but they are great enough for God, the almighty, to stop at the threshold of their freedom and ask for their collaboration in the building of the world and in its just governance.'[42] Victorio Araya echoes this point: 'The true God does not replace human beings in the task of re-creating and transforming the world.'[43] Here too Schillebeeckx's words are particularly apt: 'What is at stake here is not simply the *ethical consequence* of the religious or theological life; rather, ethical praxis becomes an essential component of a life directed to God, of "the true knowledge of God"...God is accessible above all in the praxis of justice and love.'[44] In short, it is *through* us and *with* us that God liberates others from their miserable situation just as it is *through* others and *in* others that we experience the reality of God's sympathy. How and to what extent we are called upon to participate in God's work of liberation will, of course, vary depending on our circumstances.

This question of how to talk of God's work of liberating will continue to challenge us.[45] No doubt, it is a difficult task since any attempt to answer this question seems to be betrayed by the facts. That is to say, in trying to describe God's activity we will have to reckon with the need to show plausibly and realistically that God *is actively* working for our liberation from oppression *despite* the obvious presence of so much undeserved suffering in the world. This is not, of course, a new challenge but as we become more and more aware of unjust and dehumanising situations the world over we need once again to face the issue.

THE TASK OF CONCEPTUALISING OUR IMAGES

So far we have seen some of the images of God which emerge when we reflect on our practical responses to the reality of suffering in its various forms. In the Introduction we referred to the need to develop those images. Let us now briefly examine what is involved in this task.

Just as there are different ways of expressing what someone has conveyed to us or of communicating a personal experience, so there are various ways of expressing our beliefs about God to others. Hence, the use of symbols, images, music and other non-verbal forms. But such beliefs articulated in intellectual forms result in a conceptuality. Concepts, therefore, are a further and essential stage in the articulation of religious beliefs and images. Because a concept is an intellectual expression it tends to be more coherent. A concept makes more explicit what one held implicitly or what one has experienced.[46]

Ideally, a concept should express adequately and faithfully what one grasps at the preconceptual stage. If it does, then, in the case of beliefs about God one's understanding of God becomes richer and possibly more profound. But because human thinking is involved, there is always an element in the whole process that is open to change and development. Thus, the development of these images of God, and of religious beliefs in general, is really part of a process of reflection on and a continuous search for more adequate ways of articulating one's experiences. This is because in more developed formulations there is the likelihood that certain elements do not (or may no longer) do justice to the original insights, experience, or images. Consequently, it is important to continuously take a more critical look at any development since what has resulted may in fact be a perversion of the original. Hence, the need to rethink and reinterpret any conceptualities that we formulate means that the attempt to express conceptually what we know about God is an on-going one. John Cobb shows the importance of this task:

> To reject the conceptual task of theology reflects an inade-
> quate understanding of how faith functions. It is true that we
> are more immediately affected by images than by concepts
> and that through Christian history much of the attention of
> theologians has been properly directed to the fashioning and
> refashioning of images. But images are powerful only when
> those who hold them believe, consciously or unconsciously,
> that the images are appropriate to reality. When images are
> used to move us without convincing us that they are appropri-
> ate to reality, they are felt as manipulative rather than liberat-
> ing and energising. Propaganda consists in such images.
> Theology should not. Even when images have a life and power
> of their own which cannot be exhausted by analysis, theology
> cannot avoid the conceptual and discursive questions of their
> meaning and truth.[47]

If the formation of concepts is indeed a process, and an important one as Cobb rightly maintains, then one could enlist the help of philosophical thinking for this task. It seems useful to us to think of this process as involving the stages of *rejection, recognition, adaptation*, and *response or acceptance*. In this way it is possible to liken the efforts[48] of developing our images of God to the work done by the early Christians who were faced with the task of systematising their beliefs about God.[49]

One stage before arriving at a satisfactory conceptuality or doctrine is the *rejection* of alternatives. To some extent, it may be a matter of being more clear as to what something is not than of what something is.[50] In the case of the first Christians they had the important challenge not only of formulating Christian doctrine which was faithful to what had been experienced by the believing community but also of weeding out doctrines which could not be considered part of the Christian experience. For example, they rejected the customary belief in 'gods' since 'god' was used by the popular religious cults of the day. When these Christians spoke of their God, they did not want their concept of God to be associated with the gods of popular religion. Today it is important that we do not ignore this stage lest we continue to uphold certain concepts of God which in fact do not do justice to our experience.

Another stage in the formation of concepts is that of *recognising* or becoming aware of the value of a particular conceptualisation. Here there is partial acceptance, and some similarities are noted. This stage in the process of describing God's reality reveals the reasons why the early Church opted in favour of a particular philosophical framework in its attempts to conceptualise its faith-experience. The early Church's concept of God was very much shaped by the philosophical schools of the day, especially Platonism and Stoicism. The first Christians belonged to the Graeco-Roman world and were concerned to speak to it. They wanted to convey the Christian message to their neighbours. Greek philosophy was an excellent medium. Moreover, they wanted to show the reasonableness of Christianity and the ability of Christian teachings to withstand a thorough examination by philosophy. Philosophy was then understood as a search for truth, critical of the mythical interpretation of reality. There was a parallel, therefore, between the philosophers' task and that of the first Christians. Both wanted to differentiate their beliefs about

God from those of popular religions which they regarded as superstitious. The early Christians furthermore found that philosophical categories helped them understand Christian revelation even more deeply than had been possible with biblical images. Philosophy met the need to achieve greater clarification of terms and ideas.

But one does not simply take over a favoured formulation. There is need for *adaptation*. One has to reshape what one has recognised as helpful. Thus, there is adaptation prior to adoption, transformation before acceptance.[51] Despite aligning itself with philosophy (thereby rejecting popular religion) the early Church did not completely identify its God with the God of the philosophers. The philosophers' God, in spite of its acceptability as the ground of all being, did not have any religious significance. This God was absolute perfection and the culmination of one's intellectual pursuit but one could not pray to this God nor establish a personal relationship with this God. Thus, some transformation was called for. Whether this stage was satisfactorily crossed or not is, of course, debatable. One suspects that the present demand for more relevant and adequate concepts of God harks back to this period in Christian history.

The stage of *response* or acceptance of a particular conceptuality is really a further development. But it should not be regarded as a final stage if by that is meant no improvement can be expected. As time goes by, certain expressions or formulations become irrelevant or even misleading. Thus, the search for newer formulations is in effect an attempt to recover what has been obscured. The dissatisfaction felt by some with the conceptuality worked out by the early Church has led to calls for more appropriate and contemporary expressions of the same Christian experience of God.

It will be observed that concepts of God are regarded in this interpretation as likely to develop. This is because they are seen as the results of the continued efforts by human beings, using human reason, to find more relevant intellectual expressions of their experience of God's reality. There is, therefore, the serious challenge to meet the demands for more contemporary conceptual formulations.[52]

At the same time, however, reference was made to certain concepts doing or not doing justice to our experience of God's reality. Here certain factors can guide us in our attempts to find the limits of conceptual innovation and hence of human reasoning. This is because the search for a satisfactory conceptuality, while very much a personal matter, occurs within a specific context.[53] That context is the religious community that we belong to. Insofar as that community has a history, we can and should constantly consult it. This is why scriptures occupy an important place in every religious community because they represent early and fundamental expressions of that community's faith-experience.[54] In fact, many religious believers regard scriptures as the embodiment of God's disclosure to them or to their founder. Hence, they rightly talk of *orthodoxy*. Moreover, the community's life and practices over the years resulted in certain traditions. These represent that community's *witness* to that fundamental experience. Thus, in the task of conceptualisation we must always consider whether that community's witness is being continued (here, the better term is *orthopraxis*).

To this task of exploring and developing our images of God we shall now turn in the next part of this book.

Part II

...TO GOD

Conceptualising Our

Images of God

Chapter 4

THE TASK OF
DESCRIBING GOD

OBJECTIONS TO THE USE OF HUMAN REASON

If we are to pursue the task of exploring further our images of God and if we are to move from literary descriptions to theological and philosophical development, we have to consider first the extent to which human reason can help us fulfill this task. Since the time of Hume and Kant the use of human reason in religious matters has been subjected to a number of criticisms.[1] Many theologians and philosophers claim, for instance, that even if one were to grant the possibility that from the evidences which are on hand in this world there could be some way to acquire some knowledge of God, we would still be unable to get through to this knowledge. According to them, due to the perversion of our reasoning power whatever idea of God we may arrive at would be so false and distorted that it could not be said to be knowledge *of God* at all.

Some would say that this is because human nature is in such a fallen and sinful condition that it has been stripped of sound intelligence as well as of moral integrity. It seems that they would agree with the following lines from George Herbert: 'Love bade me welcome: yet my soul drew back/ *Guiltie of dust and sinne.*'[2] In other words, this corruption of human nature has affected our intellect and our will. Thus, given our tendency to project our images and ideas, what we end up with is actually a figment of our imagination, a creation of our own making. Others, making a similar criticism, distinguish between human sinfulness and finitude. In their view, the human inability to know God arises not

75

so much because humans are sinful creatures but because they are finite. Humans are limited beings, a fact readily confirmed by everyday experiences; hence, we cannot reach out to the transcendent. Our very nature rules out any such possibility.

Related to this view on the inadequacy of human reason is one which questions the logic of a move from the empirical to the transcendent. God, this view holds, cannot be known in the same way as we would know of the existence of a plant or of an animal or even of a fellow human being. To maintain otherwise is to bring God to the level of a finite being or to speak of God as if God were a finite being. We could, for example, prove the existence of a table through empirical means, simply by looking at it or touching it (although this would not constitute a valid proof for some extreme idealists). But we cannot show that we know of God's existence in the same way because it would be illogical to move from sense experience to the transcendent. The move we make or the conclusion we draw would be valid only if God were another object among other finite beings. Humans, according to this opinion, are capable of knowledge but only of finite beings.

In contrast to the above views Charles Hartshorne, a contemporary American philosopher, has persistently claimed that human reason can know and therefore describe God. He regards it as an unfortunate and even dangerous mistake not to employ reason in thinking through our claims about God. In this chapter we want to develop further our understanding of the task, briefly discussed at the end of the previous chapter, of developing our images of God by interacting with his views.

HARTSHORNE'S GOD-TALK

Although Hartshorne accepts that there is much about God that is describable only in negative terms, he nevertheless puts much stress on the possibility of positive or affirmative God-talk not only in the form of symbols and analogy but also of literal language. He rests his claim on a certain understanding of metaphysics which for him is the search for the general traits of reality. God in this scheme of things is said to exemplify metaphysical categories.[3] It is within this metaphysical set-up that Hartshorne locates positive and literal God-talk.

Hartshorne acknowledges different ways of speaking of God: *symbolic, literal (or formal)* and *analogical*. One is talking of God in a symbolic way when one calls God a rock, a king, a shepherd or a parent. Hartshorne also refers to this kind of predication as 'material' because the implied comparison is in terms of a concrete species of reality, a particular part of the psycho-physical universe. God is being compared with a parent, a rock and so forth; but it is understood that God is not on the same level as these entities nor is God really a rock or a parent.[4]

Hartshorne explains symbolic (or material) predication by contrasting it with literal (or formal) predication. In formal predication no specific entity like parent or rock serves as a basis for comparison. Instead, purely abstract and general philosophical categories such as space, time, and becoming, are employed. Thus, symbolic predication, since it resorts to specific images, is logically in a different class from formal predication which makes use of purely abstract categories.

The two types of predication differ from each other also in their application. The categories of formal predication have a literal meaning, i.e. they may be asserted or denied of a thing in a given aspect. In contrast, symbolic terms like 'father' admit of more definite alternatives than 'not being a father.' Hartshorne explains that not being literally a father opens up all sorts of possibilities having next to nothing in common with one another such as not being alive, conscious, or sentient at all, on the one hand, or being the unsurpassable form of living, conscious creator, on the other. The alternatives to being a ruler or shepherd cover a vast number of other possibilities. But not to be necessary is simply to be contingent.[5] The same can be said about other abstract forms, e.g. finite, relative. There are not a variety of possible forms of reality which would constitute an alternative to being relative, other than to be non-relative or absolute. Thus, unlike symbolic predication, literal or formal predication is not a matter of degree but of all or none.[6]

When one comes to literal predication itself, Hartshorne talks of two forms: negative and positive. Negative God-talk uses literal language but denies its applicability to God. In saying that God is in no way corporeal or temporal, one is maintaining that these literal concepts are inadmissible in the case of God. The other type of literal God-talk, in contrast, advances farther by stating that one can speak of God not only literally but also positively. Hartshorne is convinced that literal knowledge of the positive kind can be achieved. He has persistently held this view in the face of much opposition. In his book *The Logic of Perfection* he put this on record: 'I wish now to emphasize my conviction that the formal predicates of deity are not exclusively negative, and accordingly, some positive properties of deity can be connoted by non-symbolic designations.'[7] Much of his time has been devoted to exploring the positive formal characterisations which seem to him compatible with the religious meaning of the term 'God'. It is Hartshorne's contention that the most completely abstract general terms applicable to God are quite literal and positive. True, there is a *difference in principle* between the way they pertain to God and the way they apply to others; but the difference itself can be literally stated. In other words, there does not have to be a blurring of the distinction between God and non-divine realities. Hartshorne considers it a mistake to hold that no concepts describe God at all. He argues that unless there are definite common aspects between God and creatures, there can be no definite contrasts, either. That is to say, if we do not talk of God literally and positively, we cannot talk of God even negatively for then we would have no point of reference for our negative talk.[8] He adds that the dogmatic refusal to consider positive formal properties of God results in the impossibility of making even decent symbolic sense out of such religious terms as 'love' or 'purpose' without covertly abandoning the formal negation. Unless one accepts that some categories are predicable of God in a literal and positive manner, there is no basis for either negative comparison or for symbolic talk. Both of these forms of talking about God actually presuppose literal and positive talk. Hartshorne consequently stresses that in its own interest, if not in that of religion, philosophy should not lightly renounce the hope of speaking logically and even literally of God.[9]

Besides symbolic language and literal predication (both negative and positive) there is a third type of God-talk discussed by Hartshorne. He calls it 'analogical' because here one describes God in a way which depends partly upon one's philosophical beliefs.[10] Hartshorne explains that, for instance, God is symbolically ruler, literally necessary, but analogically conscious and loving. This last description arises from our inability to say definitely how divine knowledge or love differs qualitatively from ours. We can express the difference quantitatively: God knows and loves all creatures, we know only some. But we cannot have a literal grasp of how God knows and loves creatures for we cannot know and love anything as God does. The psychological conceptions, then, such as love, will, knowledge in the context of God-talk are analogical and not literal. They rely to some extent on how we understand human knowledge, will and love.

However, Hartshorne also maintains that there is a strange sense in which analogical concepts apply literally to God and analogically to creatures. In comparing creatures with God, we come to an awareness of our defects only in so far as we know the divine standard. We do not first know our defects independently and then, by eliminating them, think of God's perfection. At times we actually use our awareness of God to furnish us with a criterion for judging our imperfections. Our understanding of human knowledge (and the same can be said of the other psychological conceptions) is a derivative one, produced by drastically restricting the idea we have of God's perfection. Given the variety of theories on the nature of human knowledge, Hartshorne is inclined to doubt whether anyone really knows what it is. 'Know' in the human case turns out to have a rather indefinite meaning whereas in the divine case one can state simply what God's infallible knowledge means: God has absolutely conclusive evidence concerning all truths. If knowledge is possession of evidence as to the state of affairs, then God simply knows. That is all there is to it, says Hartshorne, whereas no such plain definition will work for human knowledge. Thus, he insists that there is room for the belief that we are enabled to learn something about the creatures by our knowledge of the divine.[11]

METAPHYSICAL DESCRIPTIONS

As was stated previously, what provides Hartshorne with the basis for his literal descriptions of God is the way he understands the nature of the metaphysical inquiry. Metaphysics for him is the study of the general features of experience.[12] This definition in some ways resembles that given by Whitehead for speculative philosophy as 'the endeavor to frame a coherent, logical, necessary system of general ideas in terms of which every element of our experience can be interpreted.'[13] One of the first points which will be noticed in Hartshorne's understanding is that metaphysics is not, as is sometimes mistakenly conceived to be, the study of what is wholly transcendent or supersensible. It implies that what is metaphysical is not behind or above the physical or observable but is itself included in the physical and the observable as well as everything else. He has affirmed in many of his writings that the pursuit of metaphysics is rooted in experience and the analysis that metaphysicians conduct is related to experience. Hence, it is misleading to think of metaphysicians as seeking the object of their study 'behind' the objects of empirical science, if by this is meant that in their search for the ultimate causes of things or for essences, for example, metaphysicians are looking for something over and above experience.

But what distinguishes metaphysics from other disciplines which likewise take experience as their starting point is its search for strict generality or universality. Unlike other disciplines, metaphysics examines the extremely general features of experience or its universal traits. It is the attempt to clarify those ideas (or categories) which are so general that no conceivable facts and no conceivable observations could fail to illustrate them.[14] By virtue of the generality of these ideas, they are said always to be embodied in any experience; that is, they are exemplified in every experience. Any experience must not only be compatible with these metaphysical ideas but it must also corroborate them. To quote Hartshorne, 'Metaphysical truths may be described as such that no experience can contradict them, but also such that any experience must illustrate them.'[15] He cites as an example the truth, which he maintains is metaphysical, that 'the present is always influenced by the past'. No possible experience could come into conflict with it. We cannot know that we are uninfluenced by the past since to know the past is to be influenced in one's state of knowledge by it.[16]

When Hartshorne therefore states that metaphysics is the study of the general features of experience, he means not only that metaphysical ideas are derived from experience, but also that they are so general that they are true of all experience, actual or possible. This extension of the study of truly general features to include possible experience leads him to bring out another characteristic of the metaphysical task: the search for necessary truths. Metaphysical truths are necessary in that, unlike empirical truths or facts, they cannot be otherwise since they are about what is common to all possible facts. They are not just about this world but about reality in general, about any and all possible worlds. Hartshorne maintains that the validity of metaphysical ideas applies in principle to all cosmic epochs.[17] Consequently, the metaphysical search is more than the mere observation of reality (the method used by empirical sciences) since observation only shows what goes on in the actual world with its particular regularities or natural laws. Observation does not and cannot show what must go on or what principles would be valid in any viable, truly possible, world. Metaphysics, in contrast, tries to show that the features that distinguish the actual state of reality from conceivable or possible ones are not the only ones worth knowing about reality. Or to put it in another way, the universality of metaphysical truths reveals their necessity.

Since God is regarded by Hartshorne as within the metaphysical structure, these metaphysical truths apply to God although in an eminent manner.[18] This position is reminiscent of the principle of eminence used in classical tradition. But whereas that principle is employed in an analogical sense, Hartshorne's metaphysical standpoint endeavours to show which categories are applicable to God univocally or literally. In earlier writings Hartshorne referred to his use of the 'law of polarity' but he now prefers the phrase 'the principle of dual transcendence' since the latter makes explicit not only that God is to be described as embodying metaphysical opposites, e.g. relative/absolute, contingent/necessary, mutable/-immutable, etc. but also that these metaphysical pairings are true of God in a uniquely excellent form (this double predication to describe God will be discussed in a later chapter).

THE STATUS OF OUR DESCRIPTIONS OF GOD

Hartshorne's insistence on positive God-talk is understandable, given the apparently insurmountable difficulties facing the negative theologian. We have already indicated that the stage of rejection (saying what God is not) is merely a first step. What Hartshorne has shown us further is that negative God-talk is negative only on the surface, that is, it actually makes a positive or affirmative statement. A close examination of the ground on which such discourse is taking place will unearth a certain positive presupposition. For one is in a position to evaluate something negatively only if one has access to some positive understanding against which certain statements are judged inappropriate. A positive understanding of God is assumed by any talk which considers certain attributes to be incompatible with God. It could also be added that if God were to be characterised entirely in negative concepts, then God would not be discernible from pure nothingness.[19] The argument that all we can say is what God is not results in a complete blank.

Even Hartshorne's challenge that we should make the attempt to speak of God literally, while it may cause a stir, can nevertheless be appreciated. For pure symbolism in religious discourse risks being identified with meaningless chatter. The same is true of analogical language which has to be made explicit if it is to have any intelligibility at all.[20] For this reason, among others, we argued for the need to develop our images of God. This is also why it is essential for our explorations to move from the literary and the theological to the philosophical.

On the other hand, Hartshorne's turn to experience as the basis of his metaphysical descriptions of God is an attempt to take seriously those who have argued that ideas which are not grounded in experience are bereft of meaning. His approach rightly shows that we have no other way of knowing about anything, including God, except through and in human experience.[21] (For this reason, we believe that poets and other literary writers offer a rich source for a theological and philosophical reflection that is experience-based.) We have only human experience to appeal to. Even revelation, it appears, must be referred to human experience for it to be intelligible by human beings. To illustrate this claim we have turned to the experience of suffering and our practical responses to its challenge to discover what we could meaningfully say about God.

But there are areas in Hartshorne's God-talk, given his version of metaphysics, which remain problematic to us. For instance, to steer clear of gross anthropomorphism, Hartshorne depicts God as being *different in principle*. There are, we are told, qualitative differences between God and us. In fact, Hartshorne points to a 'unique form of logical type distinction' between God and any other individual being.[22] Yet in distinguishing God from us in this fashion, Hartshorne runs the risk of being accused either of equivocation or of ambiguity. He would not, of course, accept that 'different in principle' means that God has been totally set apart and that as a result no comparison with God is possible. In fact, he maintains that God-talk can only be rooted in human experience. Thus, we start with human notions which are subjected to a test to see whether any of our characteristics are shared by non-human creatures. If they are, then they are not typically human categories. Consequently, they can be said to apply to others. If they are extremely general, they could even be extended to include God. But if Hartshorne is not being equivocal, how clear are his attempts to distinguish God from us? One example he resorts to in illustrating the difference in principle between God and everyone else is to say that God and only God is unsurpassably relative. Our idea of God as being unsurpassably relative, he says, is based on our experience of being relative. The qualification attached to God's form of relativity marks God out from everyone else since the rest of us are surpassable in our relativity. But 'surpassable relativity' is the only type of relativity that we are or will ever be familiar with. We have and can have no experience of what 'unsurpassably relative' means. Although we may have some idea of it, that idea is actually that of being 'surpassably relative'. Even the attempt to define God's difference from us in terms of 'unsurpassability' is still unclear for its touchstone is our concrete experience of 'being surpassed' and its negation. In other words, there is no positive content to the idea of 'unsurpassable relativity' itself. If this is the case, then we are left wandering about in murky waters.[23]

But Hartshorne would probably counter that this is precisely why he has insisted on positive and literal descriptions of God. One suspects that this is one reason for his regarding God as also the supreme instance of metaphysical categories. For if God is indeed part of the metaphysical structure, then positive and even literal God-talk may be possible. But how does one show that God is within our metaphysical reach?

This leads us to a second problematic area in Hartshorne's God-talk. It is Hartshorne's view that concrete experiencing establishes the correspondence between God and our God-talk.

Knowledge, as he puts it, is always knowledge of something, i.e. it corresponds to something external to the knower. He maintains that metaphysical knowledge which gives us access to God, though in an abstract way, is gained through concrete experiencing. Without the latter there can be no abstract metaphysical knowledge. However, what all this amounts to in the present context is that empirical knowledge *will lead us* to an abstract knowledge of reality. To assert that it also helps us to know God is actually to pre-define the applicability of the metaphysical categories to include God. Instead of showing conclusively that it is indeed God we are talking about, Hartshorne's metaphysical route is reducible to an explanation of how we can know God, provided God is regarded as coming within metaphysics.[24]

But even if the assertion that God exemplifies the metaphysical set-up can be supported, it is still not clear how Hartshorne's understanding of metaphysics enables us to apply our metaphysical judgments to God. Hartshorne himself is aware of the problems of really achieving what he calls metaphysical judgments since they are claimed to be necessary. Although a statement such as 'something exists' may assert the existence of something particular (e.g. 'something' could refer to the chair beside me) as a strictly generalised statement it is not restricted to any one particular object. And because it applies to everything and anything, it cannot not be true. It is, in brief, necessary. Hartshorne, however, would admit that it is in all cases only probable that we have approximated to a correct understanding of necessary truth.[25] Granted that the most general ideas cannot possibly be untrue, it is nevertheless possible that we have confusedly grasped their meaning. Or as he expresses it differently, while a metaphysical judgement seeks to express something which is universally and necessarily true, our apprehension of that truth may not always be correct. Hence, mistakes can and often do occur. For this reason the metaphysical inquiry, even for Hartshorne, is an on-going process: a search to discover what is universally and necessarily true. Unlike mathematics, metaphysics cannot claim absolute certainty since the results arrived at in metaphysics lack the definiteness of purely mathematical ideas.

The above observation means, Hartshorne would say, that we can be hasty in drawing up metaphysical conclusions since what we took to be a metaphysical truth turns out not to be so. On the other hand, does it not show rather that any such conclusion can only be tentatively held and that, consequently, references to God, even those which we now regard as metaphysical ones, may not after all apply to God?

Our question should become clearer when we find out from Hartshorne how we arrive at such a generalised knowledge of reality. In his view it is not necessary to have all possible experiences but only some experiences coupled with the capacity to abstract or explicitly generalise. What creates problems for the would-be metaphysician is not the process of generalisation since even outside of metaphysics we are prone to generalise. The real difficulty in the kind of generalisation demanded in metaphysics is in distinguishing metaphysical concepts from non-metaphysical ones. Hartshorne explains this point by contrasting metaphysics with natural science. In natural science one pays attention to the details of experience and then generalises these details so as to arrive at the total system of details which distinguish the actual world from the rest in the cosmos. In metaphysics one turns to the generic traits of human experience which one then generalises in order to arrive at the generic traits of *all* experience, actual and possible, and from here to discover the abiding features of the entire cosmos.[26] But since the metaphysician must be concerned with the adequacy of his or her findings he or she must evaluate them by deducing their consequences and comparing them with the relevant data of experience. One can enlist the aid of the natural sciences in this task since they can discredit generalisations which one is claiming to be valid for all time and all existence. Natural sciences can bring up instances which would falsify such a generalisation.[27] Metaphysical ideas and judgements must be referred back to experience to test their generality. Therefore, it is important for these ideas and judgements not just to be coherently linked up but also to be adequate to other experiences, i.e. not to be falsified by them. For if they are falsified, then they are not really metaphysical.

Hartshorne's criterion then for what is truly metaphysical is: unfalsifiability. Hartshorne explains that it is doubtful, if, strictly speaking, any scientific generalisation has been verified in the sense that it has been shown to be true exactly as it stands. The really crucial experiments are those which can disprove it. As he puts it, 'One instance clearly not in accordance with a supposed law refutes the law, but many instances in conformity with the law still do not prove it.'[28] Hence, he supports Popper's view that falsification rather than direct verification is the more viable criterion, but he adds that in metaphysics falsification must be *a priori*.[29] This means, a metaphysical claim must not only be unfalsifiable by fact but also by reason.

In the attempt to discover absurdity one can turn to logic and mathematics. Hartshorne regards logic as the search for alternatives, the exploration of the possibility of formulating an alternative to one's initial idea of statement. In a way the initial idea or statement is a hypothesis which needs to be tested. By constructing a logically complete classification of possible ideas, one can avoid a question-begging procedure. In this respect mathematics too is useful because through mathematically possible combinations the definiteness and completeness of the possibilities among which the truth must lie—so far as the truth can be expressed through the concepts initially proposed—can be certified. What these mathematically possible combinations cannot certify is the truth of that statement. Hartshorne brings out the importance of conducting a mathematical survey of possibilities by making the observation that people do not adopt philosophical positions because they are beyond question nor because conclusions are deemed to be completely satisfactory but because they seem to be stronger or more satisfactory than alternative positions. It is, he believes, a matter of preference and not of absolutely sun-clear evidence and perfect understanding.[30]

Granting this way of looking at metaphysics and of testing the validity of our conclusions, one is inclined to ask Hartshorne: at what stage can we justifiably claim that our ideas or judgements are truly metaphysical, that is, universal and therefore necessary? Hartshorne's criterion of *'a priori* unfalsifiability' which leads to the elimination of alternatives merely establishes the unsoundness of those alternatives. It does not yet show that the remaining alternative possesses the characteristics of universality and necessity. To say that we can regard something as metaphysical until it is falsified is really to admit that it is provisionally held and therefore not necessary. The necessity and universality which Hartshorne recognises in metaphysical statements are logical or analytic traits. In other words, if a statement is metaphysical, then by definition it is universal and necessary. If it is universal and necessary, then it is by the same factor metaphysical. But what we need to be shown is *that* our conclusions merit the label 'metaphysical'. Until this is done then it is hard to see how one's God-talk truly applies to God since such a conclusion depends on our previous acceptance of the claim that metaphysical statements do extend to God. It is a claim by Hartshorne which remains uncertified.[31]

If the above argumentation is right, then all we can really say, despite Hartshorne's views on the ability of the metaphysical inquiry to truly describe God, is that the attempt to use human reason in developing our claims about God's reality can be justified. However, given its limitations any conceptions of God that we arrive at will remain tentative and in need of constant revision. It is a less ambitious claim regarding our descriptions of God (compared to what Hartshorne wants to say), but it seems to be a more defensible one.

Chapter 5

THE CONCEPT OF AN IMMUTABLE GOD

One of the most dominant developments of various claims about God, at least in Western thought, has been the idea of an immutable God. In this chapter we will briefly survey the development in classical theism of the belief in God's immutability. We will then discuss the reasons put forward by Charles Hartshorne, and by Latin American liberation theology for rejecting the concept of an immutable God. Throughout our presentation of classical theism and of the objections of these schools of thought our aim will be, given the focus of this exploration and the reflections in the earlier chapters, to inquire into the adequacy of this conceptuality in articulating our beliefs about God in the face of suffering.

SCRIPTURAL FOUNDATIONS

Since it is generally accepted that the belief in God's immutability has a basis in the Judaeo-Christian scriptures, let us look first at its scriptural foundations. As is usually the case with most descriptions of God found in these sources, the belief that God does not and cannot change is, however, not developed in any great detail. Given the Semitic thought pattern and linguistic expressions, which are concrete, this is not of course surprising.

Certain passages seem to provide a foundation for regarding God as immutable. For instance, in Mal 3:6 Yahweh says, 'Surely I the Lord do not change.' In Ps 101:27 the psalmist addresses Yahweh: 'Thou art the same and thy years have no end.' Moreover, Yahweh's revelation of Godself as other than the world and humans (Hos. 11:9), Lord of all creation (Is 6:5; Ps 97:5), the almighty (Ps 135) who resembles nothing in the created world (Ex 20:4, Dt 5:8) and other similar descriptions apparently support that belief since God is unlike creatures, who are subject to change.

On the other hand, the Israelites experienced Yahweh as a living God (Jdg 8:19; 1 Kgs 17:1) who is actively and personally present to the people. Yahweh was *their* Lord and Master. In fact, the Hebrew Scriptures are a record of that personal involvement of God with the people. The Israelites, therefore, believed in a God who was utterly other but who despite this status listened, talked, wept, walked, judged and loved.

With the birth of Christianity this dual conception of God gains more significance. Although one finds a reference to the 'Father of lights with whom there is no variation or shadow due to change' (Jas 1:17), the belief in God's immutability and transcendence posed certain difficulties in the light of the affirmation that the Word himself, who in the beginning was with God and is God, has become flesh and lives among men (Jn 1:1-14). For, if the Word is divine, how does one interpret his relationship with the Father and at the same time uphold God's oneness and immutability? Moreover, how should one explain the Word himself becoming man without introducing the notion of change in divinity? These were the kind of questions which confronted the early church and, more particularly, the Fathers. But the immutability of God continued to be taken for granted because of its biblical basis. Hence, the early Christian debates centred around the reconciliation of God's immutability and impassibility with the reality of the Incarnation.[1]

CLASSICAL THEISM

However, our concern here is with the conceptual development of the belief in God's immutability by certain classical theists. Let us now look briefly at how these thinkers articulated and defended the concept of an immutable God.

Philo (ca 20 BC - AD 54) is regarded by some as the founder of classical theism. In his writings one will find the double insistence upon divine absoluteness and immutability and upon

God's omniscient providence which puts God in a relation with all other beings.[2] Philo did not deviate from the Judaeo-Christian ideas of creation and providence, but at the same time he accepted the Aristotelian denial of all relativity, temporality, dependence, passivity and inner complexity in the divine. What results is a logical tension which became a characteristic of classical theism.

For Philo certain scriptural passages could be elaborated by using Aristotelian categories. Thus, the 'one God' of the Bible was translated philosophically into 'God is one entity,' i.e. without complexity; and the revelation of Yahweh's nature (Ex 3:14) was understood as the identification of essence and existence, i.e. God's very nature is to exist and God's actuality exhausts all possibilities. The biblical prohibition of idols emphasised the unlikeness of God to creatures. Since Aristotle had equated mutability with corporeality, it was inevitable that God, who stands apart from everyone else, would be depicted as immutable and as having no corporeal or spatial characteristics. As Philo puts it: 'God alone exists in a continual and unvarying existence. But those creatures which owe their existence to creation and generation all are subject to changes in time.'[3] Philo regards 'this world which is always in the same place and in the same condition,' as the most evident proof for God's unchangeableness—a view undoubtedly influenced by Aristotle's static cosmology.

In this thinker one will also discover traces of the teaching, to be explored further by other classical theists such as Boethius and Aquinas, that nothing is future to God. As creator of time, God controls its very boundaries. There is neither past nor future to God, only present. Furthermore, Philo maintained that God does not benefit from anyone since God is not in need of anything but is continually and unceasingly benefiting all things. He accepts the reality of divine love as taught by the Scriptures, but he seems to stress more the majestic power of God. Even the statement 'I am thy God,' which some would take as indicating a personal relationship between God and God's people, is interpreted by Philo to be a certain figurative misuse of language rather than a strict reference to the living God who, Philo claims, does not have any relation to anything.

Like Philo *Augustine (AD 354 - 430)* combines the vision of God captured in Sacred Scripture (now including the New Testament) with Greek philosophy. He does not question that God is a wholly immutable or non-temporal actuality. However, he does realise that that view has to be reconciled with the scriptural account of creation. The Manicheans objected to the Christian doctrine of *creatio ex nihilo* since, according to them, if one could speak of an absolute beginning, one could always ask what happened before something else. So questions arise: What was God doing before the creation? Why did God create the world when God did and not sooner or later? Augustine's response is to explain that time is merely the order of the created. Thus the problem would simply not emerge since God as Creator is outside the temporal order. Augustine writes: 'But if before *heaven and earth* there was no time, why is it demanded, what Thou then didst? For there was no "then" when there was no time.'[4] In another passage he says: 'God created the world not in time but with time.'[5]

And because for Augustine God is outside time, God is totally immutable. Augustine expresses this point succinctly: 'God is unchangeable because of his eternity, without beginning or end. Consequently, he is also incorruptible. For one and the same thing is therefore said, whether God is called eternal or immortal or incorruptible or unchangeable.'[6] Time implies change, and only the created temporal beings are changeable. The apparent change, then, from non-creator to creator does not occur in God but on the part of creatures. This is an argument that will find its way into the thinking of later defenders of God's immutability.

God's complete changelessness is also affirmed by the Jewish philosopher, *Maimonides (1135 - 1204)*.[7] Like Philo, he was influenced by Aristotle and was confronted with the task of showing the compatibility of Judaism with philosophical tenets derived from the Greeks. He is a highly systematic thinker, offering elaborate arguments for his assertions. In this sense he paved the way for that great systematiser, Thomas Aquinas.

Maimonides follows Philo in arguing that any positive predicates ascribable to God, who has absolute existence, could not possibly have anything in common with those accessible to our experience and thought. The most significant example of this is knowledge. God's knowledge of the world, in the opinion of Maimonides, is not comparable to any type of knowledge; non-divine knowledge cannot be infallibly accurate due to possible changes in the object of knowledge. Maimonides accepts that these changes are real. Hence, since he also believes that God's knowledge must be infallible, he concludes that the term 'knowledge' as applied to God has a completely different meaning. In other words, our use of that word is equivocal.

What is at the root of this assertion is the belief in the immutable perfection of God, or in God's utter simplicity. Maimonides cites the Aristotelian argument for an unmoved mover as philosophically establishing divine immutability. Furthermore, it shows God's simplicity because if there is composition in God, God could change. Religiously, Maimonides appeals to the belief that 'The Lord our God is One' as supporting the conclusion that God is one simple substance without any composition or plurality of elements. He adds that anything hinting of corporeality or passiveness is to be denied of God. All perfections must really exist in God, and none of them must in any way be a mere potentiality. He dismisses the view that God is related, despite his admission that having relations would not require a change in God's essence.

It has been said that *Aquinas (1225 - 1274)* is the most Aristotelian Christian and the most Christian Aristotelian. There is no doubting his achievement in fusing Aristotle's philosophy and Christian beliefs nor his eminent place in classical theism. Aquinas' thinking on God's unchangeableness is summed up in question 9, article 1 of the first part of his *Summa Theologiae*. It represents a succinct argumentation considerably influenced by Aristotelian metaphysics.

Aquinas provides three reasons for concluding that God must be altogether unchangeable. The first is based on the metaphysical principle that actuality precedes potentiality, that is, something must first be before it becomes. God as the first existent must therefore be regarded as sheerly actual and unalloyed with potentiality. Such a reality cannot change. The second reason is rooted in Aquinas' explanation of change: anything in change partly persists and partly passes as a thing changing from white to black. This is an example of accidental change; but the same applies to substantial change, namely, that change is possible for a reality if it is composite. But God is simple (Aquinas discusses this attribute in question 3); thus, God is not capable of change. Lastly, for Aquinas change implies imperfection since anything which changes acquires something which it did not previously have. God being limitless and perfect, cannot be said to lack nor acquire anything else. Hence, God does not need to change.

On the question of the relations between God and the world—an issue which we came across in Philo and Maimonides—Aquinas states that a relation of God to creatures is not a reality in God but in creatures.[8] It is in God only as far as God is related to us in our idea only. Aquinas is here introducing the distinction between 'real' and 'logical' relations. (Later Thomists will make much use of this). Creatures are really related to God, but in God there is no real but merely logical relation. This is because the two are of different orders: God is outside the whole order of creation whereas all creatures are directed to God and not conversely. And yet Aquinas maintains that there is nothing to prevent us from predicating of God temporally terms which suggest a relation, e.g. knowledge, to creatures. But the change occurs not in God but in creatures. As an illustration, Aquinas refers to a column which is on the right of an animal. The column has not changed its position; it is the animal which changes its position. Similarly, God is spoken of relatively inasmuch as the creature is related to God.

Aquinas explains further that God knows Godself through God's essence. However, God knows about things not in themselves but in Godself since God's essence contains the similitude of things other than Godself. Since God knows things not only in general but as they are distinct from each other, it must be said that God has proper knowledge. However, the term as applied to God is used analogically. This is because for Aquinas whatever perfection exists in any creature exists in God in an excelling manner.

But God's knowledge of created reality is from eternity. God knows all things, not only what is actual but also what is possible. The object of God's knowledge includes all contingent realities as they are in their causes and as they actually are in themselves. Contingent realities become actual successively; but, Aquinas explains, God knows them not successively but simultaneously. The reason for this is that God's knowledge, as well as God's being, is measured by eternity. Eternity, being simultaneously whole, comprises all time. All things that are in time are present to God, therefore, from eternity. That is, God has the types of are dehumanising. To try to justify them is to turn a blind eye to the hurt and pain which can sometimes lead to what can only be described as an inhuman kind of existence. This is particularly true of the misery and the degradation experienced by the poor. We may try to impart a theological, biblical or spiritual meaning to their plight, yet we cannot escape the economics of it. Nor can we ignore its psychological consequences. Poverty is extreme need or destitution. It means the way of life of the slum-dwellers or the homeless of Latin America or of the Philippines, of over-populated India, of the ghettos of America and elsewhere, of famine-stricken Ethiopia, Sudan and Somalia. Poverty hurts and oppresses people because it deprives them of the necessities of life. It creates the gap between the rich, over-fed landlord and the hungry, grief-stricken tenant. It makes a parent worry over the next crumb for the family. It forces a man or woman to stand in line at employment agencies in spite of the very slim chance of getting a job. Poverty is what causes grim-faced children to peer into restaurants to watch the more fortunate ones partake of life's bounties—as if the mere sight of food is enough to ease the hunger they feel. Poverty is certainly not a welcome word, and its effects are to be dreaded and avoided.[30] Hence, it is crucial that we work towards the removal of the causes of this kind of suffering. We ought to use every resource at our disposal to transform the situation.[31]

In claiming that we must root out the causes of this kind of suffering whenever possible—as another practical response to the challenge of suffering—we are asserting that God is not its cause. It is unfortunate when poor people are simply encouraged to 'accept their poverty' as the lot assigned to them by God. This is really to ignore that often the real causes are the actions and policies of people. The most appropriate loving response then is to identify and remove these causes as part of our struggle to construct a just and peaceful society in which all—and not just the powerful few—can live in dignity and be masters of their own destinies.

Third-world writers, for instance, are becoming increasingly conscious of the obstacles put forward by certain economic and social aspects of Western society to the complete fulfillment of their people as human beings. They are critical of the growing dehumanisation brought about by structures which are in fact structures of domination. These structures may bring about an things present within God, and God's glance is carried from eternity over all things as they are in their presentness. Aquinas resorts to an analogy of someone looking down from a height at moving traffic. From that person's perspective everything is happening simultaneously although not so from the perspective of someone below. Aquinas thus denies that God's knowledge is variable although God knows the variability of things since whatever is or can be in any period of time is known by God from eternity.

SUFFERING AND THE CONCEPT OF AN IMMUTABLE GOD

As we have seen, God is considered by the thinkers whom we have surveyed so far to be utterly changeless. There is no relativity, temporality or passivity in God. The correlative of this teaching is that there is no suffering in God either.

Anselm (1033 - 1109) appears to accept the truth of God's complete immutability in his development of the idea of divine perfection. He holds that all of us, including the fool who has said in his heart that there is no God, have an idea of God. The fool understands what the idea means although he denies that it corresponds to an objective reality. For Anselm God is 'a being than which nothing greater can be conceived.' He equates this concept with that of an absolute maximum of greatness, 'a supreme Good requiring nothing else and which all other things require for their existence and well-being.'[9] God, therefore, lacks no perfection and is thereby self-sufficient. God is outside all time—no yesterday, today or tomorrow—since these have no existence except in time. God does not exist in space or time; but all things, which God created from nothing, exist in God. Unlike created reality, which has contingent existence (with the essential precariousness, dependence, derivativeness and non-eternity) and is imperfect, God as a perfect being exists necessarily, non-dependent and eternally. Any change is thus ruled out because it would detract from God's necessity and eternity. God in no way requires change or motion, nor is God compelled to undergo change or motion.

But if God lacks no perfection, must God be said to be compassionate? Anselm accepts that to be compassionate is to feel sympathy. Yet God for Anselm is passionless; so how does one explain that God nonetheless is 'the source of so great consolation to the wretched'? Anselm resolves the difficulty by stating that God is compassionate in terms of our experience and not compassionate in terms of God's being. That is to say, we experience the effect of compassion, but God does not experience the feeling. Thus, without compromising God's utter immutability, Anselm offers an explanation of divine love. But, once again, any change which takes place does so in creatures and not in God.

This is certainly the view held by *von Hügel (1852 - 1925)*, who believed that Plato, Aristotle, Plotinus, the Old Testament, even the sayings of Jesus, imply on the whole a purely joyous deity, free from suffering.[10] This classical theist rules out any suffering in God because suffering, as von Hügel understands it, is intrinsically an evil. Although suffering cannot be regarded as identical to sin, he thinks that they are sufficiently alike for it to be exceedingly difficult to treat sin as intrinsically evil if suffering is not treated as evil at all. He claims that accordingly fundamental religious experience and apprehension do not impute the presence in God of any evil, be it sin or even only sorrow, whether actual or potential. Von Hügel is also concerned to preserve God's transcendence. In his opinion religious considerations demand that we uphold this belief. God's otherness, seen in God's utter sanctity and sheer beatitude, is as essential a part of the facts and of the power of religion as God's likeness can ever be. There is an immense contrast between God and us, who are contingent, changing and transitory.

The wish to consider God one of us has been fulfilled in the Incarnation, says von Hügel, in that like us the human nature of Jesus Christ suffered. God, however, does not suffer. Does this mean that God does not sympathise with us? On the contrary, von Hügel affirms that God's omniscience puts God in a unique position to directly reach the human heart and will. But since God is bodiless and spiritual we cannot impute physical or psychical suffering to God. Thus, like the other classical theists before him, von Hügel defends God's complete unchangeability while trying to show how we are to interpret God's love for creatures.

HARTSHORNE'S CRITICISMS OF THE
CONCEPT OF AN IMMUTABLE GOD

Within the context of this exploration, the question that has now to be asked is whether the concept of an immutable God as developed by classical theism helps us to understand meaningfully the belief in a compassionate and liberating God. To put it in another way, to what extent can one support the claim that the immutable God of classical theism is a concerned God? We have seen briefly how Anselm and von Hügel handle this problem. Nevertheless, this issue has recently become a bone of contention, particularly in the context of wide-spread suffering in the world. For it is asked, how can one continue to portray a loving God as immutable—unmoved and unmovable—with so much pain and suffering about? While maintaining that God is compassionate, classical theists have persistently denied that this means God suffers with us.

One of the most articulate critics of the classical concept of God has been Charles Hartshorne. In chapter 3 we noted briefly his criticism of Anselm's interpretation of God's compassion. Against Anselm Hartshorne argues that God's compassion must be said to imply that God does truly suffer with us. For Hartshorne God is a sympathetic participant in our sufferings. Hartshorne argues that if the nature of knowledge is such that concrete knowledge of suffering is in some sense sharing in that suffering, how much more true is this of God? God's knowledge is so concrete and intimate that God is united with the sufferings of creatures much more fully than any sympathy of ours can unite us with those suffering individuals that we care about. In Hartshorne's view, therefore, God does not simply know *that* we suffer; God is aware of our actual pain and misery in their concreteness. As he puts it, God after all cannot remain aloof in the face of real suffering.[11]

Hartshorne agrees with classical theism that if God is regarded as the object of our worship—and God is so regarded in religion—then God must be perfect for only someone who is perfect can be admired, respected and reverenced without limit.[12] But God's perfection has been interpreted by classical theism to mean 'non-relative or devoid of any relations and is therefore incapable of change or increase.' It was felt that in order to uphold God's perfection consistently, one must say that God is absolute, completely immutable and totally independent. Hartshorne admits that one can find this insistence on God's unchangeableness in religious teachings, but he points out that it is God's goodness which is affirmed never to change or to be 'without a shadow of turning.' The different religions consider God to be all-good: God is completely reliable for no matter what changes there may be in us, God will not waver in the concern for our well-being. In this sense there can be no change whatsoever in God. But this talk of God's constancy in goodness, Hartshorne argues, does not justify a general conclusion as to God's immutability or absoluteness. To support his view, Hartshorne reminds us that religion also emphasises God's social and personal nature. For religion God is the highest ruler, judge and benefactor who knows, loves and assists us with a view to sharing God's happiness with us. All this would indicate that God is definitely related to us. It is this relatedness of God that leads Hartshorne to question the classical theist's interpretation of God's nature.

How then should one understand God's worshipfulness which implies God's perfection, and at the same time take account of God's social nature? According to Hartshorne, this can be done by using the philosophical category of 'unsurpassability' rather than of absoluteness.[13] For God to be worshipful, God must be unsurpassable. God's status excludes any rivalry or superiority on the part of any other individual, actual or potential.[14] Here Hartshorne agrees with Anselm that God is a 'being than which nothing or no one is or could be greater.' Because only God is unsurpassable, God is qualitatively different from everyone else.

But while God cannot be surpassed by others, God in Hartshorne's view, unlike in Anselm's, can surpass Godself.[15] While there can be no change whatsoever in God's status, there can be change in God. God can surpass Godself, not in the sense that God can be more God but in the sense that God can be affected by what others do.

On the other hand, if God is worshipful, God must be perfect in Godself and not merely in comparison with others. Is saying that God can surpass Godself and can change not equivalent to maintaining that God can grow in perfection? If this is true, then God must not have been perfect in the first place. Accordingly, classical theism considers God's perfection to be absolute i.e., 'complete and incapable of enhancement.' Absolute perfection means the actualisation of every potentiality. In classical theism God was described as being perfect in this sense; hence, the phrase *actus purus*. Because God possesses everything that is in accordance with the nature of a supreme Being, nothing is said to contribute anything to God. God is necessarily all that God is capable of being. Unlike ordinary or imperfect individuals which fail to actualise some of their potentialities, God was conceived to be pure actuality, that is, to have no unactualised aspect of God's reality. Classical theism argued that if God did not already possess all possible values, God would not be God. God as the absolutely perfect being was considered to lack no possible value.

Hartshorne objects to this interpretation of God's perfection because he considers it contradictory. 'Absolute perfection' is contradictory, he argues, because not all values can co-exist.[16] To equate God's perfection with the idea that everything in God is fully actualised is to ignore that some values contradict one another. The claim that 'all possible values are fully actualised' is nonsensical, Hartshorne tells us. For instance, God cannot be said to know me as going out for a walk and at the same time as writing these words. Both are positive values. If I am going out for a walk, then God knows me in that state. But in knowing me in that state, God is excluding from the content of God's knowledge the other value (knowing me as writing). God cannot know me as doing the two things together at the same time—not because of any limitation on God's part, but because the two simply cannot co-exist. The second value, given the actuality of the first, is a potential value for me as well as for God. To say that all possible value is actual in God *because God is God* is to make possibility and actuality co-extensive and for all purposes identical. But this would empty 'actualisation' of all meaning whereas it means that one does or is this and for that reason *not* to do this or be that. Thus, if the notion of absolute perfection understood in the sense of *actus purus* is contradictory, then we cannot affirm it of God. Even God cannot be said to have all values actualised because this is nonsensical.

Hartshorne's other objection to the classical interpretation of God's perfection as absolute and therefore incapable of any change whatsoever is that the denial of change in any form in God makes it impossible to make sense of religious beliefs.[17] The doctrine of total immutability, he holds, cannot be reconciled with the religious stress on God's love and our duty to serve God. Religions teach that what we do makes a difference to God. Because God cares for us, what we do matters to God. But if all possible values were already actualised in God, there would be no point in our doing anything at all. There would be no sense in serving God. If God were unaffected by the acts of God's creatures, God would hardly be a sympathetic God.

Hartshorne argues that an important feature of the religious idea of God is that God is one with whom we are able to enter into a personal relationship. And this is understood as mutual relationship. Such a relationship implies that both parties are moved by whatever happens to the other. To love is to be really affected by what the other does. If God is the God of compassion and understanding, then it must mean that God really and literally responds to our feelings with sympathetic appreciation. Compassion implies that one is truly, and not merely apparently, touched by our plight. An unmoved mover or, worse still, an unmovable mover is hardly our model of love, compassion and sympathy. God's relationship with us understood religiously thus points to a certain receptivity or passivity on God's part. But this means that there must be some change *in God*. According to Hartshorne, God must therefore be regarded as capable of change.

But in conformity with God's nature as unsurpassable, God changes eminently—and only eminently. This means that one cannot attribute decay or decrease in value to God. Thus, while ordinary individuals may change by increasing or decreasing in value, God can only increase. God cannot become inferior, even to Godself, but can and endlessly does surpass Godself as well as all others.

For Hartshorne, then, God's perfection understood as 'unsurpassability' enables us to predicate change in God. Hartshorne maintains that it also leaves open the possibility of taking seriously any claim of a personal relationship with God, a relationship that means something to us as well as to God. In conformity with God's supreme nature God is supremely moved by everything that happens whereas none of us is universally nor fully moved by everything. In showing that God can and does change, Hartshorne wants to give support to the religious doctrine that God is someone personally related to us. Hartshorne is thus maintaining that the categories of *becoming* and *relatedness* also apply to God though in an eminent way.

For Hartshorne God changes, really changes. But God is also said to be immutable and absolute in some respects. For instance, God's unsurpassability is never changing. There is no question of God's identity being threatened by anyone. No matter what anyone does, God's superiority cannot be challenged. It remains constant. God possesses an absolutely immutable quality, the quality of being universally superior, of surpassing absolutely all others. Whatever non-divine beings do, they cannot alter God's being God. Thus, while God's relatedness is responsive to every item of reality, God's identity is infallibly secure or non-touchable. In this respect, God is absolute and immutable. For this reason God is different from us *in principle* and not just in degree.

In the next chapter we will have occasion to investigate more fully the conceptuality developed by Hartshorne as an alternative to the classical theistic one. But first let us examine another set of criticisms of the concept of an immutable God in the face of widespread oppression and poverty.

CRITICISMS FROM LATIN AMERICAN LIBERATION THEOLOGIANS

From another perspective the classical concept of an immutable God has also been subjected to much criticism. Victorio Araya, a liberation theologian from Costa Rica, writes in his *God of the Poor* that from the perspective of the suffering and the hope of the poor, their view of God makes a clean break with the picture of the perfect, immutable, and impassible God of the Greek tradition:

> The philosophical notions that seem most applicable to the supreme being were those of prime mover, efficient cause, almighty doer. An active love did not seem applicable. Love did not figure among the Greek categories of perfection. If God is perfect, how can God love? To the Greek mind, love is passion, *pathos*. Love means having needs, depending on someone. Consequently, if God is perfect, God cannot love. After all, God is not in need of anything. Total inability to love will entail total incapacity to suffer, or to save in suffering (not

in virtue of the suffering, but in virtue of love). The image of the liberating God of the Bible is a very different one.[18]

Thus, in Araya's view the image of God among the poor, the biblical God as Liberator, stands in contrast to that conceived by the Greek mind.

Victor Codina also attacks the concept of an impassible, triumphalistic, neutral and self-satisfied God, unperturbed by the 'damned of the earth,' as being far removed from the God who liberates. He likens the immutable God to the gods of Olympus or the mighty of this earth. Both settle down where they are beyond the reach of the starving and the oppressed masses.[19]

The inability of the classical theistic concept of an immutable God to meet the demands of the Latin American experience of impoverishment, injustice and poverty is further brought out by Jon Sobrino. He writes: 'The Greek metaphysical conception of God's being and perfection renders any theology of the cross impossible. A truly historical theology of liberation must view suffering as a mode of being belonging to God.'[20] It is for this reason that Sobrino insists that liberation theology go beyond Greek thought and inquire in what sense suffering and death can be a mode of being for God. Blaming the identification of God's perfection with immutability, Sobrino claims that it has made God ahistorical and eternal. Suffering therefore is considered alien to God since it implies passivity and mutability. As he puts it, 'Greek thought cannot picture suffering as a divine mode of being because that would imply a contradiction.'[21] One gets the impression that Sobrino believes that the only way out is to reject entirely this identification of God's perfection with immutability.

The criticisms of the concept of an immutable God by these and other Latin American liberation theologians who affirm God to be a liberator is well summed up by Peter Phan:

God the Liberator clearly is not the *Actus Purus* who is absolute, immutable, impassible, eternal, independent, all-powerful. Rather, he reveals himself as the God of love, as suffering love; the God who is crucified, who internalises all the pain, sorrow, and horrors of history, who takes the side of the poor against their oppressors, who participates in the changing process of history, who 'lets himself [be] affected by' human history; the God who is the liberator, the vindicator (*Go'el*), the God of life 'who vanquishes death and re-creates life'.[22]

JUAN LUIS SEGUNDO'S CRITIQUE

Juan Luis Segundo, another noted liberation theologian, has also some harsh words about the conception of God as some immutable, self-sufficient nature. His critique brings out another dimension of the liberationist view. Such a conception, he argues, is nothing but the rationalisation of our own alienated social relationships.[23] Segundo adds that the only valid refutations of thinkers like Marx, Freud and Nietzsche who regarded God as crippling humans is not so much proving that God exists after all but rather liberating ourselves from the alienations caused by false notions of God. He regards the concept of an immutable God as one such notion.[24] He points to the sociological impact of such an idea of God and the ideological bias of those who continue to uphold it.

Segundo explains his critique by showing that the image we have of God intimately corresponds to the image we have of our neighbours. Our treatment of other humans influences the way we think of God. As he succinctly puts it, 'Our idea of God is conditioned by our experiences of interpersonal relationships with others in this world.'[25] Segundo warns that neglecting to take into account this intimate connection between our dealings with others and our idea of God has dangerous consequences to ourselves and to others. He spells this out forcefully: 'Our falsified and inauthentic ways of dealing with our fellow men are allied to our falsifications of the idea of God.'[26]

Developing this line of argument further, Segundo also claims: 'Our unjust society and our perverted idea of God are in close and terrible alliance.'[27] Along similar lines Pablo Richard, a Chilean biblical scholar and sociologist, maintains that the practice of justice and correct thinking about God go hand in hand. He adds that conversely, to commit injustice is to necessarily think idolatrously of God.[28] Why? Because, Segundo observes, people seek to *do* something with God. He furthermore notes that people's concept of God conceals their class interests, their immaturity vis-a-vis reality, their fragility and weaknesses.[29]

Victorio Araya echoes this point when he writes that despite the claim to worship the true God and to believe in Jesus Christ, in reality we conceal under those names our own selfish group or class interests. The name of God may have been preserved, but it has been emptied of content.[30] In other words, the deformations that have occurred, and continue to occur, in our notion of God spring from the fact that we fashion God into the image and likeness not only of our personal existence but also of our society.[31]

The close connection between human beings and their concept of God has been of course a constant theme in many theological and philosophical writings (and as we saw previously, also in literature). But what makes Segundo's point particularly relevant is that he focuses on the social dimension of humanity, i.e. the individual *in society*. He regards the individualistic emphasis, which seems to perpetuate the concept of an immutable God devoid of any real relations to creatures, to have been transcended in Christianity since Christian liberty is radically social; that is to say, humanity is free when it spontaneously gives itself, in love, to other persons.[32] The social dimension of our humanity, which Christianity enables us to become much more aware of, must not be ignored.

Segundo claims that as our whole existence came to be made up of broader and more complex social relationships, the features of our *society* started to show more and more clearly in our notion of God. Hence, in his view we need to look into the interaction between our idea of God and real-life social relationships.[33] This is why he espouses the method of suspecting that anything and everything involving ideas, including theology, is intimately bound up with the existing social situation in at least an unconscious way.[34]

A good example given by Segundo of how a particular kind of society shapes our image of God can be found in what he regards as the Western concept of God. Since the West has been the milieu for the expansion of Christianity, the so-called Christian image of God quite logically reflects the conditionings of Western civilisation. Segundo is, of course, aware that this influence has not been thoroughly one-sided since Judaeo-Christianity has had a role in forming Western civilisation itself. Through a process of reciprocal influence, Western civilisation and Christianity became so closely united and identified that it was hard to distinguish the elements specific to each.

But this identity is being seriously challenged, a challenge that comes from a specific Christian awareness. Segundo's theological critique of society is done in the context of Latin America. On that continent, he writes, Christians are looking at Western society with a critical eye insofar as they see in this society obstacles to the complete fulfillment of human beings. Such a critical look, Segundo tells us, cannot avoid creating a crisis for the traditional Christian image of God.[35] Thus, in Latin America, as Philip Berryman notes, what is at stake is not simply an ethical exigency but the very nature of God.[36]

Segundo becomes more specific in his observations of Western society. Undoubtedly, due to technological developments, Western society can be characterised by the growing complexity of social structures: labour relations, commercial transactions, class relationship, power, and so on. The more these structures of domination are perfected and seemingly made more subtle, the more clearly is their inhuman character revealed.[37] But Segundo is not devaluing the progress made by Western society. He believes that the transition from feudal society to modern society was a forward step in the recognition of the rights of the individual. Nevertheless, there have been unwelcome consequences. Segundo's observations highlight an important point: the highly competitive society has benefited only a few and has dehumanised countless others. In other parts of the world the accelerated pace of development may have produced a greater distribution of wealth. Unfortunately, this is not true in Latin America.

Whenever some individuals dominate others, society is faced with a crisis when people become aware of and hostilely confront the growing dehumanisation brought about by social structures. According to Segundo, such a situation also creates, as was pointed out, a tension in Christian consciousness, particularly with respect to the image of God. As he himself puts it:

> On the one hand, once the capitalist system has revealed the full dimensions of its inhuman domination in the course of its development, the Christian finds no element in his concrete societal existence that would help him to ponder the God who revealed himself in Jesus Christ. What is more, his indictment

of the social system necessarily leads him to criticise a notion of God which is the projection of the false image created by an ideology of domination. In this sense we can say that never before has it been so difficult to conceive the Christian God in real-life terms.[38]

Segundo, therefore, points to the alienating effects of the industrial, technological and capitalist world of the West. He maintains that the history of human *dominion* over nature (which was meant to transform the world) is also the history of the *domination* of some human beings over other human beings. The aim of this process was to have the latter group assume the cost of the 'modern world' while the former group would enjoy the results. What followed was *modernisation* at the cost of *humanisation*.[39] Antonio Perez-Esclarín makes the same criticism:

> People today—even those who say they believe in God—have given over their hearts to their things and possessions. It is these that define humanity and worth. Fellow human beings are merely rungs on the ladder toward the possession of more and more things. Trodden down and turned into an anonymous mass, the vast majority of human beings look up to the top of the pyramid where a small minority enjoy the benefits of luxury, waste, and arbitrary whimsy. The law of might makes right continues to determine relationships between nations, peoples, and human groups, though it is disguised under developmentalist statistics, myths about aid, and innocuous smiles.[40]

Briefly then, what Segundo and others seem to be warning us against is a concept of God that supports a particular mentality that leads to widespread and institutionalised suffering in society. In their view the experiences of the downtrodden, the deprived, the disadvantaged should make us question the kind of society that is responsible for this situation. Moreover, it should make us suspicious of the concept of an immutable God which they claim is directly related to that kind of society.

IN SEARCH OF NEW CONCEPTUALITIES

In this chapter we have examined the concept of an immutable God with a specific purpose in mind: whether or not it enables us to speak credibly of God in the face of the challenge of suffering. Both Hartshorne and Latin American liberation theologians provide negative answers. While Hartshorne focuses on the inconsistency of such a concept given other claims about God, Latin American liberation theologians concern themselves with the inadequacy of this concept to do justice to their experience of widespread and institutionalised suffering. Peter Phan correctly notes that Hartshorne's objections stem mainly from his response to the crisis of meaning in the doctrine of God while Latin American liberation theologians' criticisms are based on their belief in the inability of the classical theistic doctrine of God to foster and sustain a liberative praxis in favor of the poor and the oppressed and to its tendency to preserve the status quo.[41] Since our methodology stresses both meaning and praxis, we have examined the two sets of criticisms. However, as we stated at the end of chapter 3, the stage of *rejection* in the process of exploring our images of God is merely a first stage. It is an important step because it enables us to clarify what we should not be saying about God. However, we need to go further in our exploration.[42] We need to search for new conceptualities that hopefully will be more compatible with our experiences of suffering and even more so with theistic responses to the challenge of suffering.

Chapter 6

REFORMULATING THE MEANING OF GOD'S COMPASSIONATE LOVE

Our reflections in Part I on various experiences of suffering and some of the practical responses by believers to its challenge yielded some images of God. One such image, we suggested earlier, is that of a God who is a co-sufferer. For many people God is experienced, despite initial feelings of abandonment, as one who is present with them in their hour of sorrow. Somehow they experience God's sympathy in the compassion shown to them by others. For this reason they also speak of a compassionate God. It is an image that gives them hope. But how is one to understand the meaning of such an image? How can one develop further the implications of believing in a God who is a sympathetic participant in our sufferings?

In this chapter we shall examine Charles Hartshorne's concept of a dipolar God.[1] We shall be primarily interested in how this conceptuality can help us reformulate the meaning of God's compassionate love. In line with the methodology presented at the end of chapter 3, we are turning to Hartshorne's concept of God because we have *recognised* its attractiveness and value in developing the image of God as co-sufferer. But as we have also stated, the process of conceptualising our images of God sometimes means an *adjustment or adaptation*. Thus, we will be suggesting that Hartshorne's conceptuality may need some modification or further development. Our intention here is not so much to justify the belief in a compassionate God as to provide a conceptual framework for articulating and developing this belief.

THE CONCEPT OF GOD AS DIPOLAR

When we examined Hartshorne's criticisms of the classical doctrine of divine immutability, we noted that for him God's perfection must be understood as worshipfulness.[2] In turn he understands this to mean unsurpassability. He claims that this category is not only more meaningful but is also consistent with many of the claims about God, including the belief that God is compassionate.

The notion of unsurpassability, according to Hartshorne, allows for change in God while preserving God's unrivalled and unchanging status. Hence, for Hartshorne God is relative and absolute, immutable and changing. That is to say, God is dipolar: God has a concrete pole (aspect) and an abstract pole. God is related and changing in God's concreteness while in the abstract aspect God is absolute and unchanging. Neither aspect can be comprehended apart from the other. The concreteness of anything (which Hartshorne refers to as its actuality) is *how* that something exists. It is to be contrasted with its abstract existence, *that* it is. *How* something exists is far richer and more complex than the bare fact *that* it is. Concrete actuality therefore is more than bare existence.[3]

This distinction between concrete actuality and abstract existence is of such vital importance in Hartshorne's doctrine of God that we should clarify it further by using the human person as an example. When I refer to John's concrete actuality, I am referring to John who is constantly changing. He grows up, he does this or that, he is affected by the things and people around him — in short, he changes in so many ways. The actual or the real John constantly changes and is related. However, if I were to exclude all these changes and the social and the personal side of John, what I have is the bare fact that there *is* a John — devoid of all the colour and the richness which make up the person John. Thus, while John is real in his concreteness, his existence is merely an abstract aspect of him.

What Hartshorne does when speaking of God is to use the same distinction between *concrete actuality* which constantly changes and is related, and *abstract existence* which does not undergo any change and is therefore outside any relationships. When Hartshorne says that God is related, changing yet absolute and immutable, he has in mind God's 'dipolarity,' i.e., the distinction between God's concrete actuality and God's abstract existence. He is referring to only one entity but is taking into account the two aspects of the same entity. There is only one God but there are two aspects in God. Thus, although Hartshorne is attributing contrasting predicates to the same God, he is predicating them in different ways. When he says that God is immutable but also changing, relative yet absolute, he means that God is immutable and absolute as far as God's abstract existence is concerned; God changes and is really related as far as God's concrete actuality is the point of reference. Since Hartshorne is attributing these contrasting predicates in diverse ways, he maintains that he is not violating the principle of non-contradiction which holds that one cannot affirm contradictory predicates of the same reality at the same time. Hartshorne says that 'absoluteness' and 'relatedness' are being predicated of God in diverse ways since these predicates refer to different aspects of God.

God's actuality puts God in a genuine relationship with us insofar as God is affected by what we do or have become. Thus, it is true to say that our woes, our grief and suffering just as our joys and happiness have a real impact on God. To a possible objection that being affected is indicative of an imperfection, Hartshorne explains that that there is an inappropriate way of responding or being affected and this is what constitutes the imperfection, rather than being affected as such. Citing the case of a father and a child, Hartshorne reminds us that a father who has no regard to the will and welfare of his child is not considered to be an ideal parent. Such a father to whom the child's plight, be it good or bad, makes no difference cannot be a father who wins our admiration. The ideal response is neither remaining unmoved nor being swayed by every whim of his child. Rather , what would be regarded as the ideal is that the father should be influenced in appropriate, and only in appropriate, ways by the child's desires and fortunes. In the same manner a person who is equally happy and serene and joyous regardless of how men and women suffer around him or her is hardly a model. But it would not be admirable either for that person to be dragged down into helpless misery by the sight of suffering in others. Such a response would be equally inappropriate. In short, what is admirable and ideal is appropriateness in one's response, not no response. Applying this to God,

Hartshorne maintains that it would not make religious sense if God is not better satisfied by our good than by our evil acts and less satisfied by the acts we do perform than God would have been by those better ones we might have achieved.[4] More to the point, it is unthinkable to Hartshorne for God to remain untouched by what happens to God's creatures.

Keith Ward sees the value of the doctrine of dipolarity in our attempt to explain God's perfection. For reasons similar to those given by Hartshorne, he finds the Thomistic identification of God's perfection with pure act unsatisfactory. Ward agrees that God's perfection is compatible with, or even requires, change of a certain sort and that God has both necessary and contingent aspects, that God is eternal yet involved in time; in short, that God is—in Hartshorne's terminology—dipolar.[5] John Macquarrie too is of the opinion that dipolarity predicated of God is a significant attempt to build a concept of God that will take account of various claims made about God[6] although he wonders whether Hartshorne's God is intellectually and religiously satisfying.[7]

However, dipolarity in God has also been subjected to much criticism. H. P. Owen finds that the distinction between God's abstract aspect and concrete aspect is unintelligible because in his view 'abstract' has a logical and not an ontological reference. It designates concepts rather than entities. If by 'abstract identity' one means God's necessity considered in isolation from all else in God's being or reality, then that notion, Owen argues, is untenable. He offers three arguments: 1) the idea of 'necessity' as a 'core' in God's being that is untouched by God's other properties is meaningless; 2) the idea of God's 'necessity' entails the identity of God's essence with existence, in which case God can be necessary if and only if God is all that God is (or could be) simultaneously; 3) what is the relation between God's non-dependent 'abstract identity' and dependent 'concrete existence'? Does the identity not 'exist'? Owen sums up his critique by accusing Hartshorne's doctrine of dipolarity as an exercise in sheer word-spinning.[8]

One gets the impression, however, that Owen is objecting to Hartshorne's use of the word 'abstract' because it differs from his own understanding of it. If this is the case, then it would be rather unfair to Hartshorne. One cannot simply reject another's use of a word just because it conflicts with one's usage of the same word unless, of course, it can be shown that the only definitive use of that word is one's own (or in Owen's case, in one's metaphysical system). But this is far from being true of the word 'abstract'. Owen's identification of it with 'logical' is not the only acceptable meaning of that word. But even if one were to accept Owen's interpretation of 'abstract' as referring to something logical, one would still have to consider what the objective referent of this logical entity or idea is. Are ideas not ideas *of* something? Logical entities, must correspond somehow to something external to the mind. The logical ultimately points to some aspect of extramental reality. Hartshorne can legitimately hold that 'abstract' is not a mere description nor a mere logical entity but an aspect of God's reality. The abstract, as he says, is something arrived at by omitting certain considerations which are true of the reality in question, by not paying attention to some aspects of the fullness of that reality. The abstract is really a partial feature of the concrete reality. Moreover, Owen seems to miss the crucial distinction (evidenced in the third reason he gives) between abstract existence and concrete *actuality* (*not* existence as Owen states) and what that distinction implies.

GOD'S LOVE AND GOODNESS

Earlier it was suggested that Hartshorne's emphasis on God's relativity or relatedness is designed to make sense of the religious claim that God's compassion means that God really loves us. In contrast, Hartshorne believes that to regard God as absolute in all respects, as classical theism does, is to violate this basic belief in God's all-pervading love. In this section we shall see how Hartshorne further develops his concept of a dipolar God in the context of his discussion of God's love.[9]

That God is love is part of Christian teaching. Arguably it can be found in the doctrines of other religions. Hartshorne aims to substantiate this teaching by defining perfect or divine love as 'absolute adequacy to the object.'[10] He understands love as acting upon adequate awareness of others, awareness at least as adequate ideally as one has of oneself.[11] Thus, divine love is essentially social because it is 'social awareness and action from social awareness.'[12]   God's love is affirmed to be the type of awareness that responds fully to what the other is.

This rather technical conception of divine love may not be particularly inspiring.[13] But it is useful in showing that God's love implies relativity or relatedness. Just as a human individual's love for another renders him or her in some genuine sense relative to the loved one[14] so love in its eminent form makes God universally relative[14] (a point already discussed in the previous section). Hartshorne is thereby refuting the view that the highest form of love will only love an object equally exalted with itself. In experience, he asserts, one discovers that the highest animals show an interest in the welfare of the low animals, sometimes even the lowest. Since love as Hartshorne understands it is adequate awareness of the value of others, everything no matter how lowly, is completely worthy of divine love in the sense of having its interests fully appreciated. God's love embraces all.

Colin Gunton, however, thinks that Hartshorne's relative God makes God a very passive lover. Gunton criticises Hartshorne's definition of love as social awareness. According to him, just because a being perceives everything does not mean that it should love everything. Undoubtedly, a supremely social knower will be impartial in that he or she knows everything, but that impartiality is no choice on his or her part. To illustrate his argument, Gunton says that one can conceive of an all-scanning computer, programmed to scan impartially the whole of a particular system. It will be related to everything in that system, but it can hardly be said to love. His point *contra* Hartshorne is not that Hartshorne may not have other reasons for characterising God as love, but that Hartshorne cannot say that God's supreme relativity entails logically that God is in some sense personal love. In other words, the doctrine that God is love does not arise directly from his metaphysical system. But due to certain metaphysical doctrines presupposed by Hartshorne, the transition from relativity to love is made easier.[15]

Gunton's argumentation is persuasive; however, it should also be pointed out that in God's case, knowledge and love are identical, unlike in any other case, including an all-scanning computer. The reason why God responds lovingly to the other is none other than the kind of knowledge only a supreme reality can possess. Gunton fails to recognise the uniqueness of 'supreme relativity.' Moreover, the awareness of the other, which relates the lover to the loved one, also provides the reason why the other or the loved one should respond to the lover. According to Hartshorne, the most sensitively and widely responsive individual is the very one who will be most readily and widely responded to. Hence, God in being uniquely good is uniquely influential. God's goodness draws creatures to God. God's worshipful excellence and beauty inspire and move creatures. Hartshorne compares God to a sensitive parent or ruler who enjoys our feelings and thoughts and responds to them. In God's case this appreciation is perfect. Because only God can appreciate us in our full worth, we unconsciously respond to this appreciation as we do not to any other.[16] The underlying argument here is that 'the influential is what is in some relevant aspect good, and goodness is socially achieved, i.e. it arises through sensitivity to others.'[17]

Previously, we noted that Hartshorne does not agree that admitting change in God militates against the belief in the unchanging character of God's love. One has only to turn to experience again, he says, to realise that one's love for one's friend is not defective because he/she must acknowledge the presence of unrealised possibilities in the friend or because they themselves change. What Hartshorne is opposing here is the argument that God must be considered *actus purus* to be morally perfect. Moreover, Hartshorne rejects the claim that any attribution of change or potentiality in God would threaten the belief in God's immutable love because in his view love has nothing to do with the possession of all possible values. In fact, when some of these possible values or unrealised capacities are actualised there is new content for the friend's love, thereby enriching the value of this love aesthetically. It would not necessarily render it more complete or perfect in the moral sense. When Hartshorne therefore talks of change in God, he means that God acquires new content which would make God happier but not that it would make God more morally perfect. Time and again one reads in Hartshorne's works, as indeed we have already seen, that the divine constancy posited by religion refers to God's unwavering benevolence. It does not allude to the fullness of *all* values: 'Clearly it is unalterableness of character, not of value, in the full sense of aesthetic enjoyment ... that is meant by "in whom is no shadow of turning".'[18]

So while it is true that God is unchangeable in that at all times God is wholly righteous and wise, it does not by any means follow that God is at all times equally and absolutely happy. To put it in another way, to affirm that God is completely good in the ethical and cognitive sense is not to claim that God is completely good aesthetically. God's love for us which puts God in a certain relationship with us changes, aesthetically, in accordance with our actions. Because our good deeds and misdeeds really affect God, God's state of happiness will vary. But God's state of righteousness remains inflexible despite the changes of pleasure and displeasure. In fact, it is because God stays equally righteous in attitude that God is said by Hartshorne to change in total value-experience in appropriate accordance with variations in the objects of God's love.[19] Here Hartshorne and the Latin American liberation theologians would be in very close agreement. The wicked, stupid or indifferent person may be unmoved by deterioration or progress in others whereas the perfectly righteous and wise individual cannot be thus insensitive. Changes which really make a difference to the value of reality must make a difference to God.[20] In other words, Hartshorne is saying that God's relativity (or changing aspect) does not endanger the belief in God's perfect love so long as the distinction is held between the moral sense of God's love and its aesthetic sense.[21] Consequently, while God's perfection excludes God's being morally depraved, it does not eliminate aesthetic or physical evil from God's reality inasmuch as God is a sympathetic participant in our sufferings.

God's love has sometimes been contrasted with non-divine love in that God's love is said not to spring from need and is consequently unselfish while non-divine love is supposed to come from need and is therefore selfish. If this were true, then Hartshorne's God would be selfish inasmuch as God needs us to be happier. If indeed genuine love overflows from a purely self-sufficient being who derives nothing from anyone else, then it would appear that the love of Hartshorne's God would be suspect. In fact, this is what leads Hugo Meynell to eye Hartshorne's God with suspicion because in his view a God who stands to gain from persuading creatures to behave in one way rather than another is more like a tyrant.[22] However, Meynell appears to forget that the same God 'who stands to gain' suffers because of the same relationship that God has with us. Meynell's criticism reflects our tendency to regard being influenced or affected by others as something imperfect or even blameworthy. 'Standing to gain' even among humans does not always make them tyrannical, however. What does turn them into tyrants is their forgetfulness of the well-being of others. This is what causes them to mistreat or utilise others. The reciprocity of relations is the consequence of the social nature of reality and of personal relationships. So why should a God who benefits from us be classed as a tyrant so long as it can be shown that such a God is not neglectful of the welfare of others? Meynell could, of course, reply that Hartshorne's God persuades creatures to behave in one way rather than another *and that in doing so* God stands to gain. But this would be true only if God were evil whereas in Hartshorne's account God is completely good. God's persuading of others is an expression of total concern for them. Besides, persuasion unlike domination *is* respecting the other's freedom. Surely, this is not the same as being tyrannical. God would be a tyrant were God always to *compel* creatures to act in one way rather than in another. Given God's unsurpassable goodness and wisdom, God would be persuading creatures in the best way possible, even if the whole activity has an effect on God.

Hartshorne would further retort that need and self-sufficiency have several senses and everything depends upon discriminating them. 'God needs only one thing from the creatures: the intrinsic beauty of their lives, that is, their own true happiness, which is also his happiness through his perfect appreciation of theirs.'[23] Such an appreciation *is* love rather than a motive to love. Harts-horne explains that God needs us not because without us God would cease to exist, but because the exact beauty of God's own life is contingent upon the amount of beauty in lives generally. The nature of love, including divine love, is social. What one does for others always affects oneself. To raise the objection which has just been referred to is, in Hartshorne's opinion, to distort the real nature of love.

Another incentive for not accepting the argument that God must be said to be 'purely' altruistic in dealing with creatures is, as far as Hartshorne is concerned, that this leads to the conclusion that creatures can love only themselves. If God does not receive any value from us, then in effect we ourselves are the object of our love. Yet the aim of creation, religiously speaking, is to glorify God, not humankind or the world. Hartshorne interprets this to mean that God *is* glorified. To construe it in any other way is to assert that our actions have no impact on God but only on ourselves. But this would amount to accepting a humanly self-regarding end as our final goal. It would make us human beings the ultimate.

It could, of course, be argued that the ultimately achieved good is not humans, but the whole of creation. But even this is to leave us with the same conclusion: creation, not God, is the long-term end. It seems as if either God or something other than God is the final beneficiary of our achievements. Hartshorne would rather have God as that beneficiary. This is why for him God is really affected by what we do and why God could not have been just as glorious had there been no creation.

Hartshorne speaks of a certain necessity in divine goodness in that God's acts are always good and must always be so. Because God possesses surpassable goodness, God has no choice between what is morally right and what is evil even if God can choose between actions all of which are morally good. God's actions, therefore, have a necessary aspect in that God must always act unsurpassably well and be at all times morally upright. But it would be false to draw the conclusion that God's acts are in their entirety necessary. The concrete acts of God are contingent insofar as God could have responded to the world differently, but not—and this is where the necessity lies—ethically better. There is never only one possible perfect solution to the problems the world poses for God. But whatever God decides on is from the moral point of view always the best. Hartshorne explains that this is so because for God, unlike for humans, knowing and deciding are mutually inseparable. God cognitively grasps all actuality as actual and all possibility as possible in the most adequate fashion; in thus knowing reality, God desires to actualise its maximal possibilities. Since God knows the end as it is, God has every motive there can be for seeking to actualise it. There can be no ethical appeal beyond the decision of someone who takes account of every actuality and possibility.[24]

Thus, God's contingent volitions are always good but are not necessary nor eternal. For instance, the divine contingent laws of nature are temporal and are accepted as good, there being no available alternatives. Moreover, any rule is preferable to chaos. Hartshorne likens God's contingent volitions to traffic regulations.

It is necessary for the cosmos to have rules. God's contingent volitions are these rules. But others would have been just as good as—to take up the simile of traffic regulations—driving on the left, if universally accepted, would have been just as good as driving on the right. Thus, any of God's volitions is good in the way that any possible acts of an ideally good and wise ruler are good. But God is not bound to one possible course of action. Despite God's inability to choose between the greater and lesser good, in Hartshorne's view, God can adopt alternative ways of willing the greatest good.

On this point one question that has troubled theists is whether God could not have created us, like God, free but necessarily virtuous beings. It has been held that although God is not free to choose between deciding rightly and deciding wrongly, God cannot be said to have less freedom. We have seen that Hartshorne concurs with this view. As he says, 'Being necessitated to these modes of action would still leave one with innumerable free decisions to make. God would be more, not less, free since his range of creative capacities is unsurpassable.'[25] So why can we not be like God in this respect? If God can be necessarily wise and good yet free to choose among ways of being good, why not we? Hartshorne's own answer is that it is not merely for the sake of ethical freedom that creatures are free. Hartshorne maintains that the basic significance of freedom is aesthetic: concrete values are aesthetic, not ethical. There can be no necessity here. Only the abstract can be necessitated. Thus virtue can be necessary in God only because of its abstract character. Only God has that abstract character which is absolute. But the particular beauty of the cosmos is concrete. Hence, it is contingent even for God, and it is in continual process of accretion. This is why the value of God's actual experience as distinguished from God's necessary virtue is likewise endlessly enriched. Furthermore, we cannot be like God because our goodness is—and here Hartshorne agrees with Neibuhr—an 'impossible possibility,' an ideal we try to live up to even if we may not manage to attain it. It is not automatic or guaranteed. God seeks the creatures' good as also good for God, but God has absolute appreciation of that good. This is divine appreciation. It *could not* be ours.[26]

God's love or goodness is unique for only God is absolutely adequate to the object. As Hartshorne puts it, in its literalness, love is God's sole privilege. There is no way anybody can outdo the absolute lovingness of God which is God's holiness. All we are capable of is to come as close as possible to the ideal of seriously caring for ourselves and others whereas God provides that ideal. In fact, God cares for us infinitely more than we do ourselves. In addition, while our love is restricted to a few, God's love is universal. God's love extends not only to all the persons there ever have been or are but also to all who will exist. God alone knows our interests, fully and concretely, and in knowing them, shares them. As has been stated previously, in God knowing and valuing are the same. In Hartshorne's words, 'To fully sympathise with and to fully know the feelings of others are the same relationship separable in our human case only because there the "fully" never applies.'[27] Such limited knowledge on our part can be no more than a rough estimate of how others feel. But in the case of God the individuality and vividness of the feeling are certainly shared.

God's goodness also stands out on its own in that God is always good, unlike us. Hartshorne explains that since we are fallible beings, our awareness of the good is not absolutely adequate. This is why we require ethical rules. They guard us against the more dangerous effects of our ignorance. These rules adopted in moments of calm and disinterested reflection protect us and others against the bias of our perception and inferences. It is easy for us to go astray because we do not always know reality in its concreteness. Our inadequate knowledge leads to inadequate response. But where knowledge can never be inadequate, as in God's case, the response will always be adequate to the reality. Hence, God alone chooses the greatest good.[28] Only God is suitably described as goodness itself.

SOME OBSERVATIONS

It should be obvious from the above discussion of Hartshorne's idea of God that we are being presented with a philosophical understanding of God which differs considerably from that of classical theism.[29] For this reason, one would really have to delve much deeper into it to do it justice. There are a number of important issues which ought to be raised in connection with such a concept of God, but which we cannot raise here.[30] Our concern here is restricted to the focus of this exploration. In his numerous writings Hartshorne has tried to elaborate on his concept of God. Others have likewise developed what to them are significant implications of this conceptuality.[31] On the other hand, critics have underlined what they consider to be its weaknesses. Some of these critics have been quite insistent in their rejection of Hartshorne's idea of God while others have been rather cautious.[32] The debate is going on, a debate which is necessary if Hartshorne's religious philosophy is to contribute anything worthwhile to the important task of speaking correctly about God today. Although there has been much critical work done in this field, more is called for.

Hartshorne claims that his God-talk stems from our experience of reality in general. As was shown in chapter 4, Hartshorne initially turns to our experience of the world around us and then to metaphysical thinking to help us understand God in a more meaningful way. The old notion of going 'beyond experience' resulted in the disrepute of metaphysics. The God-talk that Hartshorne is engaged in is one that takes serious account of this point: his concept of God is rooted in our experience of reality. In Hartshorne's metaphysics, the whole of reality is held to be constantly changing and yet as having certain unchanging aspects. Becoming and relatedness as well as being and absoluteness are universal traits. To talk of God as changing and really related to us is not to limit God but to show God's *continuity with our everyday experience.* God is the exemplification of, rather than the exception to, metaphysical principles. By metaphysical here is meant 'universally true.' Were God to be regarded as 'outside any metaphysical category,' it would be extremely difficult, if not impossible, to say anything about God that would make sense. The only consistent conclusion would be to remain silent. It should be noted, however, that in maintaining that God is the exemplification of metaphysical principles, Hartshorne also insists that God is not just another instance of these principles. God is their chief exemplification; only God has that status and this is what makes God unique. Thus, God is radically different from everyone and everything else.

In chapter 4 we noted some of the difficulties of Hartshorne's metaphysical claims and had suggested a modified version of the status of religious claims. Here we could ask further: is it true that change and relatedness are truly universal? One could argue, as indeed some have done, that to change and to be related are creaturely characteristics. God, as the classical tradition holds, is completely immutable whereas everything else changes. To predicate change and relativity of God—even if God is said to exemplify them—is ultimately to blur the distinction between Creator and creatures, to be guilty of anthropomorphism. Hartshorne is thus accused of affirming creaturely characteristics of God. What justification does Hartshorne have for predicating change and relatedness to God?

We have already encountered some of Hartshorne's reasons. But others seek further support in the doctrine of the Incarnation. It is an observation that is of particular relevance in the context of the topic of this study. According to them, Christians believe that Jesus Christ has taught us what *God is really* like: someone who is genuinely concerned with our welfare. On this point the Latin American theologians and Hartshorne certainly touch base. The teachings of Jesus describe God as a loving Father, in language that leaves no doubt as to what God's nature is. Furthermore, Christians believe that Jesus *is* God, that he is God incarnate. Whitehead once said that Jesus is the 'revelation in act' of that which Plato and other thinkers have discerned in theory. The person of Jesus discloses God not in mere speculation but in a concrete historical act. In him we have begun to appreciate the manifest expression of the character of God: that God is immanent in the world, that God is love, really related to us and is concerned with and involved in our daily lives. In Jesus we have the true key to our understanding of God and of God's way with people. If one, therefore, were to ask what God's nature is, one has only to turn to Jesus Christ. This is not to say that everything that is true of Jesus Christ can be said to apply to God. Only Jesus Christ, for instance, suffered physically. But as Daniel D. Williams explains:

> We miss what is involved in the question about God's suffering if we think primarily of physical pain, mental torment or death. These are forms of human suffering to be sure. In Christ, God has in some ways experienced them. But 'suffering' has a broader meaning. It signifies to undergo, to be acted upon, to live in a give and take with others. To say that God suffers means that he is actively engaged in dealing with a

history which is real to him. What happens makes a difference
to him. He wins an actual victory over the world through a
love which endures and forgives. It means that the world's
sorrow and agony are real to God, indeed in one way more real
to him than to us, for only an infinite love can enter completely into sympathetic union with all life.[33]

Surely, supporters of Hartshorne's conceptuality argue, the
incarnation presents us with the true picture of God. If we take
serious account of it, we should see—it is claimed—further
justification for thinking of God in the way Hartshorne conceives
God to be. Hartshorne himself mentions this Christian argument in
Philosophers Speak of God:

...The dipolar view must hold not only that God contains
suffering but that he suffers and that it is in his character to
suffer, in accordance with the suffering in the world. Here the
Christian idea of a suffering deity—symbolised by the Cross,
together with the doctrine of the Incarnation—achieves
technical metaphysical expression.[34]

Thus, by presenting us with a concept of God who is really
and truly moved by what happens to us, Hartshorne claims that
God is rightly described as compassionate. He believes that his
way of speaking of God's compassion is more credible and
consistent than that of the classical theists.

A GOD WHO LIBERATES?

But while this is an important development indeed of the
image of God as co-sufferer, in the context of some kinds of
suffering, e.g. oppression and poverty, Hartshorne's idea of a
compassionate God still has to be developed so as to address the
question of God's involvement in liberation. In the past those who
have supported Hartshorne's views appear to have concentrated
on articulating and developing important theological and philosophical doctrines rather than on specific social and ethical concerns.
There have, of course, been exceptions.[35]

And yet the question of how the dipolar God can be said 'to set the captives at liberty' is very much in line with the methodological presuppositions of Hartshorne's philosophy. In other words, Hartshorne's methodology which results in his concept of God has ethical and social implications. We have noted that Hartshorne regards the philosophical undertaking to be rooted in and starting from concrete experiencing. Furthermore, as was pointed out in the chapter 'The Task of Describing God,' although one would then generalise to arrive at a more abstract interpretation of reality, one should always return to other concrete experiences to test the validity of one's conclusions. Such methodology will alert us to the network of relationships and structures within one's experiences. Many of these, unfortunately, hinder us from developing ourselves and are consequently unjust. Thus, any attempt to understand our experiences will raise ethical problems regarding these relationships and structures, some of which will be more urgent than others depending on the situation we find ourselves in. For instance, within the context of oppression and of the struggle to assert the fundamental dignity of human beings, human rights become much more significant. Furthermore, those who seek justice and defend human rights can learn from listening to the experiences of the oppressed. Perhaps if Hartshorne had developed his idea of God in countries where there is so much deprivation, injustice and abuses of human rights, it would have taken on a different emphasis, which is now quite in evidence in the form of the active interest shown by his supporters in dialoguing with liberation theologians, feminists and black theologians.[36] This is not meant to be a criticism of Hartshorne. The point is rather that this is part and parcel of the very methodological underpinnings of Hartshorne's thought and is demanded by any attempt to take the concreteness of experience seriously. For as Whitehead once said, we do not think in a vacuum.

The task of 'describing God who sets us free' is also a logical consequence of presenting the kind of God that Hartshorne believes in. As we shall see, since Hartshorne's God relates to us as co-creators—in varying degrees, of course—this means that each and every one of us is actively involved in shaping this world. Such a God, it can be argued, would expect us to meet the challenge of uprooting the causes of injustice and oppression by exercising our creativity, a point very rightly stressed by the Latin American liberation theologians. Hartshorne's God must be said not only to suffer with us but also to actively respond to the cries of oppression of God's creatures. One needs to understand the meaning not only of God's compassionate love but also of God's activity in a world of oppression and victimisation.

Chapter 7

PARTICIPATING IN
GOD'S LIBERATIVE ACT

THE IMAGE OF A LIBERATOR GOD

Another image of God which emerged in our reflections in Part I on the theists' experiences of suffering and on their practical responses to its challenge is that of God as liberator. In the preceding chapter we noted the need to develop this image further because of the challenge of certain kinds of suffering. In this respect Latin American liberation theology has led the way in highlighting the importance of this image of God as liberator. Rebecca Chopp writes that this metaphor, which is at the centre of Latin American liberation theology, has been influenced no doubt by culture, but it is also uniquely Christian in the light of Scripture, Christian tradition, and church teachings:

> The metaphor of God as liberator provokes the movement of liberating praxis, judges historical situations, recalls the dangerous memories of Christian tradition, and gives hope for the journey to freedom. As the central metaphor, God as liberator relates to other symbols popular in Latin American liberation theology—to the suffering Christ, to the church as sacrament of history, to Christ liberating culture, and to symbols of popular religion.[1]

The metaphor of God as liberator thus signals the providential relation of God to the world: God acting in history through human activity.[2] In short, it is a metaphor that not only describes God

124

but also points to our responsibility to participate in the task of liberation.

Such a theological move on the part of Latin American liberation theologians is not meant to offer some kind of palliative to ease suffering through false hopes but to uncover the nature of God as revealed in the Bible rather than in Greek metaphysics: the God of Life that one encounters in the Bible is indeed our Liberator. In fact, the people of Israel recognised the presence of God in their very experience of liberation.[3] As Pablo Richard puts it, the people of Israel was born as a people through its liberation from slavery in Egypt. It was in this liberating action that it discovered its God.[4] But, as Gustavo Gutierrez notes, such an image of God in the Bible had implications for the way the people of Israel were to live:

> Israel's identity, or what it means to belong to the Hebrew people, consists in doing justice to the poor and restoring their trampled rights. Consequently, when the Jewish people do not do justice to the poor, they are traitors to themselves. This means that not only do they act in evil ways, but that violations of the covenant are directly contrary to what identifies them and originally gave rise to them as a people: namely, the liberating event of the exodus and the historical experience of having come forth from Egypt thanks to God's intervention.[5]

Put more succinctly, Israel's God of life established a norm.[6] In the Bible one finds that God nurtures liberties in the people but expects participation in the process of liberation. Such a God liberates by empowering others.

Juan Segundo describes the Bible as the education in faith of God's chosen people, provided by God in different stages. In the Old Testament there were, he writes, four stages: *sacral*, *covenant*, *justice*, *wisdom*. As the people of Israel moved from one stage to the next, an attempt was made to distinguish authentic religious elements from deficient or immature ones. The entire process was not a series of abrupt and unrelated transitions but a dialectical movement in the course of which previous conceptions of God were purified and then integrated into new syntheses.[7] It was, however, in the New Testament that there was a deepening of the notion of freedom and the clarification of its essential relationship to love. At this stage in the education of the chosen people they learned that it is by efficacious love that humanity shares in and reflects the inner life of God, who is love. But to accomplish this task, human beings must be free—free *from* all forms of slavery, including religious ones, and free *for* the loving service and reconciliation of their brothers and sisters. And it is precisely for such freedom, Segundo stresses, that Christ came to set us free.[8]

God's progressive revelation points to what could be called the *salvation of history*. Segundo says that when we understand what the Christian God is, then history is saved from any and all victimisation. Since this revelation of God has been gradual, progressive and spaced out over the unfolding development of humankind, it is properly *the history of salvation*. He writes, 'We could say that a presentation of Christianity is adequate only when it moves from the history of salvation to the salvation of history in man, i.e. to the buildup of history by man, whom God has prepared and commissioned for this task.'[9] This is because God encountered in Christ is the answer to the question of human liberation. In this sense the Bible is a record of the history of the human encounter with God where the human is subject, rather than an object, of that history.[10]

Given this understanding of God as liberator of humankind, as portrayed in the Bible, what task lies ahead for Latin America?[11] Segundo's answer admits of no equivocation: 'Latin America, in its struggle for liberation, is not confronted with the "death of God" but rather with the task of ensuring the "death of the idols" that hold it in bondage and that are too often confused with God.'[12] To fulfill this task the Latin American Church, in Segundo's view, will have to work for the liberation of human beings for it is only in this way that God will be experienced in an authentic way. Or in the words of Perez-Esclarín:

Authentic acceptance of God means accepting a God who impels people to construct a more humane and fraternal world and to eradicate every trace of oppression. If one worships a God who does not do that, then one is worshipping a false god, an idol. For the true God has revealed himself as our liberator. He has made it clear that faith in him must be translated into the concrete practice of service to others and love for other people.[13]

Gustavo Gutierrez would agree and would add that in Peru and in Latin America generally this task may mean confronting powerful interests, especially when the defense of basic human rights is mounted by the weakest members of society, the poor and the oppressed. Gutierrez insists that the command laid upon the Christian community, a church, is not to survive but to serve. As he puts it, 'Today the church is bringing into play the sense of its own identity as the community of disciples of him who came that we might have life and have it more abundantly (Jn 10:10). The assertion of its identity depends on its witness.'[14] The growing awareness in Latin America of exploitation and human suffering has resulted in the conviction that the work of the Church must be seen as a whole in terms of liberating people from any and every type of servitude.[15] It is as if Camus' challenge were being directed to the Latin American Church:

> What the world expects of Christians is that they should speak out loud and clear, and they should voice their condemnation in such a way that never a doubt, never the slightest doubt, could rise in the heart of the simplest man, that they should get away from abstraction and confront the blood-stained face history has taken on today. The grouping we need is a grouping of men resolved to speak out clearly and pay up personally.[16]

In short, the affirmation of a Liberator God entails that the Church in Latin America take on the challenge of working for the liberation of the people.

According to Segundo, in general the Latin American Church, far more than the European Church, does not regard the world of religion and religious realities as the necessary real-life introduction to the message of Christ. Instead, it holds that everything in the Church, absolutely everything, must be translated from 'religious' terms into the human task in history.[17] As far as Segundo is concerned then, the emerging interest of the Church in forms of society where personal fulfillment is achieved in societal work itself (in fact, he maintains that the Church should work for the development of *community*)[18] rather than in the private realm cut off from it constitutes the best way of preparing Christianity to deepen its theology of an incarnate God; that is, to solidify its theology of a divine person who 'worked with human hands...thought with a human mind, acted by human choice and loved with a human heart.'[19]   The same theological view is powerfully expressed in the words of the Nicaraguan Campesino Mass:

> You are the God of the poor,
> a God human and simple,
> a God sweating in the street,
> a God with weather-beaten face.
> And so I speak to you,
> as does this people of mine—
> because you are a worker God,
> a Christ who toils.[20]

Moreover, Segundo writes, this critical, creative and social awareness combined with a more adequate theology bodes well for the future. It will alert us to the concrete embodiments which offer more promise of authentic human relationships which in turn will be the best foundation for further purification of our notion of God.[21]

DEVELOPING THE IMAGE OF GOD THE LIBERATOR

How should we understand further this image of a God who liberates creatures from every type of oppression? In line with the aim of this exploration, how can we develop it philosophically? What understanding of God's activity will help us to conceptualise the biblical insight into God's work among us? How are we to stress even more that such a portrayal of God which calls for our active participation in the task of liberation is rooted in our very nature? How are we to show that this description of God has universal significance? To pose these questions is not to imply that Latin American liberation theologians have not taken on the task of pursuing this image much further. On a number of occasions reference was made to their recent theological writings dealing with the doctrine of God from the perspective of the poor and the oppressed. The previous emphasis on social and ethical concerns, which characterised much of Latin American liberation theologising, is now being complemented by the important work which they are doing in the area of doctrine. In the previous chapter we pointed out that Hartshorne's thought could benefit from taking into account the concrete concerns of Latin American liberation theology. What we now wish to suggest is that, given the striking similarities in this area between their form of theology and Hartshorne's philosophy, Hartshorne's conceptuality may well be a useful way of developing further some of the insights associated with the image of God as Liberator.

Intrinsic to Hartshorne's concept of a dipolar God is the idea of a God whose creativity is shared by every other reality. Hartshorne's notion of universal creativity accounts for the existence of evil in the world.[22] But since it is also the source of good as Hartshorne claims, we want to stress that the philosophical category of creativity, particularly human creativity, enables us to understand further why each and everyone of us, as the Latin American liberation theologians tell us, is called upon to participate actively in the task of transforming this world.[23] But first let us see to what extent Hartshorne's understanding of God's power is similar to what we have already noted in the image of God as liberator.

GOD'S POWER AS SUPREME CREATIVITY

Hartshorne describes God's power as 'unsurpassable power over all things' rather than total control in the way that classical theism does. This means that for Hartshorne God's power is the maximal degree or kind of power compatible with a real plurality of powers.[24] God's power is absolutely maximal, the greatest possible; but even the greatest possible is still one power among others. It is, in brief, not the only power.

Hartshorne emphasises that God's power is exercised not over the powerless but over genuine powers. A plurality of beings, therefore, connotes a plurality of powers. Supreme creativity, i.e. God's, permits and even demands a division of creative power. Or as Hartshorne expresses it: 'The creatures must determine something of their own actions, and to this extent the supreme capacity to influence others cannot be power unilaterally to determine the details of reality.'[25] Thus, realities other than God have their appropriate, non-eminent forms of creativity.

Insisting that he is not downgrading God's unique status, Hartshorne argues that God can do everything that can be done by a being with no conceivable superior.[26] This is very much in line with what we have already heard about the absoluteness of the identity of Hartshorne's God. God's is the power, which Hartshorne describes as 'adequacy of cosmic power,' to do for the cosmos what only an unmatched cosmic agent can do. In this sense God's power is absolutely adequate. Hartshorne maintains that God's power is sufficient to preserve the society of the cosmos, no matter what others may do.

But God's power does not entail power to do for the cosmos whatever could be accomplished by nondivine agents. Such deeds are really theirs, not God's. This is because God's power although perfect in form is still social. Looked at in this way, it is power to set limits to the freedom of others, but not to destroy it. Hartshorne rejects as meaningless the notion of a power that determines all decisions and controls everything. For him the perfection of God's power is shown, not by taking away or preventing the freedom of others, but by fostering and inspiring that freedom. Hartshorne likens God to the creative orator, thinker and artist who, like the biblical God of the liberation theologians cited above, inspires creative responses in others. Hartshorne's God is the supreme or perfect artist who encourages appropriate degrees of artistic originality in all creatures. 'God is the unsurpassable inspiring genius of all freedom, not the self-determining coercive tyrant, or (if possible) even worse, the irresistible hypnotist who dictates specific actions while hiding his operations from the hypnotised.'[27] God is also compared to rulers who are held in high esteem for their wisdom and benevolence in placing others in a position to make fruitful decisions of their own. All these awaken creativity in others. God then governs the world by inspiring us, by providing us with opportunities and by fostering creativity in us.[28]

If supreme power is understood in this way, it means that Hartshorne's God can only impose limits on the disagreements, conflicts or confusions among lesser powers. God cannot simply eliminate these confusions for this would require God's becoming the sole power. And yet there really is no compromising the uniqueness of God's power since, in Hartshorne's way of thinking, the ideal form of power does not monopolise power, but allots to all their due measure of creative opportunity. Hartshorne adds that not only can it be shown that there is no monopoly of power on God's part, but it can also be argued, presuming God's goodness, that God is not desirous of such a monopoly. In fact, God surpasses others in generous willingness to delegate decision-making to others. God's inspiration enables us to act freely while ensuring that a coherent and in general harmonious world comes about. To concede all power to God is not only to misunderstand God's nature but also wrong because 'unqualified monopoly is always bad, even in the eminent case.'[29] The longing to possess total control and to reduce others to powerlessness is not particularly ideal. On the contrary, such a longing is symptomatic of weakness. Hartshorne tells us that it is only the inferior, weak being who yearns to be able to manipulate everything. 'The Eternally Secure has no fear of letting others do some of the deciding. Eminent generosity in delegating decision-making to others and taking loving possession of the results, that is real Eminence.'[30] A concentration of decision-making in the one being is in principle undesirable because the values of life, as Hartshorne sees them, are essentially social, involving the interactions of more or less free individuals. Power that would violate these values is judged wrong. As he puts it, a monopoly of power is itself 'the most undesirable thing imaginable; or rather it is the most unimaginable and indeed inconceivable absolutising of an undesirable direction of thought.'[31] Power cannot therefore be maximised by supposing a being who decides beforehand or eternally what happens since this would be assigning every power to that being. That would be attributing to that being something basically immoral.

Pursuing the question of God's governance of the world, Hartshorne says that God can take each successive phase of cosmic development and make unsurpassably good use of that phase in God's own life. God provides creatures with such guidance or inspiration as will optimise the ratio of opportunities and risks for the next phase while setting the best or optimal limits to freedom. Hartshorne explains that by 'optimal limits' is meant that they are such that, were more freedom allowed, the risks would increase more than the opportunities, and were less freedom permitted, the opportunities would decrease more than the risks.[32] God's power, however, does not guarantee a perfection of detailed results for no power, as Hartshorne understands it, could ensure the detailed actions of others.

Comparing his doctrine with traditional teaching, Hartshorne says that what was traditionally known as 'general providence' is what he has in mind by his assertion that God decides the cosmic limits within which lie the possibilities for various happenings.[33] God accomplishes this through natural laws. Only God can decide natural or cosmic laws, which are the only laws which are always beneficent. This does not mean that all the results are good, but the advantages of having the laws outweigh the risks involved. Human laws do not compare favourably since some of the laws which human beings enact may create greater risks than opportunities. Hartshorne regards natural laws as the decisions God has already made and through which God exercises providence over us.[34] Humans more or less fashion their human world, but they do not and could not establish the basic general order within which their decisions could achieve anything. Only God could set up this general framework. But God does not institute natural laws once and for all. Natural laws, being definite ones, are not eternal but arbitrary. At due intervals God inspires the universe with new modes of behaviour which would exclude mere disorder and too exact a regularity or an eventually trivialising persistence in one type of order.[35]

In affirming then that God sets boundaries to the freedom of others or that God establishes a general order, Hartshorne is refuting the view that it is nature which miraculously restrains or controls whatever happens thus preserving a measure of harmony in the world. Instead, there is a superior form of freedom, God's, which furnishes a directive which ordinary forms of freedom accept or obey. God guides all of creation and through this universal guidance lines of demarcation are established to discord and confusion. Without such guidance, order would not be possible.[36] In God's benevolence God guides creation in an eloquent and appealing fashion. 'God "speaks" to creatures so eloquently, beautifully, wisely, and hence relevantly to their natures that they cannot except within narrow limits, even wish not to respond.'[37] Despite divine eloquence, however, the creatures themselves are free to follow their own initiatives. God does not coerce anything, God inspires it to act in a certain way. In short, God persuades it.

But Hartshorne does not deny either that chance plays a certain role in creation. 'Chance,' he writes, 'is just as real as some of the atheists have been telling us during the centuries.'[38] Providence is not the prevention of chance but its optimisation. It checks chance occurrences. These cannot be done by chance for chance limited by chance is the same as chance not limited at all. The end result would be total chaos. Surprisingly, Hartshorne affirms the reality of chance in order to show the significance of God's providence. Through the laws of nature God puts restrictions within which the lesser agents can effectively work out the details of their existence. These limits ensure that universal creativity does not end in universal chaos and frustration. But because of chance, there will still be elements of chaos and frustration; but they remain subordinate to the general order and harmony.

In Hartshorne's view then God's governance of the world cannot be conceived of as totally determining any part of it. In this sense he is critical of the traditional understanding of God's omnipotence. In Hartshorne's philosophy the development of the world is not a simple act of God, but a fusion of divine and lesser acts, all of which in different degrees are self-determined, creative or free. Thus, in Hartshorne's view, it is meaningless to ask why God does not control the world so that evils could not happen. Such a question would arise only if God is understood to have a monopoly of decision-making. Nor can any amount of evil prove that God has willed evil since it is the chance coming together of creaturely acts which actually produce it. This is why, according to Hartshorne, in spite of God's guidance some conflict and misfortune and thereby suffering do arise. But God's love for creatures would not allow God to deprive even the least creature of its due amount and kind of freedom. As Hartshorne expresses it: 'Love cannot be less than the wish to have others exist as genuine actualities, and this means as partly self-deciding agents, whose fortunes depend therefore in part upon themselves and their neighbors.'[39]

So far Hartshorne's philosophical development of the notion of God's power as supreme creativity would be germane to the theological views of Latin American liberation theologians.[40] We have seen how Segundo and others speak of the God of the Bible as one who fosters and nurtures the freedom of others. Such a God seeks our liberation not by reducing us to automatons but rather by empowering us even at the risk of misadventure on our part. But we still need to see how one could indeed speak of our participation in God's liberative act. Here Hartshorne's notion of creativity, particularly human creativity, can serve as a possible conceptual framework for understanding that task. At the same time it will help us appreciate more fully Hartshorne's interpretation of God's power as supreme creativity.

CREATIVITY

Creativity or, as he sometimes calls it, creative synthesis is a metaphysical description of the workings of reality. As was explained in chapter 4, Hartshorne understands by 'metaphysical' a trait that is applicable to the whole of reality. The phrase 'creative synthesis' is Hartshorne's description of every happening or event.[41] There is an old as well as a new (or creative) element. The old consists of previous happenings or experiences which gave rise to and which persist in the new. There is permanence since in the synthesis the prior data are preserved, the synthesis being the holding together of the data. The many become one which in turn produces a new many and so on. It is an accumulation of these prior acts or a 'putting together' of various factors into a whole. But the resulting synthesis is a new actuality or experience because a different kind of experience has emerged from the coming together of past experiences. Previously there was the separate existence of the included realities, but now there is a unity. Furthermore, the synthesis is spontaneous or free because none of these experiences—individually or collectively—dictated the exact unity that would arise[42]. A synthesis therefore *emerges* rather than is determined. Hence, an experience or happening cannot be fully described in its fullness merely by specifying what its constituents are. Furthermore, each experience is an addition and an enrichment of reality.

This seemingly theoretical explanation is really Hartshorne's interpretation of causality. Every act is viewed by him as creative. However, each creative act is influenced by its past acts and does require them even if it cannot be determined precisely or fully by these antecedent acts, which are simply earlier cases of freedom. These acts, those of oneself or of others, restrict the freedom of the new act, establishing and limiting the possibilities for an otherwise free and creative activity. On the other hand, they never determine them fully. Thus, Hartshorne defines causality as the way in which any given act of creativity is influenced or made possible, but yet not completely determined, by previous acts.[43] Because past free acts narrow down any creative act, there can be a certain measure of prediction. Hartshorne uses the analogy of the banks of the river which give the flowing water its direction but do not entirely determine its movement. As he puts it, 'Causality is the boundary within which resolution of indeterminacies takes place. Causal regularities mean not the absence of open possibilities but their confinement within limits.'[44]

Hartshorne thus repudiates the deterministic version of causality. In his view, absolute determinism interprets any event as having been mapped out completely in its causes. Absolute determinism does admit that no human being will ever be able to read the maps except in radically incomplete and inaccurate ways. But Hartshorne regards this doctrine as an incorrect reading of the universality of causation because it is too strict an interpretation. Causes, including God as Supreme Cause, never determine the effect in all its details. While a cause is necessary in the sense that there can be no effect without a cause, it does not follow that the event will take place in precisely the way it is predicted, even when all the necessary causes are present. All one can say is that it may take place. There will be *an* effect but it will not be a fully determinate effect. Because every effect has a creative aspect it is never literally anticipated. Causes always restrict, but never absolutely specify, the possible outcome. This lack of precision is not due to our ignorance but rather to the very meaning of creativity. According to Hartshorne, 'To ask "why may not the antecedent cases completely determine the given?" is to show that one has not grasped the meaning and pervasiveness of creativity or spontaneity.'[45] Thus, unlike absolute determinism Hartshorne holds that there is a certain originality or freshness in every effect. Inasmuch as it is creative, it is partly unpredictable, undetermined in advance. This is why for Hartshorne God's creative power is eminent and unequaled but cannot be absolute because there is a real plurality of creativities.

Hartshorne believes that his interpretation of causality is supported by contemporary science. He argues that an increasing number of scientists today, going beyond Newtonian science, regard causal laws as statistical rather than determinate.[46] Hartshorne maintains that science has grown more and more critical of the assumption that once the conditions had been arrived at the result was a foregone conclusion. Quantum mechanics strongly suggests, if not actually proves, that causality is essentially different from the older conception of it. There is more acceptance of the view that individual events happen at least in a seemingly random or fortuitous manner within certain limits. Causality is the limitation of this randomness. Only when large numbers of similar events are dealt with can there be a highly exact predictability.[47] A cause is conceived, therefore, as related to its effect not by necessity but by probability. 'In physics,' Hartshorne writes, 'this relation is even convertible, the effect necessitating, not any uniquely specifiable cause, but only a case of causes as variously probable.'[48] This is not to say that literally anything could happen in a given place and time. Rather, it means that what happens is never the only thing that could have happened.

THE CLASH OF CREATIVITIES AS AN EXPLANATION OF THE EXISTENCE OF EVIL

Since each concrete actuality (as explained in chapter 6) in the world possesses some amount of creative power or freedom, when actualities exercise their creativities, the result can be good or evil. There is genuine chance at the points of intersection between diverse free acts. What Hartshorne means is something like this: if my decisions and your decisions interconnect, the resulting situation is something neither of us can completely determine. It simply happens. Thus, for Hartshorne, evil results because of this chance coming together of various free acts, aided here and there undoubtedly by wickedness and carelessness. Since in Hartshorne's view all creatures have some freedom, evil can and should be regarded as deriving from unfortunate (and not necessarily or in general wicked) cases of creaturely creativity. Hartshorne puts it rather bluntly when he states that if what x decided harmonises with what y decided, it is good luck; otherwise, it is bad luck. It comes down to luck since neither x nor y nor a third party can simply determine that harmony shall reign. We can, of course, aim for a more satisfactory outcome, but no one ultimately can guarantee it. Hence, for Hartshorne the root of all the tragedy in the world is the clash of creativities. As he puts it, 'Evil becomes intelligible as the chance interplay of creaturely acts.'[49] He disagrees with those who cite the abuse of freedom as the real culprit, pointing instead to the unfortunate and unforeseen coming together of different creativities. In other words, each exercise of creativity can result in evil because the outcome can never be fully controlled. And because the world consists of active creative individuals, there will always be evil. As he says, it is the price we pay for creativity, ours and others.

Hartshorne's discussion of the concept of creativity rightly shows that sometimes suffering is truly the result of unforeseen and genuinely random happenings. To look for a scapegoat is to forget that chance and luck are an integral part of our lives. Thomas Hardy's poem 'Hap' expresses this point extremely well: he bemoans the fact that suffering is due to chance and claims that it would be easier to accept suffering if it were the work of a vengeful god who takes delight in our sorrow. Then he would be able to bear it and die in the knowledge that his unmerited suffering was caused by one more powerful than he:

> But not so. How arrives it joy lies slain
> And why unblooms the best hope ever sown?
> —Crass Casualty obstructs the sun and rain,
> And dicing Time for gladness casts a moan....
> These purblind Doomsters had as readily strown
> Blisses about my pilgrimage as pain.
> (lines 9-14)

Opportunities or lack of them are sometimes the real causes for the kind of lives that we live. Unfortunately, these opportunities are not always traceable to a specific agent or factor nor to ourselves. And that is what makes certain forms of suffering more tragic: we cannot even blame anyone or anything. It would be pointless to do so, as Hartshorne rightly reminds us.

CREATIVITY AS THE SOURCE OF GOOD

As was already mentioned, Hartshorne's notion of universal creativity shows why there is and will always be evil in the world. But some will find it difficult to accept Hartshorne's seemingly unconcerned explanation as to why there is much suffering in the world. It seems that Hartshorne incorrectly downplays the evil intent and sometimes deliberate calculations behind some of the suffering in the world. Individuals as well as peoples, for instance, have been victimised by the machinations of certain ambitious political leaders. However, in keeping with the focus of our explorations, our present interest in Hartshorne's concept of creativity is not to critique it (especially since we agree that some suffering is really due to circumstances beyond anyone's control) but to show how it can illuminate the claim that we are all called upon to participate in God's work of transforming this world. If Hartshorne is correct, then the good that is in the world is also due to creativity. Creaturely freedom which gives rise to evils is also what brings about good. To eliminate creativity because of the risk of evil is also to remove the possibility of good. In Hartshorne's way of thinking, the risk of evil and opportunity for good are two facets of the one thing—multiple freedom. What justifies the risk is the opportunity for good. This is why to minimalise risk by reducing freedom results ultimately in fewer opportunities for good.

We would like to draw out two implications of this claim. First, the awareness that our creativity could lead to and indeed has led to much suffering in the world requires our acknowledgement that we have had a part in much misery and pain because of the way we have exercised our creativity. In turn, this should motivate us towards transforming the situation since many times we ourselves are responsible for contributing to that unfortunate situation. Although in some cases the unwanted consequences are indeed unintended, we must nonetheless be made conscious of the effects of our actions on the lives of others and on creation in general so that where possible preventive and even corrective measures can be adopted. That is to say, the root cause of the misery of many is not that they happen to be at the wrong end of the turn of events. They have been placed there—at times deliberately, at other times less so—by the unjust actions or policies of other people.[50]

Nowhere is this more true than in the deprivation and poverty that so many in developing countries are experiencing. Aloysius Pieris rightly distinguishes between 'voluntary poverty,' which can be liberating insofar as it is a protest and a precaution against acquisitiveness and greed, and 'forced poverty' which is enslaving.[51] Many unfortunately are forced to live a life of poverty. Thus, the fate of a starving nation and the fight for the freedom to live a more humane existence by oppressed groups should remind us that we need to look much more carefully at the causes of their plight and the structures (which are the products of human creativity) which perpetuate their misery. As the Puebla bishops observed, poverty is often caused by specific factors:

> Analyzing this situation more deeply, we discover that this poverty is not a passing phase. Instead it is the product of economic, social, and political situations and structures, though there are also other causes for the state of misery. In many instances this state of poverty within our countries finds its origin and support in mechanisms which, because they are impregnated with materialism rather than any authentic humanism, create a situation on the international level where the rich get richer at the expense of the poor, who get ever poorer.[52]

This comment on the causes of poverty demands a more thorough sociological and economic analysis than is possible here.[53] The point we simply wish to make is that the realisation of the negative effects of creativity should make us much more responsible. This sense of responsibility, definitely a source of good, should make us more alert to the abuses of creativity, ours as well as that of others.

Secondly, and much more positively, the knowledge that we are indeed co-creators, as Hartshorne correctly maintains, means that we can bring about changes which hopefully will benefit all of reality. God's creativity, in which we share, does not lessen our responsibility to make this world more liveable and less tragic. In fact, it heightens it. Although our exercise of creativity, as was pointed out, may often result in undesirable suffering, foreseen or unforeseen, it is also the same creativity that can alleviate it. Often it is our creative reaction to suffering, ours or others, that helps us to rise above the absurdity of suffering. Even in the midst of the atrocities of war, the desperate plight of the starving or the undeserved poverty of whole nations one can recognise the laudable action of many to rectify the situation. We can and must do something because we are creative agents. Or to paraphrase the Latin American liberation theologians, we too are liberators. Our sharing of God's liberative act enables and challenges us to participate in God's design to free us from every type of oppression. Indeed, it is through us and with us that God transforms this world.

SOME CONCLUDING REMARKS

At the beginning of this exploration we wrote of the need to develop our images of God in the light of the challenge of suffering. In this work we have attempted to provide one such development. We based our exploration on two theistic responses to the reality of evil: sympathy and liberation. By no means are we claiming that only believers respond to suffering in these ways. However, we wanted to investigate, from the theistic perspective, what these practical responses disclose about our beliefs regarding God. In articulating our position we drew on various resources in order to sharpen our focus and to develop our thoughts. In this concluding chapter we would like to piece together, as it were, some of the lessons which we have learned from undertaking this task.

THE PROBLEM OF EVIL

Because traditionally the problem of evil has been presented as a dilemma facing the theist, it is sometimes taken for granted that one 'has not even begun to face the issue' unless one tries to resolve the belief in an all-good and all-powerful God with the existence of evil. Or sometimes the accusation is made that 'one is skirting around the problem' if one does not try to answer the question 'where does evil ultimately come from?' These issues are no doubt important and they will continue to perplex human minds. Despite the answers provided by various theodicies, including Hartshorne's, these issues will continue to be bothersome. We certainly have no intention of minimising their significance.

However, in our opinion it would be misleading to think that such issues constitute *the* problem of evil. Perhaps it would be more accurate to say that this aspect of the problem is what engages much of Western theism in its dialogue with atheism. It is for this reason that theodicies have been formulated by various Western thinkers.   But as we have tried to show in this book there is another aspect to the problem occasioned by the existence of evil insofar as it does not always deter people from continuing to believe in their God. Of course, different individuals have their own reason for so believing. It could be psychological, or even economic. It could even be due to the lack of any other perceived option. But what cannot be denied is that for many people belief in God is the most reasonable course in the midst of suffering and deprivation. Why? Does one really find God in such experiences? Or does God reveal Godself particularly in those occasions? The key question then becomes: what kind of God does one encounter in the bleak moments of life? Can it be the same God that one also meets in the more colourful and vibrant times in life? Martin Buber introduced a powerful phrase to describe the situation: 'the eclipse of God'. For many of these believers God has not really been absent, merely clouded over. And it seems that while some of us have been unable to continue to perceive God's presence (again for one reason or the other), these individuals seem to have been able to penetrate the clouds to experience God's presence. This seems to have been the message of the book of Job and to some extent the poem of Hopkins, the implication of the continued hope of Christians despite the reality of death, and the belief in a compassionate and liberating God amidst deprivation and misery.

There is another reason for insisting that the problem of evil should not be narrowed down to the way it has been interpreted in much of Western theism. For some cultures the crucial issue that emerges from the challenge of suffering is not whether atheism is the more logical option. Since in these cultures, e.g. those of Latin America, the Philippines and Africa, theistic belief is a given, the real threat is not a denial of the existence of God, but idolatry. As we have seen, theological writings coming from those parts of the world alert us to this point. Is the reality to whom we give the name 'God' really the true God? Or is it merely the summit of human wishes? Is the God we speak of not really an attempt to perpetuate the status quo? The challenge for some in the face of suffering, desperation and poverty therefore is how we can continue to speak credibly of the true God and stop talking of idols. Why should we be made to think that only when we face the atheistic challenge have we really begun to face *the* problem?

The point that we are making here is not that the traditional problem of evil is a non-issue but rather that it is not the only concern raised by the existence of evil. Exploring what we call the other dimension of the problem is not ignoring the traditional problem either. It is instead an attempt to grapple with what we maintain is the more basic and urgent issue for many. Furthermore, as we said in chapter 1, sometimes problems may not be solved, but they do 'dissolve' in the light of other more crucial considerations. Often in life we expend a lot of energy trying to tackle problems headlong, and we get nowhere. A different angle to the same set of problems sometimes produces the results. The same can be said about some theological and philosophical problems. We continue to produce 'solutions' to problems that we have made up in the first place. At times what is required is not another solution, but a different approach to the problem. Sometimes it might mean asking a different kind of question. We have suggested in this book that for some of us another question can emerge when we are faced with the challenge of suffering. It is not a completely different question, of course, but the difference in emphasis is significant. Latin American liberation theologians, shifting the focus from theodicy to anthropodicy, have rightly insisted on this other dimension of the problem of evil.

TAKING UP THE CHALLENGE

Given this question regarding our descriptions of God's nature in the midst of suffering, we have suggested in this book that the route we should take is to look at the practical responses that believers make to the existence of suffering. Our practical responses are supported by certain theoretical affirmations which remain implicit and which need to be made explicit. Starting with literary and descriptive reflections, we have pursued the task of making explicit what is more or less implicit by resorting to theological development and philosophical reasoning. Despite its limitations, human reason can help, if anything, in getting us to understand better the standpoint we have taken. It can also of course lead us to discard certain assumptions (such as distorted images of God), or to continue to believe in those assumptions but this time on more rational grounds. On the other hand, it could lead us to modify the beliefs that we have taken for granted. Our conviction that reason is beneficial to this undertaking has prompted us to explore those implicit beliefs. We have turned to literature, theology and philosophy because we think that they have much to offer to each other. This interdisciplinary approach also shows a particular understanding of their relationship to one another. Whether others agree is of course another matter.

Latin American liberation theologians, who have led the way in exploring the theological challenge of poverty and oppression, deal with the God-question by turning to what they call 'dialectical thinking'. The reality of their dehumanised, oppressed and impoverished society certainly does not lend itself to theologising based on the kind of wonder that marvels at the beauty in the world. Instead their experience and the experience of their people remind them of what God is not.

On the other hand, is dialectical thinking, despite its importance, not an early stage in thinking through our assumptions about God? Do we not have to pursue further what it is that causes us to engage in God-talk *sub specie contrarii*? What makes God so different from our experience of oppression and deprivation? As we see it, we have to develop our positive but implicit beliefs regarding God. The difficulties associated with much of Western philosophising and theologising, noted by Latin American liberation theologians in their rejection of the European approach to their problems, should not lead us to ignore the use of human reason (represented by philosophy). After all, concrete issues still require the probing of abstract reasoning.

Another reason for our suggesting that dialectical thinking is an early stage in our attempts to speak of God in the midst of suffering is the very notion of theology itself, accepted by Latin American liberation theologians, as 'theological reflection *based on praxis.*' Should theologising about God which results from praxis focus, not on the state of poverty and oppression, but on what we are doing or should do about it? Praxis is an activity, not a state. We will know more about God by examining some theistic responses to the challenge of suffering. In looking at grief, rather than wonder, Latin American liberation theologians, it seems, are still looking at what *is* rather than on praxis itself.

There is yet another reason for moving beyond dialectical thinking in our attempts to conceptualise our images of God: it is the concept of God which emerges when we examine the implications of dialectical thinking. Dialectical thinking rejects wickedness, oppression and poverty and shows what God is not. But while this way of thinking rightly claims that God is not the cause nor a supporter of such misery, does it not run the risk of leaving out the poor, the exploited and the victims from God's reality? Can dialectical thinking show that God *includes*, rather than excludes, all creation *in* their pain and misery?

If we are right then it is important for Latin American liberation theology to actively pursue the theoretical questions which emerge from the practical commitment to the poor. Is our commitment to praxis not deepened when we are clearer about the *meaning* of our claims? In this sense there is a real need to develop the implications of the powerful images of God behind their commitment to the poor. Moreover, there is the challenge to work out a conceptuality that will enable us to express more adequately than heretofore what God really means for us. Otherwise, we could be worshipping idols, more attractive and relevant perhaps compared to traditional ones, but nevertheless still false.

OUR CONCEPTS OF GOD

In this book we tried to show that our explorations of our images of God which arise from reflecting on our practical responses to suffering have led us to other conceptualities than those of classical theism. Concrete experiencing is not always served by traditional conceptualities, particularly when certain considerations become more urgent or when new ones surface. This does not always mean that one should necessarily reject those conceptualities but rather explore alternatives. No conceptuality, old or new, can fully capture concrete experiencing. A conceptuality is like a picture frame. By enclosing the picture, the frame highlights its beauty but it also restricts it since it creates a context which it did not have. Sometimes that context is the wrong one. The picture frame chosen may not always be the most suitable for the picture in question. There are situations when what we ought to do is change the frame. But more importantly, the unsuitability of a particular picture frame should make us pay closer attention to aspects of the picture which have been left out because for too long our vision had been restricted to specific parts of the picture due to the frame that it always had. What we have tried to do in this work—as far as the image of God is concerned—is to expose those parts that may have escaped our notice. What has prompted this task is the existence of suffering which challenges the way we image God.

Again we do not claim to have provided a conceptuality that does full justice to the images we looked at. We doubt whether that is possible anyway. But our explorations have led us to take serious account of what can be meant by God's compassion. It has resulted in a reformulation of what has always been said about God's goodness. But instead of merely defending the belief in God's compassionate love, we have followed through the claim that it means a God who truly participates in the grieving process, a God who is indeed moved by the suffering of all creatures. Such an image (and the concept of a dipolar God) stems from a theistic response to a lot of the suffering around us. Our explorations have also turned to the image and concept of a God who liberates. Again this has meant a different way of looking at God's power. This alternative understanding refuses to regard God as the scapegoat for many of the ills in the world. Instead it shows that in many cases we—our actions, our policies, our structures—are responsible for our own suffering and that of the innocent. It is also an understanding that demands our participation in the task of transforming this world into a more liveable one. It is a claim that just as we are the cause of the problem, we can also at times be the solution to the problem since we have been given the ability to participate in the task of liberation. Or as the poet Hoelderlin expresses it in another context: 'But where danger is, grows/The saving power also.' Once again the image of God as liberator arises from the way some believers react to certain forms of suffering.

No doubt, these explorations will lead to more questions. We certainly do not claim to have provided neat answers. We have undertaken a journey because we saw the need. We have shared the images we saw along the way. In the process of developing and conceptualising those images we made use of resources available to us. The problems which remain are due to the complexity of the task as well as our own shortcomings. But we hope the reader continues where we leave off for the task is indeed a continuous challenge. As we said at the end of chapter 3 where we discussed our view of the task of exploring our images of God, the stage of *response*, when we adopt a conceptuality that has been adapted, remains tentative. There is also the need to continually evaluate it in the light of the beliefs and practices of the community that we belong to. In short, the challenge of exploring our images of God in the light of suffering is an ongoing one.

ENDNOTES

INTRODUCTION

1. Thinking about God involves objecting to some unacceptable ideas. At times in trying to clarify something it is useful to say what that something is not since the road to the truth is littered with obstacles which are really distortions of the truth. The more we can identify them as such the clearer and more accurate the picture becomes. Hence, atheism is at times 'protest atheism'. It alerts us to the fact that in some instances the rejection of certain conceptions of God—Norman Pittenger in *Picturing God* (SCM Press, 1982) and JB Phillips in *Your God is Too Small* (N.Y.: The Macmillan Company, 1965) list some of these dubious models of God)—even to the extent of seeming indifference or open hostility to religion, can be a powerful step. It can actually be a positive stage if it spurs us on to investigate more closely what we would regard as an adequate understanding of God.

2. Victorio Araya, 'The God of the Strategic Covenant' in *The Idols of Death and the God of Life: a Theology*, trans. Barbara E. Campbell and Bonnie Shepard (Maryknoll, N.Y.: Orbis Books, 1983), p. 111. Araya paraphrases Jose Miguez Bonino, *Espacio para ser hombres* (Buenos Aires: Terra Nueva, 1975), pp. 17-18.

3. See, for instance, Juan Luis Segundo, *Our Idea of God* (Gill and Macmillan, 1980); Bishop Teodoro C. Bacani, *The Church and Politics* (Quezon City: Claretian Publications, 1987); Johannes Metz, *Theology of the World*, trans. William Glen-Doepel (N.Y.:Seabury Press, 1969); Jon Sobrino, *The True Church and the Poor*, trans. Matthew J. O'Connell (Maryknoll, N.Y.: Orbis Books, 1984).

4. Theodore Walker, 'Hartshorne's Neoclassical Theism and Black Theology' in S. Sia (ed.), *Charles Hartshorne's Concept of God: Philosophical and Theological Responses* (Dordrecht: Kluwer Academic Publishers, 1989), p. 2. According to Walker, 'black theology is defined in considerable measure by its protest against the prevailing Western theological tradition.' Ibid. See also, James H. Cone, *God of the Oppressed* (N.Y.: The Seabury Press, 1975) and William Jones, *Is God a White Racist?* (N.Y.: Doubleday, 1973).

5. Mary Daly, *Beyond God the Father* (Boston: Beacon Press, 1973), p. 19. Quoted by Sheila Greeve Davaney in 'God, Power and the Struggle for Liberation: a Feminist Contribution' in S. Sia (ed.), *Charles Hartshorne's*

Concept of God, p. 58. Davaney provides a very useful introduction to the liberationists' struggle against the traditional concept of God. See also, Rosemary Radford Ruether, *Sexism and God-Talk* (Boston: Beacon Press, 1983).

6. Sallie McFague, *Models of God: Theology for an Ecological, Nuclear Age* (SCM Press, 1987), p. ix.

7. Ibid.

8. Sheila Greeve Davaney is quite correct to note that while there is strategic importance in developing new metaphors of God, it is imperative that we clarify and develop the presuppositions 'behind' the images of God. 'God, Power and the Struggle for Liberation,' p. 73, *n*.7. This is what we have set out to do in this work.

9. Terence E. Fretheim, *The Suffering of God: an Old Testament Perspective* (Philadelphia: Fortress Press, 1984), p. 1. Masao Tanaka illustrates this point in his book, *God is Rice: Asian Culture and Christian Faith* (Geneva: World Council of Churches, 1986) which shows the implications of thinking of God 'as rice.'

10. Michael Langford, *Unblind Faith* (SCM Press, 1982), p.2.

11. We would like to add here a point made by Gustavo Gutierrez. Thinking about God should include *silence*. In fact, it is the first stage while *speech* is the second stage. Cf. his *On Job: God-Talk and the Suffering of the Innocent*, trans. Matthew J. O'Connell (Maryknoll, N.Y.: Orbis Books, 1987), pp. xiii-xiv. Aloysius Pieris also talks of the need for a harmony between *word* and *silence* in theology. Cf. *An Asian Theology of Liberation* (Maryknoll, N.Y.: Orbis Books, 1988), p. 85. To some extent this is the approach being taken in this book inasmuch as we are attempting to make explicit ('speech') the presuppositions behind the practical responses ('silence') to suffering. Furthermore, theological thinking can take place even if it is not verbalised but lives in the hearts of the people. As Carlos Abesamis rightly observed, the grassroot poor (i.e. the poor, the deprived, the oppressed masses) are doers of theology, authors of and producers of the theological formulations of which we are in search. 'Faith and Life Reflections from the Grassroots in the Philippines' in *Asia's Struggle for Full Humanity*, ed. Virginia Fabella (Maryknoll, N.Y.: Orbis Books, 1980), pp. 135f. Also, Teresa Dagdag, 'Towards the Emergence of a People's Theology in the Philippines,' *Ching Feng*, XXV (Sept. 1982), p. 140.

12. We certainly do not wish to give the impression that story-telling is only for children. After all, Jesus taught in parables. Much of the work that is being done by narrative theology and in literary writings is not only interesting but also called for. Moreover, story-telling, as shown in Minjung theology, can be an effective way of critiquing the ruling classes, gaining greater awareness of one's plight and finding release from the miserable situation. Nor do we wish

to ignore the importance of the symbolic and the poetic. Samuel Rayan, reflecting on Asian spirituality, comments on this point in 'An Asian Spirituality of Liberation,' in Virginia Fabella, et al. (eds.), *Asian Christian Spirituality: Reclaiming Traditions* (Maryknoll, Orbis Books, 1992), p. 23. Related to this is the significant role of mask dances as a satirical theological commentary on the situation. Cf. C.S. Song, *Theology from the Womb of Asia* (Maryknoll, N.Y., Orbis Books, 1986), pp. 218-219. Also, Hyun Youngchak, 'A Theological Look at the Mask-dance in Korea' in *Minjung Theology: People as Subjects of History*, pp. 43-49; David Kwang-sun Suh, *Mask Dance of Liberation*, prepared for CCA 8th General Assembly (Seoul, 26 June - 2 July 1985).

13. As the Irish Bishops' document puts it: 'many are going through adult lives with ideas about religion more suitable for primary schoolboys and schoolgirls than for modern adults.' *Handing on the Faith in the Home* (1980).

14. Gustavo Gutierrez, *On Job*, p. xv.

15. According to John Hick, the dilemma was apparently first formulated by Epicurus (341-270 BC) and quoted by Lactantius (c. AD 260- c.340). Cf. footnote 1 in his *Evil and the God of Love* (Collins, 1979), p.5. See also James L. Crenshaw (ed.), *Theodicy in the Old Testament*. Issues in Religion and Theology 4 (Fortress Press/SPCK, 1983).

16. Hick, *Evil and the God of Love*. p.3.

17. Jürgen Moltmann, *Hope and Planning* (SCM Press, 1971) p.32.

18. David Jasper, *The Study of Literature and Religion: an Introduction*. Studies in Literature and Religion (London: Macmillan Press, 1989), p. ix.

19. 'The gods are just, and of our pleasant vices
    Make instruments to plague us:
    The dark and vicious place where thee he got
    Cost him his eyes'
    　　　　　　　King Lear, Act v, Sc. 3, lines 171-173.

20. Cf. Harold S. Kushner, *When Bad things Happen to Good People* (Pan Books, 1982), p.154.

21. David Ray Griffin, *God, Power and Evil* (Westminster Press, 1976) pp. 15-16.

22. Shakespeare's sonnet 146 gives that impression.

23. Cf. Gustavo Gutierrez, *On Job*, p.7.

24. Quoted by Gustavo Gutierrez in his *The God of Life*, p. xi.

25. David Jasper, *The Study of Literature and Religion*, p. 138.

26. A. N. Whitehead, *Modes of Thought*, pp. 49-50. In his *Adventures in Ideas* Whitehead makes the same observation when he writes that philosophy expresses 'flashes of insight beyond meaning already stabilised in etymology and grammar.' (p. 291).

27. The question of the relationship between literature, theology and philosophy, is no doubt much more complex and subtle. In addition, there is the further consideration regarding the autonomy of these disciplines. We have turned to these disciplines insofar as they articulate, illuminate and develop the topic we want to explore.

28. On this point, cf. William Byron (ed.), *The Causes of World Hunger* (New York/Ramsey: Paulist Press, 1982).

29. Rebecca Chopp, *The Praxis of Suffering: An Interpretation of Liberation and Political Theologies* (Maryknoll, N.Y.: Orbis Books, 1986), p. 3. The method used by Latin American theologians is well described by Victorio Araya as 'dialectical rather than analogical.'   He explains: 'For [Latin American theology], the locus of the encounter with God appears not so much in God's analogy with the world, God's reflection in nature, but in discontinuity with a reality that must be renounced: "lived wretchedness"' *God of the Poor: The Mystery of God in Latin American Liberation Theology*. Trans. Robert R. Barr (Maryknoll, N.Y.: Orbis Books, 1983), p. 29. Cf. also Jon Sobrino, *The True Church and the Poor* (Maryknoll, N.Y.: Orbis Books, 1984), p. 27. Roger Haight discusses what he calls 'the logic of an experience of negative contrast' in his 'The Logic of the Christian Response to Social Suffering,' *The Future of Liberation Theology: Essays in Honor of Gustavo Gutierrez*. Ed. M. H. Ellis and D. Maduro (Maryknoll, N.Y.: Orbis Books, 1989), pp. 141-143.

30. Gustavo Gutierrez, *On Job*, p. xiv. In his endnote (8) Gutierrez mentions that he is 'thinking of theologies that spring from divergent racial and cultural situations—for example, those based on the situation of women' and refers to Elizabeth Schüssler Fiorenza, *In Memory of Her: a Feminist Theological Reconstruction of Christian Origins* (New York: Crossroad, 1983). A collection of essays edited by Marco Olivetti, *Theodicea Oggi? Archivio di Filosofia*, LVI, 1-3 (1988) discusses various contemporary approaches to the problem of suffering.

31. According to Latin American liberation theologians, the issue in Latin America is idolatry rather than atheism. See, for instance, 'Idolatry and Death,' in Gustavo Gutierrez, *The God of Life*. Trans. Matthew J. O'Connell (Maryknoll, N.Y.: Orbis Books, 1991).

32. Dermot A. Lane, *Christ at the Centre: Selected Issues in Christology* (Dublin: Veritas Publications, 1990), pp. 53-54.

33. Aloysius Pieris, *An Asian Theology of Liberation*, p. 9. Jon Sobrino also talks of the cross as a *locus theologicus* that reveals God's love in 'The Death of

Jesus and Liberation in History,' *Christology at the Crossroads: a Latin American Approach* (Maryknoll, N.Y.: Orbis Books, 1978).

34. Lane's essay 'The Cross of Christ as the Revelation of God' is particularly illuminating. He offers helpful insights into a rethinking of God in the light of the cross, *Christ at the Centre*, pp. 55-79.

CHAPTER 1

1. Allowance must, of course, be made for fluency and a good grasp of the nuances of the language.

2. The point we are making here is that every question implies some knowledge of the answer. Otherwise, the questioner would not have been able to raise the question in the first place. Questions are asked against a 'background' or 'horizon' of implicit knowledge rather than of ignorance.

3. *Hamlet*, Act IV, Scene 4, lines 33-35.

4. Henry Vaughan's poem 'Man' captures this sentiment.

5. Some, like Kai Nielsen, argue that there is no evidence that there is a purpose *of* life, but that we can fashion for ourselves purposes *in* life, e.g. freedom from pain and want, security and emotional peace, human love and companionship, creative employment and meaningful work. These can be sources of happiness and therefore provide some meaning to life. Cf. his *Ethics Without God* (Prometheus Books, 1973). This argument, however, fails to recognise that having only relative purposes in life is giving purpose to life. That is to say, there is a tacit acceptance of the ultimate significance of possessing a number of relative goals in life.

6. Cf. James Fowler, *Stages of Faith* (Harper and Row, 1981).

7. See note 2. The methodology we are following will be explained in later chapters.

8. This discussion of Job is limited to a consideration of the message he has for us today in the light of the topic of this book. Therefore, no persistent attempt has been made to distinguish between the author of Job, the book itself or the character Job. Nor has there been an effort on our part to take note of the two portraits of Job presented in the book—Cf. Bernhard W. Anderson, *The Living World of the Old Testament*, 2nd ed. (London: Longman, 1971), pp. 507-508—or to avail of more detailed exegetical studies of this book. Our reflection on the Book of Job is indebted to the following: Peter Ellis, *The Men and Message of the Old Testament* (Minnesota: The Liturgical Press, 1963); Gerhard von Rad, *Wisdom in Israel* (London: SCM Press, 1972); John L. McKenzie, *The Two-Edged Sword* (London and Dublin: Geoffrey Chapman,

1965); Bernhard W. Anderson, *The Living World of the Old Testament*; and Gustavo Gutierrez, *On Job: God-Talk and the Suffering of the Innocent* (Maryknoll, N.Y.: Orbis Books, 1987).

9. 'Nature's Questioning' lines 13-16.

10. Morris West, *Lazarus* (N.Y.: St. Martin's Press, 1990), p. 164.

11. *King Lear*, Act IV, Sc. 1, lines 36-37.

12. According to Gustavo Gutierrez, God's answer to Job is 'a forceful rejection of a purely anthropocentric conception of creation.' *The God of Life* (Maryknoll, N.Y.: Orbis Books, 1991), p. 160.

13. See, for instance what P. Ellis wrote: 'His work has been called the greatest poem of ancient or modern times, the most wonderful poem of any age or language, one of the grandest things ever written with pen. The author himself has been ranked with Homer, Dante, and Shakespeare, and his language and theme have fascinated and stimulated readers down the centuries.' *The Men and Message of the Old Testament*, p. 478.

14. Gustavo Gutierrez, *On Job*, p. 11.

15. The speaker or *persona* in many of Hopkins' poems, especially those written during his stay in Ireland, can be said to be no other than the Jesuit Gerard Manley Hopkins himself. Support for this interpretation (which underlies the following explication) can be found in the letters which Hopkins wrote to his friend, Robert Bridges. In some of these letters he comments on the content of his poems and the frustration, doubts and difficulties which he was experiencing. In 'Thou art indeed just, O Lord,' there are references in his own prose which will throw light on this interpretation of his work. In a letter dated Sept. 1, 1885 Hopkins wrote: '...So with me, if I could but get on, if I could but produce work I should not mind its being buried, silenced, and going no further; but it kills me to be time's eunuch and never to beget.' In another letter on January 12, 1888, he again describes himself as a eunuch: '...Nothing comes:I am a eunuch—but it is for the kingdom of heaven's sake.' A third reference can be found in notes made at a New Year's Day retreat: 'I was continuing this train of thought this evening when I began to enter on that course of loathing and hopelessness which I have of often felt before, which made me fear madness, and led me to give up the practice... I am like a straining eunuch.' Cf. Jeffrey B. Loomis, 'Chatter With a Just Lord: Hopkins' Final Sonnets of Quiescent Terror,' *The Hopkins Quarterly*, VII, 2 (Summer 1980), pp. 54-55. Hopkins' sonnet 'To R.B.' also lends itself to this interpretation: 'Sweet fire the sire of Muse, my soul needs this;/I want one rapture of an inspiration' (lines 9-10). The following explication is thus based on the understanding that the *persona* of the poem is Hopkins himself. The edition used here is taken from *Chief Modern Poets of Britain and America, Vol. I: Poets of Britain*, ed. Gerald DeWitt Sanders et al, 5th ed. (Macmillan, 1970).

This explication is indebted to: Kunio Shimane, 'The Sonnet of 'Endeavour': 'Thou art indeed just, Lord,' *The Hopkins Quarterly*, VII, 2 (Summer, 1980), pp. 65-81; Peter Milward, *Landscape and Inscape: Vision and Inspiration in Hopkins' Poetry* (Grand Rapids, Michigan: William B. Eerdmans Publishing Co., 1975); Norman H. MacKenzie, *A Reader's Guide to Gerard Manley Hopkins* (Ithaca, N.Y.: Cornell University Press, 1981); W. H. Gardner, *Gerard Manley Hopkins (1844-1889): A Study of Poetic Idiosyncracy in Relation to Poetic Tradition*, Vol. II (London: Martin Lecker & Warburg, 1949). For a different reading of the poem, see Jeffrey B. Loomis, 'Chatter with a Just Lord: Hopkins' Final Sonnets of Quiescent Terror,' *The Hopkins Quarterly*, VII, 2 (Summer, 1980), pp. 47-64; Jeffrey B. Loomis, *Dayspring in Darkness: Sacrament in Hopkins* (Lewisburg: Bucknell University Press, 1988).

16. This quotation gives us the title which is usually rendered in English. The first three lines of the poem are a paraphrasing of the Latin quotation: 'Justus quidem tu es, Domine, si disputem tecum: verumtamen justa loquar ad te: Quare via impiorum prosperatur?'.

17. Paul L. Mariani, *A Commentary on the Complete Poems of Gerard Manley Hopkins* (Ithaca & London: Cornell University Press, 1970), p. 302. According to W. H. Gardner, 'Hopkins complains to God of his crippling sterility in lines of taut and impressive poetry.' Cf. his *Gerard Manley Hopkins*, p. 364.

18. Lines 5-7 rely on antithesis (enemy-friend), strange syntax, and alliteration (wouldst, worse, wonder) for their effect.

19. The word 'lust' may be significant given Hopkins' priestly vocation and the demands of celibacy. He refers to himself as 'Time's eunuch' (line 13) so that perhaps sexual frustration is added to his complaints. Certainly the debauched ways of the wicked are implied in lines 7-8. The positioning of 'Sir' (line 9), stressed as it is, re-emphasises a formal appeal and recalls line 2. It also draws attention to the alliterative value of this word and the word 'See,' which is also in a stressed position in this line. Cf. Kunio Shimane, 'The Sonnet of "Endeavour",' p. 73. Hopkins makes good use of alliteration ('s' sounds, 'b' sounds and 'th' sounds) in this poem, thus giving the impression that the poem is to be heard and not just read. He also repeats words like 'just,' 'Lord,' 'sir,' and 'thou,' thereby helping us to focus on the object of his address and maintain the dramatic situation created in the opening line of the sonnet.

20. According to W. H. Gardner, with these lines '[Hopkins] drops into a more subdued but richly figurative and allusive style.' *Gerard Manley Hopkins*, p. 364. The style is less detached and more emotional than the octave. The fruitfulness and fertility of nature add to his misery since they uncover his own sterility. In his own harsh view of himself, he has produced nothing of real value or worth. The use of the word 'See' (line 9), followed by the comma, is interesting as it reveals how much force Hopkins can get from a simple monosyllabic word. It is comparable to the force with which evidence, e.g. exhibit A, is shown in court. In addition, it draws attention to the 'banks and

brakes' (line 9) which have rich, luscious growth. Again alliteration is employed and lends forceful emphasis to the things of nature. Not only are the banks and thickets thickly 'leaved' (line 10) but they are also covered with intertwining herbs and cow-parsley, 'fretty chervil' (line 11), as if to add insult to his injury. The use of 'fretty' (line 11) recalls Hopkins' predilection for coined words, one of the innovative techniques which he used as he broke away from the traditional 19th-century stanza forms and developed his system of Instress/Inscape and Sprung rhythm. In line 11 the arresting position of 'look' recalls his earlier use of 'See' (line 9).

21. John Pick, *Gerard Manley Hopkins: Priest and Poet* (London: Oxford University Press, 1943), p. 152.

22. In W. H. Gardner's view, the abrupt pause after 'Them;' (line 12) ushers in the climax of the poem. Cf. *Gerard Manley Hopkins*, p. 364. Line 12 continues the constructive energy referred to earlier and concretises it with the alliterative 'birds build' in contrast to Hopkins' own state—'but not I build.' The use of plosive labials adds force to the climax.

23. Hopkins had referred to this in letters to his friend, Robert Bridges. He may have in mind the sexual restraints of celibacy (not being able to reproduce or give life to a child) or he may be using the image of slavery (since eunuchs were frequently used as servants or slaves) to show his own enslavement. Cf. John Robinson, *In Extremity: a Study of Gerard Manley Hopkins* (Cambridge University Press, 1978), pp. 156-158.

24. Perhaps since he is a poet and priest the words 'one work that wakes' means a good poem or some satisfying result of his ministry. Norman H. MacKenzie observes that ironically, this poem is one of his most enduring sonnets in a form for which he is renowned. Cf. *A Reader's Guide to Gerard Manley Hopkins*, p. 204. Be that as it may, he longs for a more tangible, visible reward from his life of dedication and hard work.

25. The pause at the end of line 13 is dramatically effective. It prepares us for the final plea and request of line 14. The final line of the sonnet extends the nature-fertility metaphor and links it with religion.

26. It is interesting to note what Aldous Huxley wrote: 'Never, I think has the just man's complaint against the universe been put more forcibly, worded more tersely and fiercely than in Hopkins' sonnet. God's answer is found in that most moving, most magnificent and profoundest poem of antiquity, the Book of Job.' Quoted by John Pick, *Gerard Manley Hopkins*, p. 153.

27. Morris West, *Lazarus*, p. 164.

28. This should not, however, be taken to mean that God deliberately causes suffering as if God were a sadist.

CHAPTER 2

1. 'Do not go Gentle into that Good Night,' lines 18-19.

2. This song is from Shakespeare's play *Cymbeline*, Act IV, Scene 2.

3. *Julius Caesar*, Act II, Scene 2. In his book *Human Immortality and the Redemption of Death* (London: Darton Longman and Todd, 1990), Simon Tugwell discusses various ancient attitudes to death and mortality found in a number of literary and philosophical writings. He also traces the evolution of Christian eschatology from its beginnings up to the end of the Middle Ages.

4. 'Holy Sonnets' 10 Lines 13-14.

5. The versions of Vaughan's, Donne's and Herbert's poems being used here are those which are included in *English Seventeenth-Century Verse*, Vol. I, ed. Louis L. Martz (New York: W. W. Norton & Co., 1969). In his book, *Language Recreated: Seventeenth-Century Metaphorists and the Act of Metaphor* (Athens: University of Georgia Press, 1992) Harold Skulsky shows how figurative language is used in that century, particularly in the poetry of John Donne, George Herbert and Henry Vaughan.

6. Cf. S. Sandbank, 'Henry Vaughan's Apology for Darkness,' *Essential Articles for the Study of Henry Vaughan*. Ed. Alan Rudrum (Archon Books, 1987), p. 129; James D. Simmonds, *Masques of God: Form and Theme in the Poetry of Henry Vaughan* (University of Pittsburgh Press, 1972), p. 54.

7. S. Sandbank, 'Henry Vaughan's Apology for Darkness,' p. 129.

8. Cf. James D. Simmonds, *Masques of God*, p. 54.

9. Ibid., p. 55.

10. John Donne, 'Death be not proud,' 'Holy Sonnets' 10, lines 7-8.

11. E. C. Pettet, *Of Paradise and Light: a Study of Vaughan's Silex Scintillans* (Cambridge University Press, 1960), p. 158.

12. Henry Vaughan, 'The Retreate,' lines 11-14, 19-20.

13. In his '[Joy of my life! while left me here]' (line 17) Vaughan regards 'God's Saints' as 'shining lights'). Included in Mario A. Di Cesare, ed. *George Herbert and the Seventeenth-Century Religious Poets* (N.Y.: W.W. Norton & Co., 1978)

14. E. C. Pettet, *Of Paradise and Light*, p. 161.

15. George Parfitt, *English Poetry of the 17th Century* (London and New York: Longman, 1985), p. 104.

16. It is worth quoting Pettet at length on this point: 'There is no other short poem in the language more brightly and continuously luminous. From the dazzling impact of its opening lines, through images that interpenetrate, are modified, and are sometimes repeated, it evokes the earthly, visible light of sunset, stars, and jewels (produced, according to hermetic theory, by the action of the sun), the strange radiance of "some brighter dreams", visited by shining Angels, the divine, ultimate light, kindling as well as illuminating, that links life and death, heaven, the departed spirits, and the human soul. And all this pervasive luminosity is emphasised by Vaughan's typical, Rembrantesque chiaroscuro—of stars against "some gloomy grove", of the heavenly "world of light" over and against the dull glimmering of mortal life, and most striking of all, of light in darkness, light triumphant over darkness, at the moment of death.' *Of Paradise and Light*, p.162.

17. In this essay the death of Jesus is seen in its soteriological significance. For an account on what is discovered about God from the fact that Jesus was executed, see Jon Sobrino, 'The Epiphany of the God of Life in Jesus of Nazareth' in *The Idols of Death and the God of Life: a Theology* (Maryknoll, N.Y.: Orbis Books, 1983), pp. 88f. See also, Dermot Lane, 'The Cross of Christ as the Revelation of God,' in his *Christ at the Centre: Selected Issues in Christology* (Dublin: Veritas Publications, 1990), pp. 53-79. Also, William A. Beardslee et al., 'Preaching on the Death of Jesus' in their *Biblical Preaching on the Death of Jesus* (Nashville: Abingdon Press, 1989), pp. 75-205.

18. In pointing out that Christ's death gives meaning to our own since it gives us a focus and a participatory role, we are not implying that we should be obsessed with death the way that some people in the past were. Cf. Norman Pittenger, *After Death: Life in God* (SCM 1980), p. 2. Michael Wheeler writes about the literary and theological evidence of the Victorians' obsessive interest in death in his *Death and the Future Life in Victorian Literature and Theology* (Cambridge University Press, 1990), pp. 25-68.

19. John Donne captures this sentiment well. In his 'To Christ' (also known as 'A hymne to God the Father') he expresses ultimate fear that he would not be saved:

'I have a sinn of feare, that when I have spunn
     My last thred, I shall perish on the shore;
Sweare by thy self, that at my Death thy Sunn
     Shall shine as it shines now, and heretofore;
And, having done that, Thou hast done,
     I feare no more.' (lines 13-18).

20. W. Abbott (ed.), *The Documents of Vatican II.* 'The Church in the Modern World,' art. 18.

21. Cf. Murray Roston, *The Soul of Wit: A Study of John Donne* (Oxford: Clarendon Press, 1974), p. 205.

22. Commenting on the poem itself, Barbara Kiefer Lewalski writes that Louis Martz in his *Poetry of Meditation* notes that 'it is a classic Ignatian meditation: the extended comparison in the opening lines presenting the preparatory stage; the long central section constituting an intellectual analysis of the crucifixion in terms of its manifold paradoxes; and the final lines containing a heartfelt colloquy or prayer to Christ emerging from the meditative exercise.' *Protestant Poetics and the Seventeenth-Century Religious Lyric* (Princeton University Press, 1979), p. 278.

23. According to A. C. Partridge, this conceit is based on the Ptolemaic cosmology with the ultimate support of Plato's *Timaeus*: 'In Plato's cosmology the Creator imposed on his universe a certain order, the first being a division of heavens into inner and outer spheres, namely, those of the planets, and those of the supposedly fixed stars. The earth was regarded as the centre around which all moved, once in twenty-four hours. The orbits of the fixed stars took a different direction from those of the planets. The sphere of the fixed stars (called the Same) moved in a circle from left to right; the seven planets (called the Other) had contrary motion from right to left.' *John Donne—Language and Style* (Andre Deutsch, 1978), p. 143.

24. Helen Gardner explains the basis for the comparison: 'The spheres had more than one motion. Their own natural motion, each being guided by an Intelligence, was from West to East; but the motion of the Primum Mobile hurled them against this, from East to West, everyday. Other motions, such as the trepidation of the ninth sphere, prevented the separate spheres from obeying their "natural forme", or directing Intelligence.' *The Metaphysical Poets* (Penguin, 1970), p. 87.

25. This pun on Sun/Son is also seen in 'To Christ' (also known as 'A Hymn to God the Father'): 'Sweare by thy self, that at my Death, thy Sunn/ Shall shine as it shines nowe, and heretofore;' (lines 15-16).

26. A. C. Partridge, *John Donne—Language and Style*, p. 145.

27. As Donne puts it in another work, 'They killed once an inglorious man, but I/ Crucifie him daily. . .' ('Holy Sonnets' 11 lines 7-8).

28. In another work of his, Donne makes the same point: 'That I may rise, and stand, o'erthrow mee, and bend/ Your force, to breake, blowe, burn, and make me new.' ('Holy Sonnets' 14 lines 3-4). The same sentiment is expressed by Ben Jonson: 'Use still Thy rod,/ That I may prove/ Therein, Thy Love.' ('A Hymn to God the Father,' lines 4-6). This poem illustrates the significance of

Christ's death and resurrection, as Jonson sees it, for humankind but also raises the question of human sinfulness despite God's generosity.

Our reference to Donne and Jonson on this point does not mean agreement with their image of a God who punishes. One of the reasons for exploring our images of God is precisely to bring out not only what is tenable but also what must be rejected. We are grateful to Julie Morris for pointing this out.

29. In fact, in another poem 'Love (III)' George Herbert shows the significance of the crucifixion and death of Jesus Christ. In the final stanza of that poem Herbert offers assurance that Christ's sacrifice redeems us.

30. In John Wall's edition, the two parts are separated. However, he explains that in *1633* (i.e. 1633 edition of Herbert's religious poetry) the two are printed as one poem. This editor favors the division found in MS Jones B., 62 (in Dr. Williams' library, London) since critics agree that the second part is the speaker's response to his call in the first part. Cf. John Wall, *George Herbert: The Country Parson and the Temple* (Paulist Press, 1981), p. 155. The argument for regarding the two as really one is precisely that the two parts (call-response) form a unity.

31. Ibid., p. 63.

32. There is another sense in which one can see a connection between the two movements thus pointing to a much closer unity of the two parts than Wall is prepared to acknowledge. From the content of the first movement, one can imagine it to be the preparation and tuning up of the musical instruments for a performance and the second movement as the recital itself.

33. Chana Bloch, *Spelling the Word: George Herbert and the Bible* (University of California Press, 1985), p. 249.

34. This comparison is particularly striking since Herbert played the lute and used it to achieve the musical quality, so obvious in his poems. In fact, many of his poems are sung and have been set to music. For instance, the first 18 lines of 'Easter' have been set to music by George Jeffreys in 'Rise, heart, thy Lord is risen: Verse anthem for Easter day,' for STB soli, SSATB chorus and organ. See, also, Vaugh Williams' musical settings for Easter.

35. Structurally, this is an important development as it helps to summarise stanza 1 and stanza 2, thus preparing for the conclusion (in this stanza) of the first movement (it also introduces the second movement).

36. Anthony Low, *Love's Architecture: Devotional Modes in Seventeenth-Century English Poetry* (New York University Press, 1978), p. 85.

37. Ibid., p. 86.

38. Ibid.

39. In describing this second movement, Low says that Herbert appeals to more than one of the senses. The poet, he claims, employs a meditative technique by situating his singer in the Palestinian landscape where he gathers flowers for his offering. There is no conscious effort nor strain such as that which characterise a 'Holy Sonnet' or a formal Ignatian exercise. Instead, it is done with ease, allowing the meditation to blend with harmony. The result is a small but perfect specimen of the meditative hymn. Ibid., pp. 86-87.

40. Cf. Richard Strier, *Love Known: Theology and Experience in George Herbert's Poetry* (Chicago & London: University of Chicago Press, 1983), p. 59.

41. Along the same lines he bemoans in his poem 'Miserie' (lines 31-36) the fact that imperfect humans are not capable of praising the perfect God.

42. Richard Strier, *Love Known: Theology and Experience in George Herbert's Poetry*, p. 60.

43. David Jasper, *The Study of Literature and Religion: an Introduction*. Studies in Literature and Religion (London: Macmillan, 1989), p. 35.

44. Ibid., pp. 35-36.

45. E. Schillebeeckx, 'The Death of a Christian,' *Vatican II: The Struggle of Minds and Other Essays* (Dublin: Gill and Son, 1963), p. 68. In this chapter we explore the Christian meaning of death. For a discussion on how death is viewed by different religious traditions, see John Bowker, *The Meanings of Death* (Cambridge University Press, 1991).

46. Ibid., p. 74.

47. Karl Rahner, 'Death,' *Sacramentum Mundi*, p. 61.

48. Christian theological thinking on the significance of the death and resurrection of Jesus Christ is much more profound than what we can discuss here. Our focus in this chapter is dictated by the approach we have adopted in this work.

49. Donal Dorr, 'Death,' *The Furrow* (March, 1968), p. 146.

CHAPTER 3

1. Theists have felt particularly vulnerable on this point. Consequently, various theodicies have been developed.

2. According to John Bowker, in Christian tradition the reality of suffering has constantly attracted a theoretical and practical response. However, Jesus and Paul seemed to have been more concerned with dealing with the realities of

suffering rather than with offering an explanation as to why suffering should exist. Later developments paid more attention to providing a theoretical explanation. Cf. his *Problems of Suffering in Religions of the World* (Cambridge University Press, 1970), pp. 42-98.

3. Richard Creel, *Divine Impassibility: An Essay in Philosophical Theology* (Cambridge University Press, 1986), p. 146f.

4. Bishop Leonard Wilson's testimony which told of his experiences as a Japanese prisoner of war is only one of many. Quoted by John Bowker, *Problems of Suffering*, pp. 96-98. For another account of a faith-filled attitude to suffering, see *The Witness of Edith Barfoot: The Joyful Vocation to Suffering* (Oxford: Basil Blackwell, 1977). Our own encounters with several such people have led to the formulation of the question we are seeking to explore. For these people God was real despite all their suffering.

5. Cf. Introduction.

6. This is certainly the more important issue in Latin America today. Cf. *The Idols of Death and the God of Life* (Orbis, 1983) and Juan Segundo, *Our Idea of God* (Orbis Books, 1974). Also, Philip Berryman, *The Religious Roots of Rebellion: Christians in the Central American Revolution* (SCM, 1984), p. 377f.

7. See, for example, Antonio Perez-Esclarín, *Atheism and Liberation* (SCM, 1980). This is not to claim that the question of God's nature and of God's existence are two completely separate issues.

8. For a discussion of the status of descriptions of God see the next chapter.

9. Although we claim that the present work is not a theodicy (in the usual sense of the word), we are by no means undermining the effort that has led to the formation of various theodicies.

10. David Hume, *Dialogues Concerning Natural Religion* (the edition we have used is David Hume, *Writings on Religion* edited by Anthony Flew and published by Open Court, 1992), p.261.

11. Ibid., p. 264.

12. Ibid. See also p. 274. The following quotation makes the same point even more clearly: 'In short, I repeat the question: Is the world, considered in general, and as it appears to us in this life, different from a man or such a limited Being would, *beforehand*, expect from a very powerful, wise, and benevolent Deity? It must be strange prejudice to assert the contrary. And from thence I conclude that, however consistent the world may be, allowing certain suppositions and conjectures, with the idea of such a Deity, it can never afford us an inference concerning his existence. The consistence is not absolutely denied, only the inference. Conjectures, especially where infinity is

excluded from the Divine attributes, may perhaps be sufficient to prove a consistence; but can never be foundations for any inference.' (p. 268).

13. Ibid., p. 264.

14. Ibid., p. 267.

15. Ibid. p. 268.

16. Cf. Ibid. pp. 268-274.

17. Ibid. p. 275.

18. Philo's argumentation deals with natural evils, but he claims that the same applies to moral evil, cf.Ibid. We believe, however, that Hume does not do full justice to the sphere of human activity, which is where we want to explore a possible alternative. Hume's other challenge in this context is of course the principle of causality (see also his *An Enquiry Concerning Human Understanding*, Part XI). We discuss this point in Chapter 7.

19. Cor Traets shows how the church community deals with the sick in a liturgical/sacramental way and discusses the image of God portrayed in such a ritual, 'The Sick and Suffering Person: a Liturgical/Sacramental Approach,' in Raymond Collins and Jan Lambrecht (eds.), *God and Human Suffering* (Leuven: Peters, 1990), pp. 183-210.

20. Harold S. Kushner, *When Bad Things Happen to Good People* (Pan Books, 1982), pp. 126-127. Simone Weil analyses suffering in terms of its three essential dimensions: physical, psychological and social. The third dimension which turns suffering into affliction is isolation. 'The Love of God and Affliction,' *Waiting for God*, trans. Emma Craufurd (N.Y.: G.P. Putnam's Sons, 1951), p. 117f. Quoted by Dorothee Soelle, *Suffering* (London, DLT, 1973), pp. 13-14. In his book, *Understanding Grief* (SCM Press, 1957), Edgar N. Jackson, shows how religious practices sustain the grief-stricken.

21. On this point, cf. William J. Hill, 'Does Divine Love Entail Suffering in God?' in Bowman L. Clarke and Eugene T. Long, *God and Temporality* (N.Y.: Paragon House Publishers, 1984), pp. 55-71.

22. St. Anselm, *Proslogium; Monologium; An Appendix on Behalf of the Fool by Gaunilo; and Cur Deus Homo*, trans. S. N. Deane (La Salle, Ill.: Open Court Publishing Co., 1903, 1945), pp. 13-14.

23. Charles Hartshorne and William L. Reese, *Philosophers Speak of God* (University of Chicago Press, 1953) Midway 12 Reprint, pp. 103-106. Charles Hartshorne has been one of the leading and most articulate advocates of God's passibility.

24. Harold S. Kushner, *When Bad Things Happen to Good People*, pp. 92-93.

25. Dorothee Soelle's remark is enlightening: 'Gratuitous solidarity with the afflicted changes nothing; precise knowledge that such suffering could be avoided becomes our defense against addressing it. Only our own physical experience and our own experience of social helplessness and threat compel us "to recognise the presence of affliction."' *Suffering*, p. 15.

26. Richard Swinburne argues that there is a logical connection between love, loss and suffering. God, as a loving person must experience suffering because of the sufferings of God's creatures. Cf. his, 'The Problem of Evil,' in *Reason and Religion*, ed. Stuart Brown (Ithaca, N.Y.: Cornell University Press, 1977), pp. 81-102. This is a main tenet in process thought, some of its representatives being Charles Hartshorne, John Cobb, Schubert Ogden, Lewis Ford, David Griffin and others.

27. It is *not* specific forms of sympathetic suffering which are at issue but simply being touched or moved. How God will be touched or moved will depend on God's nature.

28. This understanding of God's nature as worshipful follows Hartshorne's. That is to say, only God is worthy of total devotion. This is what constitutes God's perfection. Cf. S. Sia, *God in Process Thought*, p. 35f.

29. E. Schillebeeckx, *For the Sake of the Gospel* (London: SCM Press, 1989), p. 90. Schillebeeckx's criticism is directed against those who, following Bonhoeffer, stress God's defenselessness and powerlessness. He prefers to speak of God's vulnerability, arguing that experience shows us that those who make themselves vulnerable can sometimes disarm evil (p. 93). John Cobb offers what could be another answer but from a Whiteheadian perspective: 'Whitehead was sensitive to an objection that might be raised at this point. What would it really mean for God to include forever all the suffering and sin of human history? Would it mean that even in God there is no redemption? Whitehead's response was to consider how in human experience there can be a kind of redemption of past suffering and sin. The consequences of my past suffering and sin remain in my experience now, but it is possible that they have been so transmuted through my growth and repentance as to enrich rather than degrade my present life. Whitehead envisions that in the divine life, far more than in the human, there is redemption which does not remove its evil, but which includes it within a whole to which even human evil can make some positive contribution, however limited. God suffers with us, but the suffering does not destroy God as it can destroy us.' *Process Theology as Political Theology* (Manchester University Press/ Westminster Press, 1982), pp. 79-80.

30. Two qualifications are necessary here. One is the observation by some Latin American liberation theologians that poverty is an abstract word. They rightly claim that what is at issue are poor people. Cf. Victorio Araya, *God of the*

Poor, pp. 114f. The other qualification is the distinction made by Aloysius Pieris in *An Asian Theology of Liberation* (Maryknoll, N.Y.: Orbis Books, 1988) between 'voluntary poverty' and 'forced poverty,' pp. 20f. What we have in mind is 'forced poverty.'

31. Aloysius Pieris notes that in an Asian situation the issue is not so much poverty vs wealth as much as acquisitiveness or avarice. Thus, he claims, 'The primary concern, therefore, is not eradication of poverty but struggle against mammon—that undefinable force that organises itself within every person and among persons to make material wealth antihuman, antireligious, and oppressive.' *An Asian Theology of Liberation*, p. 75.

32. See, for example, Juan Luis Segundo, *Our Idea of God*.; Gustavo Gutierrez, *A Theology of Liberation* (Maryknoll, N.Y.: Orbis Books, 1973).

33. Gustavo Gutierrez, 'Faith as Freedom: Solidarity with the Alienated and Confidence in the Future,' in *Living with Change, Experience, Faith*, ed. Francis A. Eigo (Villanova, Pa.: Villanova University Press, 1976), p. 25.

34. Gustavo Gutierrez, 'Speaking about God.' *Concilium*, 171 (January 1984), p. 30.

35. Cf. *The Idols of Death and the God of Life*, p.1.

36. *Theology of the Pain of God*, p. 64.

37. *God Suffers*, p. 81. Lee's use of the terms 'sympathy' and 'empathy' is the opposite to our definitions given in the text.

38. This is usually said of Asian thinking. However, this is not true of Minjung theology which speaks of 'dan' which is used to resolve 'han' described by David Kwang-sun Suh as 'the feeling of anger of the people brought by injustice inflicted upon them' in his 'Shamanism and Minjung Liberation' *Asian Christian Spirituality*, p. 33. Cf. *Minjung Theology* (Maryknoll, N.Y.: Orbis Books, 1983) and Jung Young Lee's introduction to *An Emerging Theology in World Perspective: Commentary on Korean Minjung Theology* (Twenty-third Publications,1988).

39. Virginia Fabella et al., *Asian Christian Spirituality: Reclaiming Traditions* (Maryknoll, N.Y.: Orbis Books, 1992), p.8.

40. Ibid., pp. 1-2.

41. Theodore Walker, 'Hartshorne's Neoclassical Theism and Black Theology,' *Charles Hartshorne's Concept of God*, Ed. S.Sia, p. 1.

42. Gustavo Gutierrez, *On Job*, p. 79.

43. Victorio Araya, *God of the Poor*, p. 150.

44. E. Schillebeeckx, *For the Sake of the Gospel*, pp. 101-102.

45. Victorio Araya provides a helpful answer to this question of how God can be described as a God of the Poor in his *God of the Poor: the Mystery of God in Latin American Liberation Theology* (Maryknoll, N.Y.: Orbis Books, 1983), pp. 125-152.

46. Our approach follows the distinction between *experience* and *conceptuality* as discussed by John Cobb and David Griffin in *Process Theology: An Expository Introduction* (Belfast: Christian Journals, 1977), ch. 2.

47. John B. Cobb, Jr., *Process Theology as Political Theology*, pp. 72-73.

48. It may also be possible to understand in this way what many young people and believers from different cultural backgrounds are experiencing when confronted with particular forms or expressions of religious beliefs with which they cannot identify. It is perhaps important to note that rejection of certain doctrinal beliefs does not necessarily mean abandonment of religiosity but a quest for a different way of expressing it.

49. This discussion on the use of philosophy by the early Christians draws heavily on J. Ratzinger, 'The God of Faith and the God of the Fathers,' *Introduction to Christianity* (Burns & Oates, 1968) and on M. Wiles, *The Christian Fathers* (SCM, 1977).

50. An interesting correlative to this, given the existence of suffering and oppression, is the development of the 'dialectical method' in Latin American liberation theology. See, Victorio Araya, *God of the Poor* (Maryknoll, N.Y.: Orbis Books, 1987), pp. 29-31; Roger Haight, 'The Logic of the Christian Response to Social Suffering,' *The Future of Liberation Theology: Essays in Honor of Gustavo Gutierrez*. Ed. M. H. Ellis and D. Maduro (Maryknoll, N.Y.: Orbis Books, 1989), pp. 139-153. See, 'Some Concluding Remarks' for our reaction to this method.

51. 'Adaptation' is sometimes taken to mean that particular teachings are merely to be adapted to relevant cultural settings; for instance, reinterpreting Western thought from an Asian perspective. While there is room for talking about such a step, one should not ignore the specific contribution made by traditional cultures to the whole process of formulating Christian doctrines.

52. The concept of 'contemporariness' is an elusive one. Nevertheless, in this respect we ought to pay particular attention to present-day cultural and social issues when we formulate religious doctrines today (such as the concerns being brought to our attention by liberation theologians and Third-World theologians). Nor should we overlook the key role played by inter-religious dialogue today.

53. Although we have identified the context to be the religious community, it can also be said that the knowing process itself is contextualised. One's culture too provides a context for one's theologising. See, for instance, Masao Tanaka, *God is Rice: Asian Culture and Christian Faith* (Geneva: World Council of Churches, 1986). On this point, the debate between the inculturationists and the liberationists in Asia is of particular relevance. Cf. Aloysius Pieris, *An Asian Theology of Liberation*.

54. Biblical hermeneutics has rightly alerted us to the problems involved in biblical interpretation. In turning to the Bible for doctrine, therefore, we should have due regard for the findings of biblical scholarship as well as literary theory.

CHAPTER 4

1. The objections that are mentioned here are those which John Macquarrie discusses in his *Principles of Christian Theology* (SCM Press, 1966), pp. 42-48. Cf. also, James Richmond, *Theology and Metaphysics* (SCM Press, 1970), pp. 1-47.

2. George Herbert, 'Love (III),' lines 1-2. The rest of Herbert's poem provides in figurative language a possible answer to how one is enabled to know God.

3. Hartshorne describes God as having an abstract pole and a concrete one. It is Hartshorne's contention that many of the contradictions associated with the traditional notion of an absolute God can be resolved by conceiving of God as dipolar. For an account of this reinterpretation of God's reality, see among others, his *Creative Synthesis and Philosophic Method* (SCM Press, 1970), chapter XIII. His recent book, *Omnipotence and Other Theological Mistakes* (SUNY Press, 1984), written for a more general readership continues to defend the notion of a dipolar God. Cf. also S. Sia, *God in Process Thought: a Study in Charles Hartshorne's Concept of God* Vol. 7 Studies in Philosophy and Religion (Martinus Nijhoff, 1985), Chapter III.

4. *The Logic of Perfection and Other Essays in Neoclassical Metaphysics* (Open Court, 1962), p. 134.

5. Hartshorne, however, adds that 'not contingent' may mean necessary or impossible (necessarily false or non-existent), 'not finite' can have several meanings as mathematicians know. But all of these are *very* abstract, not like being a mother or brother as cases of not being a father.

6. 'Tillich and the Non-theological Meaning of Theological Terms,' *Religion in Life*, XXXV, 5 (Winter, 1966) p. 677. See also, 'Tillich and the other Great Tradition,' *Anglican Theological Review*, XLIII, 3 (July, 1961), p. 251; 'The Idea of God—Literal or Analogical?' *Christian Scholar*, XXIX, 2 (June, 1956), p. 134.

7. pp. 134-135.

8. Hartshorne's main criticism of negative theology is that it is being one-sided in negating only some, instead of all, concepts in their application to God. We are grateful to Prof. Ogden for pointing this out. See, for example, 'Love and Dual Transcendence,' *Union Seminary Quarterly Review*, XXX, 2-4 (Winter-Summer, 1975), p.96.

9. 'The God of Religion and the God of Philosophy,' in *Talk of God: Royal Institute of Philosophy Lectures*, Vol. II, 1967-68 (Macmillan, 1969) p. 162. This statement implies a certain understanding, which as was stated earlier guides our exploration, on the relationship between literary descriptions and philosophical development.

10. *LP*, p. 134f, In Hartshorne's case these philosophical beliefs refer to his pansychism or psychicalism, a view which holds that all of reality 'feels' or 'prehends', each in its own way. He expounds and defends this view in many of his writings. See, among others, 'Pansychism: Mind as Sole Reality,' *Ultimate Reality and Meaning*, I,2 (1978), pp.115-129.

11. 'Are Religious Dogmas Cognitive and Meaningful?' *Journal of Philosophy*, LI, 5 (March 4, 1954), p. 149. See also *LP*, p. 141; 'Tillich and the Other Great Tradition,' p. 255; 'God and Man not Rivals,' *Journal of Liberal Religion*, VI, 2 (Autumn, 1944), p. 11. In 'True Knowledge Defines Reality: What was True in Idealism,' *Journal of Philosophy*, XIII, 21 (1946), p. 573, Hartshorne explains further his reason for saying that we know more of God's reality than our own, inasmuch as God is the ideal.

12. This definition of metaphysics is a paraphrased one. That it is definitely Hartshorne's understanding of metaphysics can be concluded from his various writings on this subject. See, for instance, *CSPM*, chapters II-VIII. Metaphysics for Hartshorne serves an important function as far as religious beliefs are concerned: it is important in clarifying and purifying those beliefs. See, *Insights and Oversights of Great Thinkers: an Evaluation of Western Philosophy* (Albany, N.Y.: SUNY Press, 1983), p. xiv.

13. A. N. Whitehead, *Process and Reality* (corrected ed. The Free Press, 1978), p. 13. There are, however, important differences between Hartshorne's and Whitehead's understanding of metaphysics, Cf. David Griffin, 'Hartshorne's Differences from Whitehead,' in Lewis S. Ford (ed.), *Two Process Philosophers: Hartshorne's Encounter with Whitehead*, AAR Studies in Religion, No. 5, (1973), pp. 45-48.

14. *CSPM*, pp. 20-22.

15. *LP*, p. 285.

16. Ibid.

17. *Beyond Humanism: Essays in the New Philosophy of Nature* (Bison Book Edition, 1968), p. 260. Also, 'Can Man Transcend his Animality?' *Monist*, LV, 2 (April, 1971), pp 210-211.

18. Hartshorne, however, also insists that there is an important sense in which God is and must be an exception to metaphysical categories. Again, our thanks to Prof. Ogden for drawing this to our attention. See, *A Natural Theology for Our Time* (Open Court, 1967), pp. 33-65 and *CSPM*, p. 140, 144.

19. Anthony Flew makes this point in his *God and Philosophy* (Harcourt, Brace & World, Ltd., 1967), p. 118.

20. This is because when one uses symbolic or metaphorical language one is not yet telling us what one really means. What is required is that we try to spell out the exact sense of the symbols if they are to have any communicable meaning at all. It is for this reason that symbolic language really presupposes the use of literal language. Otherwise, it would have no meaning even for those using it. As regards analogy, if a term means something partly different when applied to God and if we cannot through literal language state how different its meaning then becomes, any argument in which analogy plays a part is unreliable.Cf. H. Palmer, *Analogy: a Study of Qualification and Argument in Theology* (Macmillan, 1973), p. 26. Schubert Ogden identified certain difficulties with this aspect of Hartshorne's God-talk and suggested a way forward in his article, 'The Experience of God: Critical Reflections on Hartshorne's Theory of Analogy' in *Existence and Actuality: Conversations with Charles Hartshorne* edited by John B. Cobb, Jr., and Franklin I. Gamwell (University of Chicago Press, 1984), pp. 16-37. See also Hartshorne's reply in the same publication.

21. 'The Centrality of Reason in Philosophy,' *Philosophy in Context* Suppl. to Vol. 4 (1975), p. 6. Cf. also 'Can We Understand God?' *Louvain Studies*, VII, 2 (Fall 1978), p. 82.

22. *CSPM*, p. 140, 144. Hartshorne has been criticised for being anthropomorphic in his God-talk. See Colin Gunton, *Being and Becoming: The Doctrines of God in Charles Hartshorne and Karl Barth* (OUP, 1978), p. 222; H. P. Owen, *Concepts of Deity* (Macmillan, 1971) p.85. The problem, however, is not anthropomorphism because Hartshorne does distinguish God from non-divine realities.

23. In a letter to the authors John Cobb defends Hartshorne. He writes that 'Hartshorne never meant to say that we cannot think things greater or less than our own experience. We have within our experience more and less. We can think of something as more than what is within our experience. For example, our experience of empathy enables us to imagine more and more up to the limit of complete empathy, even though we do not experience complete empathy ourselves.' We agree with this point, especially since empathy is a

positive experience. Nor are we denying that Hartshorne claims that God has positive qualities which are unsurpassable. Our difficulty with the concept of 'unsurpassability' is not that we do not have some basis for it, but rather that as a negative concept, it goes contrary to what Hartshorne claims should be the ultimate basis for metaphysical God-talk: positive and literal claims about reality. In other words, 'unsurpassability' in Hartshorne's own scheme, would seem to stand on the same level as 'infinity.' If 'finite' is more inclusive than 'infinite,' then 'surpassable' is more inclusive than 'unsurpassable.' For this reason while we may have *some* idea of infinity and unsurpassability, this is ultimately based on the positive experience and conception of finitude and surpassability.

24. Hartshorne's answer to this, one suspects, is that God is an all-inclusive reality. Therefore, in knowing any instance of reality, we already know God. But again this is really to pre-define God's nature to meet the difficulty.

25. 'Metaphysics for Positivists,' *Philosophy of Science*, II, 3 (July, 1935), p. 293.

26. *BH*, p. 268; Also, 'The Structure of Metaphysics: a Criticism of Lazerowitz's Theory,' *Philosophy and Phenomenological Research* XIX, 2 (Dec., 1958), p. 226.

27. *BH*, p. 292.

28. 'The Modern World and a Modern View of God,' *Crane Review*, IV, 2 (Winter, 1962), p. 76.

29. 'Twelve Elements of My Philosophy,' *The Southwestern Journal of Philosophy*, V, 1 (Spring, 1974), p. 10. See also *CSPM*, ch. 2, and 'The Development of my Philosophy,' in John E. Smith (ed.), *Contemporary American Philosophy: Second Series* (Allen & Unwin, 1970), p. 220.

30. *Man's Vision of God and the Logic of Theism* (Archon Books, 1964 rep.).

31. In the same letter to the authors, John Cobb writes: 'You point out at some length that Hartshorne believes that metaphysical judgments remain uncertain. That is fine. I have been bothered at times by his tendency to seem more certain than I believe to be possible for any creature about anything. You conclude from this that all metaphysics can do is to tell us what is the best way to think about God. That is not wrong, but in your formulation it seems to stand in contrast with telling us what is probably true about God. For Hartshorne, and for me, there is no such contrast. If you and I were discussing Hartshorne's meaning in a certain passage, I trust neither of us would claim inerrancy. We could only be proposing the best way of interpreting the passage. But my proposal would be at the same time that that is what Hartshorne probably meant when he wrote the passage. Otherwise, it would not be the best interpretation.' We agree with Cobb here. Our reservations are probably due to the significant role which we see played by subjective factors

when we make and justify even metaphysical judgements. The 'best interpretation' is still governed by certain subjective criteria. The 'social theory of knowledge' alerts us to the social factors which determine our evaluations.

CHAPTER 5

1. For a historical and systematic study of the doctrine of God's immutability within a theological and christological context, see Thomas G. Weinandy, *Does God Change? The Word's Becoming in the Incarnation* Vol. IV in Studies in Historical Theology (St. Bede's Publications, 1985). Also, Herbert Mühlen, *Die Veränderlichkeit Gottes als Horizont einer zukunftigen Christologie* (Münster Ascherndorff, 1969). For a more biblical orientation, cf. Martin McNamara, 'Process Thought and Some Biblical Evidence,' *Charles Hartshorne's Concept of God: Philosophical and Theological Responses*, ed. S. Sia (Dordrecht: Kluwer Academic Publishers, 1989), pp. 197-218. Terence E. Fretheim in his *The Suffering of God: an Old Testament Perspective* (Philadelphia: Fortress Press, 1987) argues, however, that it is not the biblical sources, but churchly and scholarly neglect of OT images which portray God in nonmonarchical terms that has resulted in the depiction of God as remote, cold, stern and even ruthless. According to him, in the Old Testament there are images which show God as one who suffers and who has entered deeply into the human situation.

2. *Works of Philo Judaeus*, trans. C. D. Younge (George Bell & Sons, 1890).

3. Ibid. IV, 458.

4. St. Augustine, *Confessions*, trans. E. H. Pusey (E. P. Dutton & Co., 1907), p. 261. The idea that God is timeless was taken up and defended by other theists. Cf. Nelson Pike, *God and Timelessness* (Routledge & Kegan Paul, 1970). See also, W. Norris Clarke, *The Philosophical Approach to God: a Neo-Thomistic Perspective* (Wake Forrest Univ., 1979), pp. 93-96.

5. St. Augustine, *De Civitate*, XI, vi.

6. St. Augustine, *De Trinitate*, Bk. XV, ch. 5, sec. 7.

7. Cf. Maimonides, *The Guide of the Perplexed*, trans. M. Friedlander (Trubner & Co., 1985).

8. St. Thomas Aquinas, *Summa Theologiae*, la, pp. 2-26, F. T. T. Gilby, gen. ed., vols. 2-5 (Blackfriars, Eyre & Spottiswoode and McGraw-Hill, 1964-6).

9. St. Anselm, *Proslogium; Monologium; An Appendix on Behalf of the Fool by Gaunilo; Cur Deus Homo*, trans. S. N. Deane (Open Court, 1945), p. 1.

10. Cf. F. von Hügel, *Essays and Addresses on the Philosophy of Religion*, second series (E. P. Dutton & Co., 1926).

11. Charles Hartshorne, 'A New Look at the Problem of Evil.' *Current Philosophical Issues: Essays in Honor of Curt John Ducasse*, ed. Frederick C. Dommeyer (Springfield, Ill.: Charles C. Thomas, 1966), p. 207. Hartshorne's criticism is based on his metaphysical method which maintains that for an idea to be humanly intelligible, some human experience must provide its meaning. See, *Creativity in American Philosophy*, p. 15. For a very readable presentation of his criticisms of the classical theistic concept of God, see his *Omnipotence and Other Theological Mistakes* (Albany, N.Y.: SUNY, 1984), pp. 1-49.

12. Cf. Hartshorne, *Man's Vision of God and the Logic of Theism* (Chicago: Willett, Clark & Co. 1941; N.Y.: Harper and Brothers Publishers, 1948; rep. Hamden, Conn.: Archon Books, 1964), p. 158.

13. Hartshorne, 'Divine Absoluteness and Divine Relativity,' *Transcendence*, eds. Herbert W. Richardson and Donald R. Cutler (Boston: Beacon Press, 1969) p. 164; 'The Idea of a Worshipful Being,' *Southern Journal of Philosophy*, II, 4 (Winter, 1964), p. 165.

14. Hartshorne, 'Love and Dual Transcendence,' *Union Seminary Quarterly Review*, XXX, 2-4, (Winter and Summer, 1975) p. 97; also, 'Eternity,' 'Absolute,' 'God,' *Prophetic Voices: Ideas and Words on Revolution*, ed. Ned O'Gorman (N.Y.: Random House, 1969; N.Y.: Vintage Books, 1970), p. 141; 'Twelve Elements of My Philosophy,' *The Southwestern Journal of Philosophy*, V, 1 (Spring, 1974), p. 9.

15. Hartshorne, *Insights and Oversights of Great Thinkers: an Evaluation of Western Philosophy* (Albany, N.Y.: SUNY Press, 1983), p. 100.

16. Hartshorne, *Aquinas to Whitehead: Seven Centuries of Metaphysics of Religion. The Aquinas Lecture, 1976*, (Milwaukee: Marquette University Publications, 1976), p. 31. Hartshorne uses the word 'incompossible' (a term he borrows from Leibniz) more often than 'incompatible'.

17. See, among others, his 'The God of Religion and the God of Philosophy,' *Talk of God: Royal Institute of Philosophy Lectures* (London: Macmillan, 1969), pp. 152-167; *Man's Vision of God and the Logic of Theism* (Chicago: Willett, Clark & Co., 1941; N.Y.: Harper and Brothers Publishers, 1948; rep. Hamden, Conn.: Archon Books, 1964); *Divine Relativity: A Social Conception of God* (New Haven: Yale University Press, 1948). For an excellent brief theological discussion of Hartshorne's reasons for rejecting divine immutability, see John B. Cobb, Jr., 'Hartshorne's Importance for Theology,' *The Philosophy of Charles Hartshorne, The Library of Living Philosophers Vol. XX*, ed. Lewis Edwin Hahn (La Salle, Ill.: Open Court, 1991), pp. 176-179.

18. Victorio Araya, *The God of the Poor* (Maryknoll, N.Y.: Orbis Books, 1987), p. 61. In comparing Greek philosophy and Latin American theology, Araya makes a further point: 'In Latin America, it is not *wonder* at the positive structure of reality that motivates theological cognition, as it was for the ancient Greeks. The process is precisely the contrary. It is wonder—astonishment, awe, bewilderment—concretized as *grief*—the grief of the oppressed (the negative structure of reality)—that moves one to think theologically' Ibid., p. 30.

19. Victor Codina, *Renacer a la Solidaridad* (Santander, 1982), p. 105. Quoted by Victorio Araya, *God of the Poor*, p. 36.

20. Jon Sobrino, *Christology at the Crossroads* (Maryknoll, N.Y.: Orbis Books, 1978), p. 195.

21. Ibid., p. 196.

22. Peter C. Phan, 'The Dipolar God and Latin American Liberation Theology,' *Charles Hartshorne's Concept of God: Philosophical and Theological Responses*, ed. S. Sia (Kluwer Academic Publishers, 1989), p. 31.

23. Juan Luis Segundo, *Our Idea of God*, trans. John Drury (Dublin: Gill and Macmillan, 1980) p. 133.

24. Ibid., p. 14.

25. Ibid., p. 133.

26. Ibid., p. 7.

27. Ibid.

28. Pablo Richard, 'Biblical Theology of Confrontation with Idols' *The Idols of Death and the God of Life* (Maryknoll, N.Y.: Orbis Books, 1983), p. 17.

29. Segundo, *Our Idea of God*, p. 14.

30. Victorio Araya G., 'The God of the Strategic Covenant,' *The Idols of Death and the God of Life*, p. 111.

31. Alfred T. Hennelly, *Theologies in Conflict: the Challenge of Juan Luis Segundo* (Maryknoll, N.Y.: Orbis Books, 1979), p. 149.

32. Juan Luis Segundo, 'The Christian Understanding of Humanity,' quoted by Hennelly, *Theologies in Conflict*, p. 53.

33. Segundo, *Our Idea of God*, p. 7.

34. Juan Luis Segundo, *The Liberation of Theology*, trans. John Drury (Dublin: Gill and Macmillan, 1977), p. 8.

35. Segundo, *Our Idea of God*, p. 35.

36. Philip Berryman, *The Religious Roots of Rebellion: Christians in Central American Revolutions* (SCM Press, 1984), p. 380.

37. Segundo, *Our Idea of God*, pp. 35-36. One is reminded of Gandhi's criticism of the effects of the British way of life on India and its people.

38. Ibid., p. 36.

39. Ibid., p. 126.

40. Antonio Perez-Esclarín, *Atheism and Liberation* (SCM Press, 1974), p.1.

41. Peter C. Phan, 'The Dipolar God and Latin American Liberation Theology,' *Charles Hartshorne's Concept of God*, p. 27.

42. One difficulty with the stage of *rejection* is that one may not have done full justice to the conceptuality that is being rejected. This is always of course a risk when one is criticising a certain standpoint. One this point, see, for instance, Michael Dodds, O.P., *The Unchanging God of Love: A Study of the Teaching of St. Thomas on Divine Immutability* (Fribourg, 1986). Given the limitations of this exploration, to develop further the classical theistic position and to evaluate the criticisms of Hartshorne and the liberation theologians is, however, to write another kind of book. Our intention in turning to other conceptualities will, we hope, be clear in the following chapters. This is not to say that Hartshorne's and the liberationist's conceptualities are not themselves open to certain criticisms.

CHAPTER 6

1. For a more detailed and systematic presentation of Hartshorne's concept of God, see S. Sia, *God in Process Thought: a Study in Charles Hartshorne's Concept of God* (Martinus Nijhoff, 1985).

2. He continues to uphold this view in his later writings. See, his *Wisdom as Moderation: a Philosophy of the Middle Way* (Albany, N.Y.: SUNY, 1987), pp. 83-94.

3. See, among others, his *Insights and Oversights of Great Thinkers: an Evaluation of Western Philosophy* (Albany, N.Y.: SUNY Press, 1983), p. 99.

4. Hartshorne, 'Philosophy and Orthodoxy,' *Ethics*, LIV, 4 (July 1944), p. 295; 'Equality, Freedom and the Insufficiency of Empiricism,' *Southwestern Journal*

of Philosophy, I, 3 (Fall 1970), p. 23; *A Natural Theology for Our Time* (La Salle: Open Court, 1967), p. 134.

5. Keith Ward, *The Concept of God* (Fount Paperbacks, 1977), pp. 157-158. There is a difference, however, between Hartshorne and Ward regarding God-talk. For Ward God-talk is limited to what evokes an appropriate attitude in humans rather than in describing God's inner being. For an interesting and insightful discussion on why and how God should be described in 'tripolar' terms, Cf. Paul Fiddes, *Creative Suffering of God* (Oxford University Press, 1992).

6. John Macquarrie, *Thinking about God* (London: SCM Press, 1975), p. 115.

7. John Macquarrie, *Twentieth-Century Religious Thought* (N.Y.: Harper, 1963), p. 277. Schubert Ogden replied to Macquarrie's criticism in his contribution to *Process Theology: Basic Writings*, ed. Ewert Cousins (N.Y.: Newman Press, 1971).

8. H.P. Owen, *Concepts of Deity* (London: Macmillan, 1971), p. 83.

9. Hartshorne's idea of a dipolar God invites comparisons with the doctrine of God formulated recently by Latin American liberation theologians. As was previously noted, Latin American liberation theologians have argued that the locus of their God-talk is not a world full of beauty and order which evokes wonder in us as it did for the ancient Greeks. Rather it is a world full of misery, impoverishment and suffering. Their reflections have led them to maintain that access to God is with the poor and the oppressed and to hold that God must be described in bipolar language: as Diós Menor and Diós Mayor. Cf. Jon Sobrino, *Christology at the Crossroads: a Latin American Approach* (Maryknoll, N.Y.: Orbis Books, 1978); Victorio Araya, *God of the Poor* (Maryknoll, N.Y.: Orbis Books, 1983), pp.34f. For a helpful comparison, see Peter C. Phan, 'The Dipolar God and Latin American Liberation Theology,' *Charles Hartshorne's Concept of God: Philosophical and Theological Responses*, ed. S. Sia (Kluwer Academic Publishers, 1989), pp. 23-39.

10. Hartshorne, *Man's Vision of God and the Logic of Theism* (Chicago: Willett, Clark & Co., 1941), p.165.

11. Ibid.

12. Ibid. p.173.

13. This is a comment we got from the college students with whom we discussed this section! The actual response was: 'how unromantic!'.

14. Hartshorne, 'Whitehead in French Perspective,' *Thomist*, XXXIII,3 (July, 1969), p.580.

15. Colin Gunton, 'Process Theology's Concept of God: an Outline and Assessment,' *The Expository Times*, LXXXIV (1972-73), p. 294. See also, his *Becoming and Being: The Doctrine of God in Charles Hartshorne and Karl Barth* (Oxford University Press, 1978).

16. Hartshorne, 'Religion and Creative Experience,' *Unitarian Register and Universalist Leader*, CXLI, 6 (June, 1962), p.10.

17. Hartshorne, 'Religion in Process Philosophy,' *Philosophical and Cultural Perspectives*, ed. J. C. Feaver and W. Horosz (Princeton: D. van Nostrand, 1967), p.261.

18. Hartshorne, *MV*, p.158.

19. Ibid., p. 110.

20. Ibid.; cf. also his 'Reflections on the Strengths and Weaknesses of Thomism,' *Ethics*, LIV,1 (October, 1943), p.54.

21. In many of his writings Hartshorne seems to equate God's righteousness with God's love. But in *MV*, p.130, he states that 'love' implies the final concrete truth. By this he means that God *is* love and not just loving, as God is merely righteous or wise (though in the supreme or definitive way). Hartshorne's reason for this qualification is that in love the ethico-cognitive and aesthetic aspects of value are both expressed.

22. Hugo Meynell, 'The Theology of Hartshorne,' *Journal of Theological Studies*, N.S. XXIV, 1 (April, 1973), p. 150.

23. Hartshorne, *MV*, p.163.

24. Hartshorne, *The Divine Relativity: A Social Conception of God* (Yale University Press, 1948), pp.124-125. Hartshorne's doctrine of dipolarity means that there is a necessary aspect and a contingent aspect of God's goodness and love.

25. Hartshorne, 'Divine Absoluteness and Divine Relativity' *Transcendence*, ed. H. W. Richardson and D. Cutler (Boston: Beacon Press, 1969), p.166.

26. Ibid.

27. Hartshorne, *MV*. p.162.

28. Hartshorne, *DR*. p.126. It appears that what Hartshorne means by 'the greatest good' is what God *actually* chooses. Only in this way is it reconcilable with God's freedom to choose among alternative ways. If what God *could have chosen* can still be described as 'the greatest good,' then God, given God's unsurpassable knowledge, would have chosen it. Thus, Hartshorne

could be interpreted as saying that the standard of goodness is identified with God's actual choice.

29. There have been a number of writings comparing Hartshorne's concept of God with the Thomistic one. See, among others, Illtyd Trethowan, 'God's Changelessness', *The Clergy Review* (January, 1979), pp.15-21; John C. Moskop, *Divine Omniscience and Human Freedom: Thomas Aquinas and Charles Hartshorne* (Mercer University Press, 1984); W. Norris Clarke's essay 'Charles Hartshorne's Philosophy of God: A Thomistic Critique' and Hartshorne's reply, *Charles Hartshorne's Concept of God: Philosophical and Theological Responses*, ed. S. Sia (Dordrecht: Kluwer Academic Publishers, 1989), pp.103-123, 269-279. See, also, J. Norman King and Barry L. Whitney, 'Rahner and Hartshorne on Divine Immutability,' *International Philosophical Quarterly*, XXII, 3 (Sept., 1982), pp. 195-209. For a survey of the debate between Hartshorne and classical theists, see Barry L. Whitney, 'Divine Immutability in Process Philosophy and Contemporary Thomism,' *Horizons*, VII (1980), pp. 49-68, and S. Sia. 'The Doctrine of God's Immutability: Introducing the Modern Debate', *New Blackfriars*, LXVIII, 805 (May, 1987), pp.229-232. Also listed in the bibliography are writings dealing with the debate between these two schools of thought. We are grateful to Prof. Piet Schoonenberg for his helpful comments and for a copy of his 'God as Relating and (Be)Coming: a MetaThomistic Consideration' which appeared in *Listening*, XIV, 3 (1979), pp. 365-278.

30. Some of the criticisms of Hartshorne's concept of God have already been noted in the text. See further, E. Mascall, *The Openness of Being* (Darton, Longman & Todd, 1971). To be fair to classical theists, one would need to examine much more extensively than we have been able to do both their development of the classical theistic position and their responses to the criticisms of it. See note 42 of chapter 5. There have also been criticisms of Hartshorne's conceptuality from the point of view of the theology of the Trinity. Cf. for instance, John O'Donnell, *Trinity and Temporality: The Christian Doctrine of God in the Light of Process Theology and the Theology of Hope* (Oxford University Press, 1983); Paul Fiddes, *Creative Suffering of God* (Oxford University Press, 1992).

31. Among the more readily available sources for this concept of God, aside from Hartshorne's own works are: Norman Pittenger, *God in Process* (SCM, 1967) and *Picturing God* (SCM, 1982); Schubert Ogden, *The Reality of God and Other Essays* (Harper & Row, 1966); John Cobb and David Griffin, *Process Theology: An Introductory Exposition* (Belfast: Christian Journals, 1976).

32. A list of secondary writings on Hartshorne's thought was published by Dorothy Hartshorne in *Process Studies*, III,3 (Fall, 1973), pp.178-227, and brought up to date in *Process Studies*, XI,2 (Spring, 1981), pp.112-120. Hartshorne has recently been honoured with a volume in the Library of Living Philosophers. This contains a nearly complete listing of Hartshorne's writings. Among recent secondary sources on Hartshorne's philosophy are: J. B. Cobb,

Jr. and F. I. Gamwell (eds.), *Existence and Actuality: Conversations with Charles Hartshorne* (Chicago and London: The University of Chicago Press, 1984); John C. Moskop, *Divine Omniscience and Human Freedom: Thomas Aquinas and Charles Hartshorne* (Mercer University Press, 1984); D. Viney, *Charles Hartshorne and the Existence of God* (SUNY Press, 1985); S. Sia, *God in Process Thought: a Study in Charles Hartshorne's Concept of God* (Martinus Nijhoff, 1985); Barry Whitney, *Evil and the Process God* (Toronto: Edwin Mellen Press, 1985; D. Dombrowski, *Hartshorne and the Metaphysics of Animal Rights* (SUNY Press, 1987); R. Kane and S. H. Phillips (eds.), *Hartshorne, Process Philosophy, and Theology* (SUNY Press, 1989); ; S. Sia, (ed.), *Charles Hartshorne's Concept of God: Philosophical and Theological Responses* (Kluwer Academic Publishers, 1989); R. C. Morris, *Process Philosophy and Political Ideology: The Social and Political Thought of A.N. Whitehead and Charles Hartshorne* (SUNY, 1991); and the entire issue of *The Modern Schoolman*, LXII, 4 (May, 1985).

33. Daniel D. Williams, *What Present-Day Theologians are Thinking* (Harper, 1952). Quoted by Bernard E. Meland. 'The New Creation' *Process Theology: Basic Writings*, p.198. In an interesting and informative study, Marcel Sarot shows the need for and the possibility of a theory of divine embodiment. Cf. his *God, Possibility and Corporeality* (Kampen: Kok Pharos Publishing House, 1992).

34. Hartshorne (with William L. Reese), *Philosophers Speak of God* (University of Chicago Press, 1953), p.15. Latin American liberation theologians also cite the doctrine of the Incarnation to support the way they depict God. Cf. for instance, Jon Sobrino, *Christology at the Crossroads*.

35. See Schubert Ogden, *Faith and Freedom: Toward a Theology of Liberation* (Nashville: Abingdon, 1979); Delwin Brown, *To Set at Liberty: Christian Faith and Human Freedom* (Orbis Books, 1981); L. Charles Birch and John B. Cobb, Jr., *The Liberation of Life* (Cambridge University Press, 1981); John B. Cobb, Jr. and W. Widick Schroeder, (eds.), *Process Philosophy and Social Thought* (Chicago: Center for the Scientific Study of Religion, 1981); John B. Cobb, Jr. *Process Theology as Political Theology* (The Westminster Press, 1982), and the special issue of *Process Studies*, XIV,2 (Summer, 1985), devoted to liberation theology with articles by Joseph A. Bracken, Marjorie Suchocki, Schubert Ogden, Matthew L. Lamb and John B. Cobb, Jr. An international conference on 'Process, Peace and Human Rights' was organised in Kyoto, Japan in 1987.

   Process theologians have been critical of Latin American liberation theology for its failure to address metaphysical issues. Ogden, for instance, writes that, Latin American liberation theologians 'focus on the existential meaning of God for us without dealing at all adequately with the metaphysical being of God in himself.' *Faith and Freedom*, p. 34. See also, Delwin Brown, 'Thinking about the God of the Poor: Questions for Liberation Theology from Process Thought,' *Journal of the American Academy of Religion*, LVII, 2 (Summer 1989), pp. 267-281. On the other hand, it is important to realise that

Latin American liberation theologians are not dismissive of the attempt to think through their faith. They are, however, prompted by different concerns. As Gustavo Gutierrez explains: 'The challenges posed by concrete human situations take us to the sources of Christian life. Conceptual distinctions and theological developments do not there disappear, as a pedantic anti-intellectualism would have it; on the contrary, they take on meaning and vitality. A concern for where the poor are to sleep will make us realize that it is in fact not possible to separate love of God and love of neighbor; that is, that we must live both aspects as intertwined with each other.' *The God of Life* (Maryknoll, N.Y.: Orbis Books, 1989), p. 138.

36. See the essays by Theodore Walker, Jr., Peter C. Phan, Sheila Greeve Davaney, *Charles Hartshorne's Concept of God: Philosophical and Theological Responses.* John Cobb accepts that Hartshorne somehow separated theology from its socio-political matrix and established it instead in the context of the history of ideas. Cf. *Process Theology as Political Theology* (Manchester University Press/The Westminster Press, 1982), p. 65. In addition, one cannot help but wonder whether Hartshorne's belief that the ultimate value is beauty rather than justice does not have a strong bearing on his solution to the problem of evil. Cf. his *The Darkness and the Light: a Philosopher Reflects Upon His Fortunate Career and Those Who Made it Possible* (SUNY Press, 1990). It is also instructive to take into account Hartshorne's reply to Peter Phan's essay: 'I have stressed the idea of divine love and objected to what has sometimes been meant by divine 'justice,' taking this word in its legal sense of rewards and punishments' (p. 247). This understanding of justice may account for Hartshorne's relative neglect of the kind of issues that concern liberationists.

CHAPTER 7

1. Rebecca S. Chopp, *The Praxis of Suffering: An Interpretation of Liberation and Political Theologies* (Maryknoll, N.Y.: Orbis Books, 1986), p. 24. In making use of the symbol of God as liberator as developed by Latin American liberation theology we are not suggesting that it has been found totally acceptable. As is well known, this form of theology—like every other school of thought—has its critics. However, insofar as this symbol helps us to show that we are called upon to participate in God's liberative act, we find it useful to refer to it here.

2. Ibid., p. 25.

3. Cf. Alfred T. Hennelly, *Theologies in Conflict: The Challenge of Juan Luis Segundo* (Maryknoll, N.Y.: Orbis Books, 1979), pp. 52f.

4. Pablo Richard, 'Biblical Theology of Confrontation with Idols' *The Idols of Death and the God of Life: A Theology* (Maryknoll, N.Y: Orbis Books, 1983), p. 10. See, also, chapter 5 of Antonio Perez-Esclarín, *Atheism and Liberation* (SCM Press, 1980). An interesting discussion on how God's liberating power

was experienced by the Biblical women is provided by Teresa Okure in her 'Women in the Bible,' *With Passion and Compassion: Third World Women Doing Theology*, ed. Virginia Fabella and Mercy Amba Oduyoye (Maryknoll, N.Y.: Orbis Books, 1989), pp. 47-59.

5. Gustavo Gutierrez, *The God of Life* (Maryknoll, N.Y.: Orbis Books, 1991), p. 22.

6. Ibid., p. 28.

7. Hennelly, *Theologies in Conflict*, pp. 52-53.

8. Ibid.

9. Ibid., p. 37.

10. As Schubert Ogden notes, 'With the emergence of historical consciousness came the ever-clearer realisation that to be fully human is to be an active *subject* of historical change, not merely its passive *object*. The clearer this realisation became, however, the clearer it also became that most human beings, in most of the important aspects of their lives, neither are nor can be the active subjects of their history.' *Faith and Freedom: Toward a Theology of Liberation* (Nashville: Abingdon, 1979), p. 22. In Minjung theology the idea of the oppressed as subjects of their history is particularly central. See, *Minjung Theology: People as the Subjects of History*, ed. Commission on Theological Concerns of the Christian Church Conference of Asia (Orbis Books, 1983) and *An Emerging Theology in World Perspective: Commentary on Korean Minjung Theology*, ed. Jung Young Lee (Mystic, Conn.: Twenty-third Publications, 1988). Gustavo Gutierrez has focused on the need for the poor and the oppressed to be active subjects: 'They are less and less willing to be the passive objects of demagogic manipulations and social or charitable welfare in varied disguises. They want to be the active subjects of their own history and to forge a radically different society.' 'Liberating Praxis and Christian Faith,' *Frontiers of Theology in Latin America*, ed. Rosino Gibellini, trans. John Drury (Maryknoll, N.Y.: Orbis Books, 1974), p. 1.

11. An observation made by Leonardo Boff is worth noting: 'The common point of departure of all the various tendencies within the one theology of liberation is ethical indignation at the misery of social reality, and the demand for a process of liberation that will overcome this contradiction. But there are different ways of developing this basic experience, and this is where a variety of accents can be identified.' 'Integral Liberation and Partial Liberations,' Leonardo and Clodovis Boff, *Salvation and Liberation: In Search of a Balance between Faith and Politics* (Maryknoll, N.Y.: Orbis Books, 1984), p. 25. It would seem then that there are different tasks but one common goal for the Church in Latin America.

12. Juan Luis Segundo, *Our Idea of God* (Dublin: Gill and Macmillan, 1980), p. 49.

See also, Victorio Araya, *The God of the Poor: The Mystery of God in Latin American Liberation Theology* (Maryknoll, N.Y.: Orbis Books, 1983), pp. 91-104.

13. Antonio Perez-Esclarín, *Atheism and Liberation*, p. 2.

14. Gustavo Gutierrez, *The God of Life*, 63. Also, p. 138. See also Leonardo Boff's interpretation of the Puebla document (p. 39f) and the mediation of pastoral practice (p. 55f) in his 'Integral Liberation and Partial Liberations,' in Leonardo and Clodovis Boff, *Salvation and Liberation*.

15. Much of what is said of Latin America is applicable elsewhere. Pieris, however, sees the Asian context somewhat differently. Understanding the issues in Asia to revolve around *poverty* and *religiosity*, he interprets the local church's mission to the poor in Asia as 'total identification (or "baptismal immersion"...) with monks and peasants who have conserved for us, in their *religious socialism*, the seeds of liberation that *religion* and *poverty* have combined to produce. It is the one sure path opened for the local church to remove the cross from the steeples where it has stood for four centuries and plant it once more on Calvary where the prophetic communities die victims of politics and religion in order to rise again as local churches *of* Asia.' *An Asian Theology of Liberation* (Maryknoll, N.Y.: Orbis Books, 1988) p. 45. On how the church of Asia is to respond to the Asian context, see chapter 9 of his book.

16. Quoted by Hennelly, *Theologies in Conflict*, p. xxiii.

17. Segundo, *Our Idea of God*, p. 76. One controversy that has arisen in this respect is whether liberation theologians are not confused about the meaning of 'liberation' itself within the context of the work of the church in Latin America. Here Leonardo Boff and Clodovis Boff's book, *Salvation and Liberation,* is particularly enlightening.

18. Segundo, *Our Idea of God*, p. 81. See also, Gutierrez, *God of Life*, pp. 105-108. Leonardo Boff observes that the church has always come to the aid of the poor but what is needed is to make use of the resources of the poor in instituting change. Cf. *Salvation and Liberation*, p. 3.

19. Segundo, *Our Idea of God*, p. 69.

20. Quoted by Araya, *The God of the Poor*, p. 52.

21. Segundo, *Our Idea of God*, p. 69.

22. By explaining evil and suffering as the unfortunate consequence of creative acts and reformulating the meaning of God's power, Hartshorne wants to argue that the classical problem of evil is a pseudo-problem. It is based on a misconception of omnipotence. He believes that God's power ought not to be

considered as absolute control.

'Creativity' itself is rather ambiguous since as Hartshorne points out it could mean 'originality'. Hartshorne uses and develops it as a philosophical category as explained in the text. In his *Creativity in American Philosophy* (Albany, N.Y.: SUNY, 1984), he discusses the treatment of this central category by various American philosophers.

23. Our concern here is limited to showing how Hartshorne's concept of creativity can be useful in understanding further the image of God as liberator. There are some issues, e.g. whether depicting God's power as persuasive is completely adequate, which we do not deal with. On this point, see David Basinger, *Divine Power in Process Theism: a Philosophical Critique* (SUNY, 1988); S. Sia, 'Suffering and Creativity,' *Ultimate Reality and Meaning*, XII, 3 (Sept., 1989), pp. 210-219.

24. Hartshorne, 'Process and the Nature of God,' *Traces of God in a Secular Culture*, ed. G. McLean (Alba House, 1973), p. 136.

25. Hartshorne, 'Tillich and the Other Great Tradition,' *Anglican Theological Review*, XLIII (1961), p. 248. Cf. also, *Creativity in American Philosophy*, p. 56; 'God and the Meaning of Life,' *On Nature*, ed. Leroy Rouner (University of Notre Dame Press, 1984), p. 156.

26. Hartshorne, *Divine Relativity: A Social Conception of God* (Yale University Press, 1948), p.138.

27. Hartshorne, 'Divine Absoluteness and Divine Relativity,' *Transcendence*, eds. H. Richardson and D. Cutler, (Beacon Press, 1969), p. 169. On this point, see our reply to Meynell's criticism in ch. 6.

28. Hartshorne uses a number of analogies to illustrate this conception of power: the wise and unselfish love in parents, the unselfish love of Jesus and of Buddha, Plato's idea of the World Soul. Cf. 'God and the Meaning of Life,' *On Nature*, ed. Leroy S. Rouner (University of Notre Dame Press, 1984), p. 160. In this way, he believes he answers the questions: how does God influence the world? is God influenced by the world?

29. Hartshorne, 'The Dipolar Conception of God,' *Review of Metaphysics*, XXI (1967), p. 281. Cf. also, *Creativity in American Philosophy*, p. 36.

30. Hartshorne, 'Religion in Process Philosophy,' *Religion in Philosophical and Cultural Perspectives*, eds. J. Feaver and W. Horosz, (Princeton: D. van Nostram, 1967), p. 281.

31. Hartshorne, 'A New Look at the Problem of Evil,' *Current Philosophical Issues: Essays in Honor of Curt John Ducasse*, ed. F. Dommeyer (Charles C. Thomas, 1966), p. 202.

32. Hartshorne, *Divine Relativity*, p. 142.

33. Hartshorne, 'Religion in Process Philosophy,' p. 263; 'The Dipolar Conception of God,' p. 283.

34. Hartshorne, 'A New Look at the Problem of Evil,' p. 206.

35. Hartshorne, 'Order and Chaos,' *The Concept of Order*, ed. P. Kuntz (Univ. of Washington Press, 1968), pp. 253-267.

36. Hartshorne, 'Religion and Creative Experience,' *Unitarian Register and Universalist Leader*, CXLI (1962), p. 10.

37. Hartshorne, 'Religion in Process Philosophy,' p. 261. John Cobb clarifies further the reason for preferring to understand God's power as persuasion. Cf. *Process Theology as Political Theology* (Manchester University Press/The Westminster Press, 1982), pp.106-108.

    In his book *The Darkness of God: Theology After Hiroshima* (SCM Press, 1982), Jim Garrison discusses Hartshorne's theodicy. While agreeing with process thinkers that the universality of creaturely freedom leads to a reinterpretation of God's power, he takes their understanding of the divine lure within us to task for being too passive or not adequately spelled out. Garrison's own claims are: 1) the divine lure 'is at times overwhelming, at times subtly suggestive, at times brutally violent.' 2) 'God must be understood to be the chief instance of the freedom to commit good and evil' and human beings do experience what is defined as intrinsic evil at the hands of God 3) God 'can use those intrinsically evil and good acts committed by God and humanity alike instrumentally for a higher purpose' (p. 53). Garrison's position, despite making it clear that he is talking not about God's being but about the way God is experienced, leaves one wondering whether he has not compromised God's absolute goodness. See also, Barry L. Whitney, *Evil and the Process God* (Toronto: Edwin Mellen Press, 1985), p. 145.

38. Hartshorne, *Divine Relativity*, p. 137.

39. Hartshorne, 'Love and Dual Transcendence,' *Union Seminary Quarterly Review*, XXX (1975), p. 96.

40. While we have limited our treatment of this point to Latin American liberation theology, one could also compare it to feminist theological thinking. On this issue, cf. Sheila Greeve Davaney, 'God, Power and the Struggle for Liberation: a Feminist Contribution,' *Charles Hartshorne's Concept of God: Philosophical and Theological Responses*, ed. S.Sia (Kluwer Academic Publishers, 1989), pp. 57-75; Anna Case-Winters, *God's Power: Traditional Understandings and Contemporary Challenges* (Westminister/John Knox Press, 1990).

41. In Hartshorne's metaphysical scheme, reality is composed of events, not substances. Hartshorne also espouses a psychicalist view of reality.

42. Hartshorne, 'Religion and Creative Experience,' *Unitarian Register and Universalist Leader*, CXLI (1962), pp. 9-11; *Creative Synthesis and Philosophic Method* (SCM, 1970), pp. 62-74. For Hartshorne creation is first of all self-creation. See, *Creativity in American Philosophy*, p. 19.

43. Hartshorne, 'Philosophy After Fifty Years,' *Mid-twentieth Century American Philosophy: Personal Statements*, ed. P. Bertocci (Humanities Press, 1974), p. 143. Hartshorne explains human creativity or freedom in this way: 'The emergent synthesis of data into a new unitary experience is the ultimate emergence, the ultimate freedom. Freedom of behavior is derivative from that. Just how we remember or perceive what has been happening is our present decision.' 'God and the Meaning of Life,' p. 161.

44. Hartshorne, 'Can Man Transcend his Animality?' *Monist*, LV (1971), p. 216.

45. Hartshorne, 'Philosophy After Fifty Years,' p. 143.

46. Hartshorne, 'Real Possibility,' *Journal of Philosophy*, LVI (1963), p. 599.

47. Hartshorne, *The Logic of Perfection And Other Essays in Neoclassical Metaphysics* (Open Court, 1962), p. 223.

48. Hartshorne (with W. Reese), *Philosophers Speak of God* (Midway Reprints, 1976) p. 501. On Hartshorne's reference to quantum physics on this point, see Robert H. Kane, 'Free Will, Determinism, and Creativity' (pp. 139-140) and Hartshorne's response (p. 607), *The Philosophy of Charles Hartshorne*, *The Library of Living Philosophers Vol. XX*, ed. Lewis Edwin Hahn (La Salle, Ill.: Open Court, 1991).

49. Hartshorne, *Creativity in American Philosophy*, p. 20.

50. In a letter to the authors, John Cobb points out, that most of the economic injustices are caused by *competing* creativities, e.g. First World groups seeking to expand their markets and profits do untold harm in the Third World. He adds that 'Generally this harm is the incidental result of achieving their own purposes. Rarely is it sought for its own sake.' While we would agree with Cobb that in some cases this may well be the case, it is hard to ignore the factor of deliberateness in some cases, e.g. when certain developments are forced through contrary to the wishes of the affected party or, worse, at the cost of their lives or their well-being. When these developments meet with opposition, then sometimes the harm that occurs has been sought for its own sake.

51. Aloysius Pieris, *An Asian Theology of Liberation*, p. 37.

52. Quoted in Leonardo and Clodovis Boff, *Salvation and Liberation*, p. 4. As Samuel Rayan explains, how one understands poverty will determine one's approach to it. Cf. his, 'An Asian Spirituality of Liberation,' *Asian Christian*

Spirituality: Reclaiming Traditions, eds. Virginia Fabella et al., (Maryknoll, N.Y.: Orbis Books, 1992), pp.26-28.

53. This is where the 'socio-analytical mediation' of Latin American liberation theology is particularly valuable.

SELECT BIBLIOGRAPHY

Abbot, W. ...

Anderson, G H, ed., ...
1975.

Augustine, Confessions ...

Anselm, Proslogion ...
... Cur Deus Homo ...
... c. 1803-1534.

Aquinas, Thomas, Summa Theologiae ...
McGraw Hill, 1964-66.

Araya, Victorio, God of the Poor ...
Theology Press, Book ... 5 ...

Baccei, Bishop ... The ...
Publications, 1987.

Badham, Paul, ...

Balasuriya, Tissa, ...

Baradale, W ... et al ...
Abingdon Press, 1989.

Berryman, Philip, ...
American Revolution SCM, 19 ...

Birch ..., Charles, ... Christian ... Life ...
Press, 1981.

Bloch, Ernst, ... Spirit ...
Capstone Press, 1985.

Boff, Leonardo, ... Ecclesio-Genesis ...
between Reformation ...

Boff, Leonardo and Virgil ...
Edinburgh: T. & T. Clark, ...

Bowker, John, Meanings of Death ...
... Problems of Suffering ...
Press, 1970.

Brown, Delwin, Thinking about the ...
Theology ...
Religion, LVII, 2 ... 1989.

... To Set at Liberty Christian ...
... 1981.

Brümmer, Vincent, What are ...
London SCM Press, 1984.

Buber, Martin, Between Man and ...
Kaufmann, New York, Kegan ...

SELECT BIBLIOGRAPHY

Abbot, W. (ed.). *The Documents of Vatican II*. N.Y.: Guild Press, 1966.

Anderson, G. H. (ed.). *Asian Voices in Christian Theology*. N.Y.: Orbis Books, 1976.

Augustine. *Confessions*. trans. E. H. Pusey. E. P. Dutton & Co., 1907.

Anselm. *Proslogium: Monologium: An Appendix on Behalf of the Fool by Gaunilo: and Cur Deus Homo*. trans. S. N. Deane. La Salle, Ill.: Open Court Publishing Co., 1903, 1945.

Aquinas, Thomas. *Summa Theologiae*. Blackfriars, Eyre & Spottiswoode and McGraw-Hill, 1964-66.

Araya, Victorio. *God of the Poor: The Mystery of God in Latin American Liberation Theology*. trans. Robert R. Barr. Maryknoll, N.Y.: Orbis Books, 1983.

Bacani, Bishop Teodoro C. *The Church and Politics*. Quezon City: Claretian Publications, 1987.

Badham, Paul. *Christian Beliefs About Life After Death*. Macmillan, 1976.

Balasuriya, Tissa. *Jesus Christ and Human Liberation*. Colombo, 1981.

Beardslee, William A. et al. *Biblical Preaching on the Death of Jesus*. Nashville: Abingdon Press, 1989.

Berryman, Philip. *The Religious Roots of Rebellion: Christians in the Central American Revolution*. SCM, 1984.

Birch, L. Charles and John B. Cobb. Jr. *The Liberation of Life*. Cambridge University Press, 1981.

Bloch, Chana. *Spelling the Word: George Herbert and the Bible*. University of California Press, 1985.

Boff, Leonardo and Clodovis. *Salvation and Liberation: In Search of a Balance between Faith and Politics*. Maryknoll, N.Y.: Orbis Books, 1984.

Boff, Leonardo and Virgil Elizondo (eds.). *The People of God Amidst the Poor*. Edinburgh: T. & T. Clark Ltd., 1984

Bowker, John. *Meanings of Death*. Cambridge University Press, 1991.

_____. *Problems of Suffering in Religions of the World*. Cambridge University Press, 1970.

Brown, Delwin. 'Thinking about the God of the Poor: Questions for Liberation Theology from Process Thought.' *Journal of the American Academy of Religion*, LVII, 2 (Summer 1989), pp. 267-281.

_____. *To Set at Liberty: Christian Faith and Human Freedom*. N.Y.: Orbis Books, 1981.

Brümmer, Vincent. *What are We Doing When We Pray: a Philosophical Inquiry* London: SCM Press, 1988.

Buber, Martin. *Eclipse of God: Studies in the Relation between Religion and Philosophy*. New York: Harper and Row Publishers, 1957.

Byron, William (ed.). *The Causes of World Hunger*. New York/ Ramsey: Paulist Press, 1982.

'Charles Hartshorne,' *Louvain Studies*, VII, No. 2 (Fall 1978).

Chopp, Rebecca S. *The Praxis of Suffering: An Interpretation of Liberation and Political Theologies*. Maryknoll, N.Y.: Orbis Books, 1986.

Clarke, Norris. *The Philosophical Approach to God: A Neo-Thomistic Perspective*. Wakeforest University Press, 1979.

Cobb, B. John, Jr. *Process Theology as Political Theology*. Manchester University Press/ The Westminster Press, 1982.

_____ and W. Widick Schroeder, (eds.). *Process Philosophy and Social Thought*. Chicago: Center for the Scientific Study of Religion, 1981.

_____ and F. I. Gamwell (eds.) *Existence and Actuality: Conversations with Charles Hartshorne*. Chicago and London: The University of Chicago Press, 1984.

Collins, Raymond and Jan Lambrecht (eds.). *God and Human Suffering*. Leuven: Peters, 1990.

Cone, James H. *God of the Oppressed*. N.Y.: The Seabury Press, 1975.

Cousins, Ewert (ed.). *Process Theology*. Newman Press, 1971.

Creel, Richard. *Divine Impassibility: An Essay in Philosophical Theology*. Cambridge Unversity Press, 1986.

Crenshaw, James L. (ed.). *Theodicy in the Old Testament*. Issues in Religion and Theology 4. Fortress Press/ SPCK, 1983.

Dupré, Louis. 'Evil—a Religious Mystery: a Plea for a More Inclusive Model of Theodicy,' *Faith and Philosophy*, VII, 3 (July 1990), pp. 261-280.

Enright, D. J. (ed.). *The Oxford Book of Death*. Oxford University Press, 1983

Fabella, Virginia et al. *Asian Christian Spirituality: Reclaiming Traditions*. Maryknoll, N.Y.: Orbis Books, 1992.

_____ and Mercy Amba Oduyoye (eds.). *With Passion and Compassion: Third World Women Doing Theology*. Maryknoll, N.Y.: Orbis Books, 1989.

Ferm, D. W. (ed.). *Third World Liberation Theologies: A Reader*. Maryknoll, N.Y.: Orbis Books, 1986.

Fiddes, Paul S. *Creative Suffering of God*. Oxford University Press, 1992.

Fiorenza, Elizabeth Schüssler. *In Memory of Her: A Feminist Theological Reconstruction of Christian Origins*. New York: Crossroad, 1983.

Flew, Anthony. *God and Philosophy*. Harcourt, Brace & World, Ltd., 1967.

Ford, Lewis. 'The Immutable God and Father Clarke,' *The New Scholasticism*, XLIX, 2 (Spring 1975), pp. 189-199.

_____. 'Process And Thomist Views Concerning Divine Perfection'; W. Norris Clarke, SJ. 'Comments on Professor Ford's Paper.' *The Universe as Journey: Conversations with W. Norris Clarke, SJ*. Ed. Gerard A. McCool, SJ. (N.Y.: Fordham University Press, 1988).

Fowler, James. *Stages of Faith*. Harper & Row, 1981.

Fretheim, Terence E. *The Suffering of God: An Old Testament Perspective*. Philadelphia: Fortress Press, 1987.

Galot, J., SJ. 'La Realité de la souffrance de Dieu.' *Nouvelle Revue Théologique*, CI (March 1979), pp. 224-245.

Gardner, Helen. *The Metaphysical Poets*. Penguin, 1970.

Garrison, Jim. *The Darkness of God: Theology After Hiroshima*. SCM Press, 1982.

Gibellini, Rosino (ed.). *Frontiers of Theology in Latin America*. trans. John Drury. Maryknoll, N.Y.: Orbis Books, 1974.

Griffin, David Ray. *God, Power and Evil*. Westminster Press, 1976.

Gutierrez, Gustavo. *The God of Life*. trans. Matthew J. O'Connell. Maryknoll, N.Y.: Orbis Books, 1991.

_____. *On Job: God-Talk and the Suffering of the Innocent*. trans. Matthew J. O'Connell. Maryknoll, N.Y.: Orbis Books, 1987.

_____. 'Faith as Freedom: Solidarity with the Alienated and Confidence in the Future,' *Living with Change, Experience, Faith*. ed. Francis A. Eigo. Villanova University Press, 1976.

Hahn, Lewis Edwin (ed.). *The Philosophy of Charles Hartshorne*. The Library of Living Philosophers Vol. XX. La Salle, Ill.: Open Court, 1991.

Hartshorne, Charles. *Aquinas to Whitehead: Seven Centuries of Metaphysics of Religion*. Milwaukee: Marquette University Publications, 1976.

_____. 'Can We Understand God?' *Louvain Studies*. VII, 2. (Fall 1978), pp. 75-84.

_____. *Creative Synthesis and Philosophic Method*. SCM Press, 1970.

_____. *Creativity in American Philosophy*. Albany: State University of New York Press, 1984.

_____. *Divine Relativity: A Social Conception of God*. Yale University Press, 1948.

_____. 'God and the Meaning of Life.' *On Nature*. ed. Leroy S. Rouner. Notre Dame: University of Notre Dame Press, 1984, pp.154-168.

_____. 'The God of Religion and the God of Philosophy,' *Talk of God: Royal Institute of Philosophy Lectures*. Macmillan, 1969.

_____. *The Logic of Perfection and Other Essays in Neoclassical Metaphysics*. Open Court, 1962.

_____. *Man's Vision of God and the Logic of Theism*. Archon Books, 1964 rep.

_____. 'Metaphysics and the Dual Transcendence of God.' *Tulane Studies in Philosophy*, XXXIV (1986), pp. 65-72.

_____. 'The Modern World and A Modern View of God,' *Crane Review*. IV, 2 (Winter 1962), pp.73-85.

_____. *A Natural Theology for Our Time*. Open Court, 1967.

_____. 'A New Look at the Problem of Evil,' *Current Philosophical Issues: Essays in Honor of Curt John Ducasse*. ed. F. Dommeyer. Charles C. Thomas, 1966, pp. 201-212.

_____. *Omnipotence and Other Theological Mistakes*. Albany: State University of New York Press, 1984.

_____. 'Process and the Nature of God,' *Traces of God in a Secular Culture*. ed. G. McLean. Alba House, 1973, pp. 117-141.

_____. 'Love and Dual Transcendence,' *Union Seminary Quarterly Review*. XXX (1975), pp. 94-100.

_____. (with W. Reese). *Philosophers Speak of God*. Midway Reprints, 1976.

Hennelly, Alfred T. *Theologies of Conflict: The Challenge of Juan Luis Segundo*. Maryknoll, N.Y.: Orbis Books, 1979.

Hick, John. *Evil and the God of Love*. Collins, 1979.

Hill, William, O.P. 'Does Divine Love Entail Suffering in God?' in Clarke L. Bowman and Eugene T. Long, (eds.). *God and Temporality*. N.Y.: Paragon Publishers, 1984, pp. 55-71.

_____. 'Does the World Make a Difference to God?' *The Thomist*, XXXVIII, 1 (January 1974), pp. 146-164.

_____. 'Two Gods of Love: Aquinas and Whitehead.' *Listening*, XIV (1976), pp. 249-264.

Hume, David. *Writings on Religion*. Ed. Anthony Flew. Open Court, 1992.

Hyun, Younghak. 'Minjung Theology and the Religion of Han.' *East Asia Journal of Theology*, III (1985), pp. 350-360.

Jackson, Edgar N. *Understanding Grief*. SCM Press, 1957.

Jasper, David. *The Study of Literature and Religion*. Studies in Literature and Religion. London: Macmillan, 1989.

Jonas, Hans. 'A Concept of God after Auschwitz: a Jewish Voice.' *The Journal of Religion*, LXVII, 1 (January 1987), pp. 1-13.

Josephson, Eric. *Man Alone: Alienation in Modern Society*. N.Y.: Dell Publishing Co., Inc. 1966.

Kaneko, Keichi. 'The Compassionate God.' *North East Asia Journal of Theology* (March-September, 1982), pp. 170-176.

Kasper, Walter. *The God of Jesus Christ*. London: SCM Press, 1984.

Kim, Yong-Bok. *Minjung Theology: People as Subjects of History*. Maryknoll, N.Y.: Orbis Books, 1983.

King, J. Norman and Barry L. Whitney. 'Rahner and Hartshorne on Divine Immutability,' *International Philosophical Quarterly*. XXII, 3 (September, 1982).

Kitamori, Katzoh. *Theology of the Pain of God*. John Knox Press, 1965.

Kondoleon, Theodore. 'The Immutability of God: Some Recent Challenges,' *New Scholasticism*, LVIII (1984), pp. 293-315.

Kushner, Harold S. *When Bad Things Happen to Good People*. Pan Books, 1982.

Lane, Dermot A. *Christ at the Centre: Selected Issues in Christology*. Dublin: Veritas Publications, 1990.

Langford, Michael. *Unblind Faith*. SCM Press, 1982.

Lee, Jung Young. *An Emerging Theology in World Perspective: Commentary on Korean Minjung Theology*. Twenty-Third Publications, 1988.

_____. *God Suffers for Us*. Martinus Nijhoff, 1974.

Loomis, Jeffrey B. *Dayspring in Darkness: Sacrament in Hopkins*. Bucknell University Press, 1988.

Low, Anthony. *Love's Architecture: Devotional Modes in Seventeenth-Century English Poetry*. New York University Press, 1978.

Lucas, George R. Jr. *The Genesis of Modern Process Thought: a Historical Outline with Bibliography*. N.J.: Scarecrow Press, 1983.

Martinez, Salvador (ed.). *The Mission of God in the Context of the Suffering and Struggling Peoples of Asia: Biblical Reflections*. Hongkong: Christian Conference of Asia, 1988.

Martz, Louis. *Poetry of Meditation*. New Haven: Yale University Press, 1955.

McFague, Sallie. *Models of God: Theology for an Ecological, Nuclear Age*. SCM Press, 1978.

Metz, Johannes. *Theology of the World*. trans. William Glen-Doepel. N.Y.: Seabury Press, 1969.

Meynell, Hugo. 'The Theology of Hartshorne,' *Journal of Theological Studies*. N.S. XXIV, 1 (April, 1973).

Miller, J. Hillis. *The Disappearance of God: Five Nineteenth-Century Writers*. Cambridge, Mass.: The Belknap Press of Harvard University Press, 1963.

Milward, Peter. *Gerard Manley Hopkins 1844-1889*. New Haven: Yale University Press, 1949.

_____. *Landscape and Inscape: Vision and Inspiration in Hopkins' Poetry*. Grand Rapids, Michigan: William B. Eerdmans Publishing Co., 1975.

The Modern Schoolman, LXII, 4 (May 1985). Papers presented at a conference on Process Philosophy and Theology at St. Louis University.

Moltmann, Jürgen. *The Crucified God*. London: SCM Press, 1976.

Morris, R.C. *Process Philosophy and Political Ideology: The Social and Political Thought of A.N. Whitehead and Charles Hartshorne*. SUNY, 1991.

Moskop, John C. *Divine Omniscience and Human Freedom: Thomas Aquinas and Charles Hartshorne*. Mercer University Press, 1984.

Mühlen, Herbert. *Die Veränderlichkeit Gottes als Horizont einer Zukunftigen Christologie*. Münster Ascherndorff, 1969.

Muñoz, Ronaldo. *God of the Christians*. Maryknoll, N.Y.: Orbis Books, 1992.

Neville, Robert C. *Creativity and God: a Challenge to Process Theology*. N.Y.: The Seabury Press, 1980.

O'Donnell, John. *Trinity and Temporality: The Christian Doctrine of God in the Light of Process Theology and the Theology of Hope*. Oxford University Press, 1983.

Ogden, Schubert. *Faith and Freedom: Toward a Theology of Liberation*. Nashville: Abingdon, 1979.

_____. *The Reality of God and Other Essays*. N.Y.: Harper & Row, 1966.

O'Hanlon, Gerard F., SJ. *The Immutability of God in the Theology of Hans Urs von Balthasar*. Cambridge University Press, 1990.

Olivetti, Marco M. (ed.). *Theodicea Oggi? Archivio di Filosofia*, LVI, 1-3 (1988).

Osthathios, Geevarghese Mar. 'Solidarity with the Poor, but How?' *Indian Theological Studies*, XVIII (December, 1981), pp. 323-331.

Owen, H. P. *Concepts of Deity*. Macmillan, 1971.

Pailin, David A. *God and the Processes of Reality: Foundations of a Credible Theism*. London and N.Y.: Routledge, 1989.

Palmer, H. *Analogy: A Study of Qualification and Argument in Theology*. Macmillan, 1973.

Partridge, A. C. *John Donne—Language and Style*. Andre Deutsch, 1978.

Perez-Esclarín, Antonio. *Atheism and Liberation*. SCM Press, 1980.

Pettet, E. C. *Of Paradise and Light: A Study of Vaughan's Silex Scintillans*. Cambridge University Press, 1960.

Phillips, J. B. *Your God is Too Small*. N.Y.: The Macmillan Company, 1965.

Pieris, Aloysius. *An Asian Theology of Liberation*. Maryknoll, N.Y.: Orbis Books, 1988.

Pike, Nelson. *God and Timelessness*. Routledge & Kegan Paul, 1970.

Pittenger, Norman. *God in Process*. SCM Press, 1967.

_____. *Picturing God*. SCM Press, 1982.

Ratzinger, J. *Introduction to Christianity*. Burns & Oates, 1968.

Richard, Pablo et al. *The Idols of Death and the God of Life: A Theology*. Maryknoll, N.Y.: Orbis Books, 1983.

Richmond, James. *Theology and Metaphysics*. SCM Press, 1970.

Ruether, Rosemary Radford. *Sexism and God-Talk*. Boston: Beacon Press, 1983.

Sandbank, S. 'Henry Vaughan's Apology for Darkness,' *Essential Articles for the Study of Henry Vaughan*. ed. Alan Rundrum. Archon Books, 1987.

Sarot, Marcel. *God, Possibility and Corporeality*. Kampen: Kok Pharos Publishing House, 1992.

Schillebeeckx, E. *For the Sake of the Gospel*. London: SCM Press, 1989.

_____. 'The Death of a Christian,' *Vatican II: The Struggle of Minds and Other Essays*. Dublin: Gill and Son, 1963.

Schoonenberg, Piet. 'God as Relating and (Be)Coming: a Meta-Thomistic Consideration.' *Listening*, XIV, 3 (1979), pp. 265-278.

Segundo, Juan Luis. *The Liberation of Theology*. trans. John Drury. Dublin: Gill and Macmillan, 1977.

_____. *Our Idea of God*. Gill and Macmillan, 1980.

Sia, Santiago (ed.). *Charles Hartshorne's Concept of God: Philosophical and Theological Responses*. Kluwer Academic Publishers, 1989.

_____. *God in Process Thought: A Study in Charles Hartshorne's Concept of God*. Martinus Nijhoff, 1985.

Simmonds, James D. *Masques of God: Form and Theme in the Poetry of Henry Vaughan*. University of Pittsburgh Press, 1972.

Skulsky, Harold. *Language Recreated: Seventeenth-Century Metaphorists and the Act of Metaphor*. Athens: University of Georgia Press, 1992.

Smith, Huston. 'Has Process Theology Dismantled Classical Theism?' *Theology Digest*, XXXV, 4 (Winter 1988), pp. 303-318.

Sobrino, Jon. *Christology at the Crossroads: A Latin American Approach*. Maryknoll, N.Y.: Orbis Books, 1978.

_____. *The True Church and The Poor*. trans. Matthew J. O'Connell. Maryknoll, N.Y.: Orbis Books, 1984.

Soelle, Dorothee. *Suffering*. London: DLT, 1973.

Song, Choan-Seng. *The Compassionate God*. Maryknoll, N.Y.: Orbis Books, 1982.

_____. *Theology From the Womb of Asia*. Maryknoll, N.Y.: Orbis Books, 1986.

Surin, Kenneth. *Theology and the Problem of Evil*. Oxord: Blackwell, 1986.

Strier, Richard. *Love Known: Theology and Experience in George Herbert's Poetry*. The University of Chicago Press, 1983.

Tanaka, Masao. *God is Rice: Asian Culture and Christian Faith*. Geneva: World Council of Churches, 1986.

Thomas, T. K. (ed.). *Testimony amid Asian Suffering*. Singapore, 1979.

Tugwell, Simon. *Human Immortality and the Redemption of Death*. London: Darton, Longman & Todd, 1990.

Von Hügel, Baron Friedrich. *Essays and Addresses on the Philosophy of Religion*. Second Series. N.Y.: E. P. Dutton & Co., 1926.

Wall, John. *George Herbert: The Country Parson and the Temple*. Paulist Press, 1981.

Ward, Keith. *The Concept of God*. Fount Paperbacks, 1977.

Weinandy, Thomas G. *Does God Change? The Word's Becoming in the Incarnation*. Vol. IV in Studies in Historical Theology. St. Bede's Publications, 1985.

Wheeler, Michael. *Death and the Future Life in Victorian Literature and Theology*. Cambridge University Press, 1990.

Whitehead, A. N. *Process and Reality*. Corrected Ed., The Free Press, 1978.

Whitney, Barry L. *Evil and the Process of God*. Toronto: Edwin Mellen Press, 1985.

_____ and Norman King. 'Divine Immutability in Process Philosophy and Contemporary Thomism,' *Horizons*, VII (1980), pp. 49-68.

Wiesel, Elie. *Night*. N.Y.: Bantam Books, 1986.

Wiles, M. *The Christian Fathers*. SCM Press, 1977.

The Witness of Edith Barfoot: The Joyful Vocation to Suffering. Oxford: Basil Blackwell, 1977.

Yap, Kim Hao (ed.). *Asian Theological Reflections on Suffering and Hope*. Singapore, 1977.

Yewangoe, A. A. *Theologia Crucis In Asia: Asian Christian Views on Suffering in the Face of Overwhelming Poverty and Multifaced Religiosity in Asia*. Amsterdam: Rodolphi, 1987.

INDEX